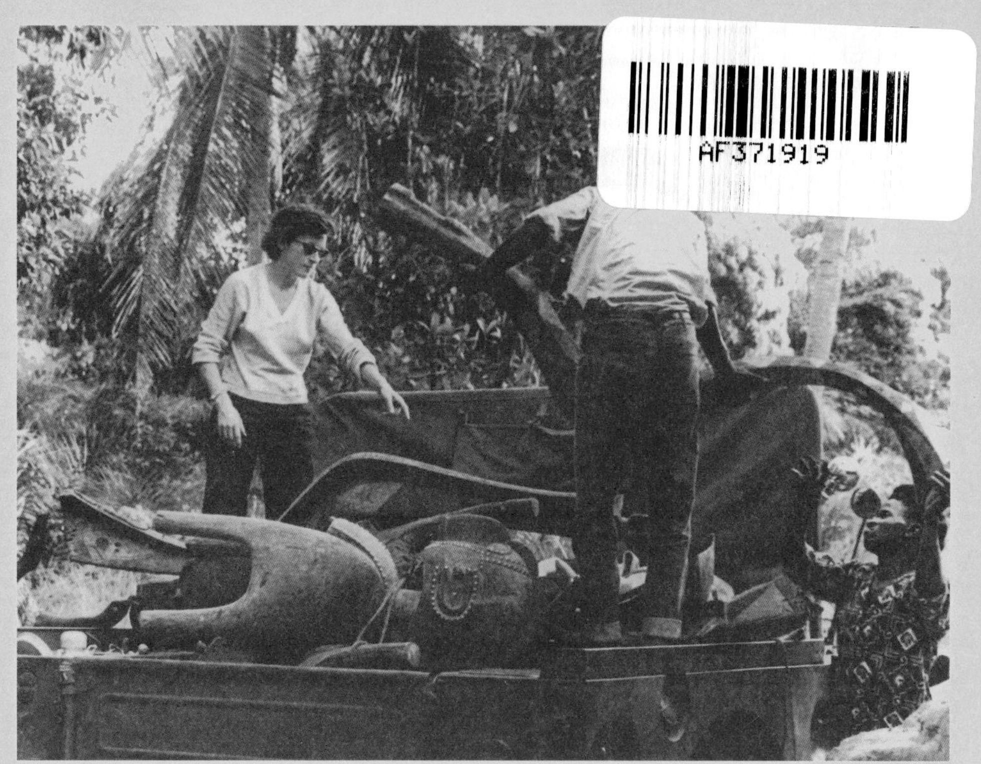

Migrating Objects

Migrating Objects

Arts of Africa, Oceania, and the Americas in the Peggy Guggenheim Collection

With contributions by
Christa Clarke
R. Tripp Evans
Ellen McBreen
Fanny Wonu Veys

Edited by
Vivien Greene

PEGGY GUGGENHEIM COLLECTION

Marsilio

Editor's Note

Scholarly terminology is always advancing. Certain
descriptors employed throughout the catalogue are
discussed and defined in the following essays on the
pages cited below. In the essays, the terms are enclosed
in quotation marks at times to indicate that their use is
undergoing critical re-evaluation in current scholarship.

Ancient American, *pre-Columbian*, and *pre-Conquest*:
See R. Tripp Evans, p. 58 and p. 64, n. 2.

Art and *artifact*:
See Fanny Wonu Veys, p. 46.

Ethnography and *ethnographic*:
See Fanny Wonu Veys, p. 46.

Non-Western and *Western*:
See Ellen McBreen, p. 18 and p. 33, n. 4, and
Christa Clarke, p. 43, nn. 2 and 14.

Primitive and *"modern primitivism"*:
See Ellen McBreen, pp. 20–21 and p. 33, nn. 9 and 14, and
Christa Clarke, pp. 36–41 and p. 43, n. 4.

See also *Note to Reader* in the Selected
Bibliography, p. 154.

In the discussions of Peggy Guggenheim's collection and
its cultures, the authors use the terms *Mesoamerican* and
Mexican; *Andean* and *Peruvian*; and *Amazonian*. African
and Oceanic cultures are also typically paired with a
country's contemporary name. Titles of modern art are
generally given in English, and in the original language
in parenthesis, depending on how they are most often
cited in fields of study.

All objects reproduced in the Plates are in the Peggy
Guggenheim Collection, Venice. Dimensions are given
by height, width, and depth in that order. Most have been
reproduced at 20% scale; objects in plates 1, 10, 12, 15–20,
26, and 30–32 have been reproduced at 25% scale.

Contents

7
Directors' Foreword

8
Acknowledgments

12
Introduction
Vivien Greene

17
Migrating Objects:
From Maker to Museum
Ellen McBreen

35
"Fantastic Artifacts":
Peggy Guggenheim and
African Art at Mid-Century
Christa Clarke

45
Peggy Guggenheim and
the Pacific
Fanny Wonu Veys

57
Guises of Commemoration:
Peggy Guggenheim and
the Funerary Arts of
the Americas
R. Tripp Evans

67
Plates

154
Selected Bibliography

155
Contributors

Directors' Foreword

Peggy Guggenheim challenged boundaries as a patron of the arts and collector, and she is celebrated for her collection of modern art from Europe and the United States. *Migrating Objects*, an exhibition and its accompanying collection publication, focuses on a lesser-known but crucial episode in her own migratory path: her turn to the arts of Africa, Oceania, and the indigenous Americas. Guggenheim had already shown interest in such works thanks to her personal connections and particularly her brief marriage to the artist Max Ernst, who collected pre-Columbian, Oceanic, and especially Native American art. However, it was not until 1959 and well into the 1960s that Guggenheim began to acquire objects created by artists from cultures worldwide, including sculpture from Mali, Côte d'Ivoire, and Papua New Guinea, as well as examples from Mexico and Peru. Guggenheim displayed them in Palazzo Venier dei Leoni, her Venetian home and museum on the Grand Canal, juxtaposing them in dialogue with her collection of paintings and sculpture, glass objects, and antique and modern furniture. Exhibited now for the first time in Venice as a whole, in conversation with several modernist works by Ernst, Alberto Giacometti, Tancredi Parmeggiani, and Pablo Picasso, among others, these holdings represent a remarkable occasion to appreciate Guggenheim's broader collecting interests.

The realization of *Migrating Objects* was guided by the expertise of the Curatorial Advisory Committee, whose members oversaw every stage of its development. We extend our sincere thanks to Christa Clarke, Independent Curator and Scholar, Arts of Global Africa, and Affiliate, Hutchins Center for African & African American Research, Harvard University, Cambridge, Mass.; R. Tripp Evans, Professor, History of Art, Wheaton College, Mass.; Ellen McBreen, Associate Professor, History of Art, Wheaton College, Mass.; and Fanny Wonu Veys, Curator, Oceania, National Museum of World Cultures, The Netherlands; as well as to Vivien Greene, Senior Curator, 19th- and Early 20th-Century Art, Solomon R. Guggenheim Museum, to whom we are especially grateful for insightfully managing the project and bringing it to fruition.

Our gratitude extends to the staff of the Opificio delle Pietre Dure, Florence, and Marco Ciatti, Soprintendente, for the treatment of several sculptures from the collection.

We are delighted to acknowledge the invaluable support of the Peggy Guggenheim Collection exhibitions provided by its Institutional Patrons, Lavazza, EFG, and Sanlorenzo; the Guggenheim Intrapresæ, whose corporate assistance allows the museum to develop its long-term exhibition program; as well as valued members of the Peggy Guggenheim Collection Advisory Board. We are thankful to the Fondazione Araldi Guinetti, Vaduz, for underwriting the educational activities of the museum. As always, we are most appreciative of the staff listed elsewhere in the book for their diligent efforts in ensuring the successful outcome of the exhibition.

Peggy Guggenheim's personal migration is well documented, from her childhood in New York City to her adult life spent largely in Paris and London, followed by her later decision to settle in Venice. In her care, the objects highlighted in this exhibition thus also found a permanent home in Italy. The conclusion of their journeys and the subsequent presentation of these objects offer the unique opportunity to open dialogue and foster exchange about the complex, global nature of migration today.

Richard Armstrong
Director, Solomon R. Guggenheim Museum and Foundation

Karole P. B. Vail
Director, Peggy Guggenheim Collection

Acknowledgments

The *Migrating Objects* exhibition and publication had a long journey of their own, and many fellow travelers were intrinsic to their successful realization. Karole P. B. Vail, Peggy Guggenheim Collection Director, first suggested this project over two years ago, when surveying her institution's holdings and recognizing that this rich trove of African, Oceanic, Mesoamerican, Andean, and Amazonian material had yet to undergo much close examination, particularly through a revisionist lens. Her vision is to be commended in launching this important and complex endeavor and all that it encompasses.

When we first considered this idea, it was immediately apparent that external specialists were crucial to bring this exhibition and collection book to fruition. We owe the exhibition's Curatorial Advisory Committee more thanks than mere words can express for what has been a truly seamless collaboration. The erudite members of this indispensable team are Christa Clarke, R. Tripp Evans, Ellen McBreen, and Fanny Wonu Veys. They perceptively, cogently, and—yes—patiently guided the long process of giving voice to these thirty-five objects, taking them on yet another migratory trip from art storage to the temporary galleries in Venice and the lasting pages of this book. Their careful research yielded not only the enlightening essays herein, but culturally sensitive frameworks through which to better understand these works and their layered meanings. It was a privilege to work with this scholarly and collegial group, whom I am now proud to also call my friends.

Neil Donnelly is responsible for the sophisticated and evocative look of this book. We salute him and Ben Fehrman-Lee of his studio for their design, which conceptually and physically responds to the content of *Migrating Objects* and conveys the ideas of the project in ways both subtle and overt. We are deeply grateful to the freelance editor of the English-language edition, Anne Barriault. Her commitment to this publication was admirable, and extended beyond perfecting prose to an overall engagement with every aspect of its content. Chiara Barbieri, Director of Publications at the Peggy Guggenheim Collection, along with overseeing the Italian edition, capably steered the book through the involved process of transforming manuscript to print. We are also appreciative of Barbieri's, Elena Cimenti's, and Roberta Cimenti's attentive translations, and Simone Bottazzin, Digital Media Manager, for the high production values of this catalogue.

A number of colleagues were extremely generous with their time, advice, and expertise. We are indebted to Paz Núñez-Regueiro for her input on the indigenous Americas works in the earlier stages of this exhibition. Henry John Drewal was responsible for proposing that the Yoruba headdress (*Ago Egungun*) is by the workshop of Oniyide Adugbologe (ca. 1875–1949) from Abeokuta, Nigeria—an exciting discovery for which we will always be thankful (Pl. 15). In addition we acknowledge the following individuals: Emily Braun, Laure Moure Cecchini, Bernard de Grunne, Teresa Fiore, Silvia Forni, Elizabeth Franzen, Giovanna Ginex, Francesco Guzzetti, Ruth Iskin, Hélène Joubert, Jacopo T. Monti, Lisa Panzera, Lucia Piccioni, Dorit Shafir, Zafrira Shoher, Debora Silverman, and Andrea Volpe.

At the Solomon R. Guggenheim Museum in New York many of my cohort imparted their wisdom, lent a helping hand, served as soundboards, and provided general encouragement along the way. Richard Armstrong, Museum and Foundation Director, and Nancy Spector, Artistic Director and Jennifer and David Stockman Chief Curator, endorsed *Migrating Objects* from its inception. Further, we express our gratitude to: Indira Abiskaroon, Curatorial Assistant, Collections; Tracey Bashkoff, Director of Collections and Senior Curator; Jennifer Blessing, Senior Curator, Photography; Minjee Cho, Senior Production Manager; Lauren Hinkson, Associate Curator, Collections; David Horowitz, Assistant Curator, Collections; Jaime Krone, Director, Exhibition Design; Ryan Newbanks, Senior Editor; Nathan Otterson, Senior Conservator, Objects; and Terra Warren, Curatorial Assistant. Our interns Allison Carey, Cassandra Kessler, Johanna Rietveld, Yubai Shi, 2019–20 Hilla Rebay Fellow Eugenia Delfini, and 2019 Philip Rylands Curatorial Intern Elisabetta Zeni were integral to the completion of this exhibition and book, as were Ellen McBreen's student assistants Eliza Browning and Anne Tucker of Wheaton College, Mass.

The exceptional staff members of the Peggy Guggenheim Collection, listed on p. 11, merit accolades for their heartfelt efforts to realize *Migrating Objects*. In particular, Siro De Boni, Technical Services and Art Handling; Sandra Divari, Manager for Collections and Exhibitions, and Luciano Pensabene Buemi, Conservator—responsible for the safety, care, and installation of the objects— helped make the exhibition itself possible. We are also grateful to the conservators from the Opificio delle Pietre Dure, Florence, Sara Bassi and Claudia Napoli, who ensured the stable condition of the works.

On a final, personal note, for their unconditional companionship, support, and love throughout this incredible, though sometimes arduous, journey, I thank my husband, David Johnson, and Dolcetto.

Vivien Greene
Senior Curator
19th- and Early 20th-Century Art
Solomon R. Guggenheim Museum

Introduction

The "non-Western" objects in Peggy Guggenheim's collection have migrated great literal and metaphorical distances from their origins. In a concatenation of events embedded in conquest, colonialism, and commerce, these and many other works like them were removed from their homelands. Dislocated from their customary environments, upon their arrival in Europe and the United States, they were drastically repositioned, their sources obfuscated, and their intended purposes largely ignored. For Western viewers they conveyed a seductive unfamiliarity, a romanticized aura of "exoticism," the otherworldly, and an authenticity unspoiled by the pitfalls of modernity. By the late nineteenth century, avant-garde artists were capitalizing on non-Western objects and their real and imagined attributes, appropriating from them in multiple senses.

Although Peggy Guggenheim acquired her African, Oceanic, Mesoamerican, Andean, and Amazonian works starting in 1959 and into the 1960s, they have languished in relative obscurity.[1] This is particularly evident when compared to the attention, both popular and scholarly, lavished on much of her Western collection, a celebrated cornucopia of twentieth-century art, especially in the areas of Surrealism and European and U.S. abstraction. Yet, a survey of the many photographs taken during her lifetime, in Guggenheim's Palazzo Venier dei Leoni and *barchessa*, reveals that her non-Western sculptures are ever present among her modernist icons. Larger-scale examples, such as a Papuan Asmat soul canoe (*wuramon*) and a Guinean Baga *D'mba* headdress, make appearances alongside paintings by Max Ernst or Pablo Picasso, an Alexander Calder mobile, or an Alberto Giacometti bronze. In one instance, in a scheme possibly echoing Surrealism's plumbing of the psyche, sexuality, and violence, Guggenheim located her Senufo two-faced helmet mask (*wanyugo*) between two canvases of enigmatic female nudes by American self-taught painter Morris Hirshfield and Belgian Surrealist Paul Delvaux (opposite page). In the new conceptual role it has been assigned, the Côte d'Ivoire sculpture is situated so its toothy mouths (perhaps a sly nod to the Surrealist trope of the *vagina dentata*) look as though they are about to bite the women's exposed flesh.

In many of her installations Guggenheim was loosely following historical conventions codified by a number of the prominent Western artists exhibited in her house/museum. Picasso, Ernst, and Henry Moore, among a multitude of others, collected what was imperfectly classified earlier in the twentieth century as "primitive" art and borrowed quite liberally from these models to advance their own explorations of reductive form, abstracted representation, and theoretical underpinnings unfettered by Western mores. Moreover, collectors before Guggenheim, from Albert C. Barnes to Helena Rubinstein to Nelson A. Rockefeller, had amassed African, Oceanic, and, later, indigenous Americas pieces and integrated them into their own corpuses of modern art. These long-standing precedents were grounded in the then-dominant, but specious, "affinities" model, which projected Western values upon the works. Associations were based primarily on formal qualities, misconstrued meanings, and false universalities. But these may not have been the only strategies informing Guggenheim's curatorial choices. In the living spaces of her residence, these objects from far afield were arranged in elegant combinations with furniture, on fireplace mantels, or atop bookshelves. Unlike the smaller-scale Western sculptures that sometimes were relegated to these sites, the ancient Mexican Nayarit terracotta woman and man, the carved wood Senufo male (*pombia*) from Côte d'Ivoire, or the Western Iatmul suspension hook from Papua New Guinea seemed to function as foils for her Western art. Perhaps the positioning of these works—interpreted as decorative elements more in line with her Venetian glass, rather than as "high" art—also contributed to the lack of scholarly and critical focus conferred upon them until recently.

This publication and exhibition strive to address the above lacunae. When embarking upon *Migrating Objects*, a timely idea conceived by Peggy

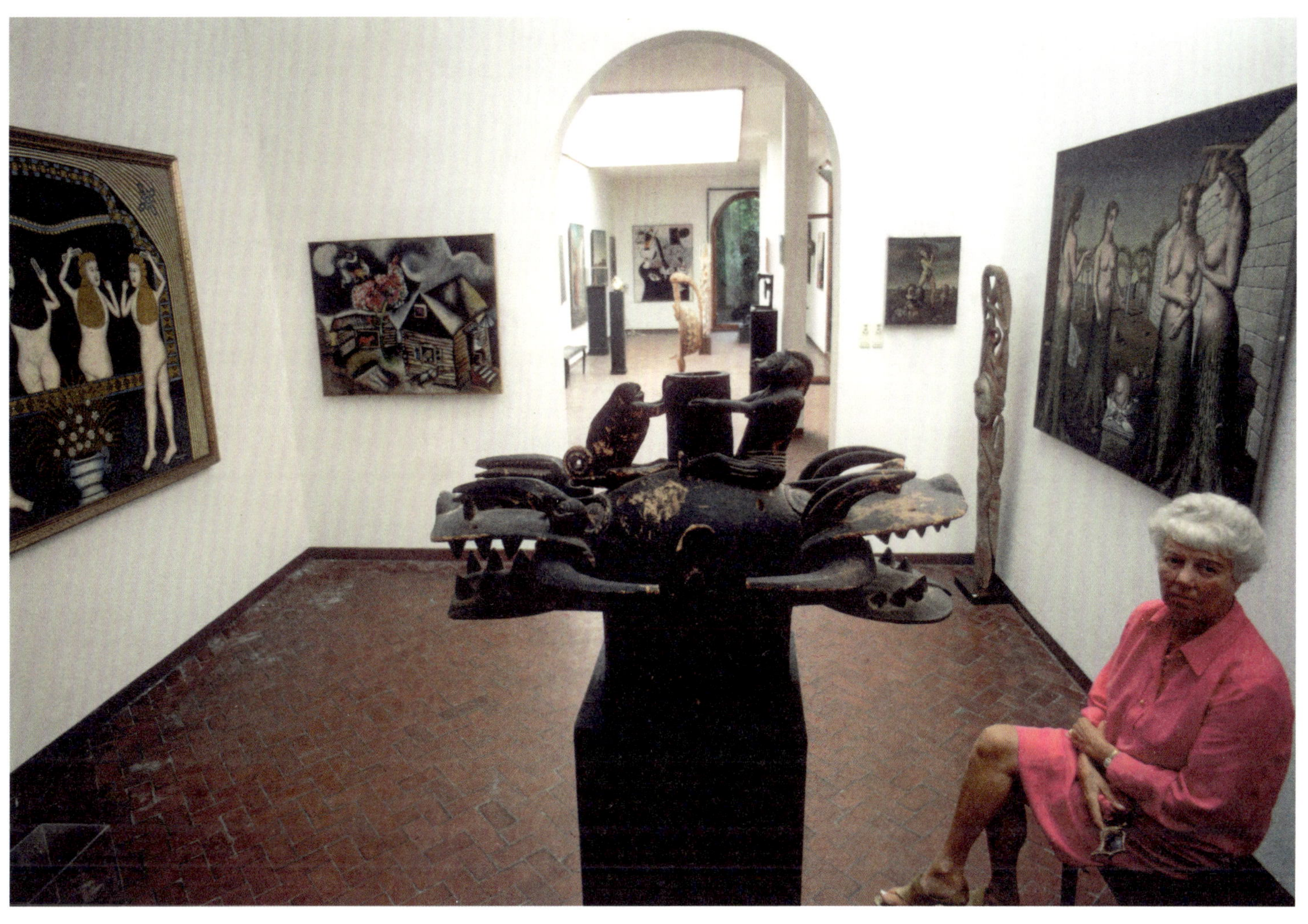

Peggy Guggenheim in the *barchessa* of Palazzo Venier dei Leoni, Venice, 1968. From left: *Two Women in Front of a Mirror*, 1943, Morris Hirshfield; *Rain* (*La Pluie*), 1911, Marc Chagall; *The Shepherdess of the Sphinxes*, 1941, Leonor Fini; ancestor figure (*miamba maira*), mid-20th century, unrecorded Wosera artist, Southern Abelam, Bobmagum (or Bogmuken) village, East Sepik Province, Papua New Guinea (Pl. 27); *The Break of Day* (*L'Aurore*), July 1937, Paul Delvaux. Center: Two-faced helmet mask (*wanyugo*), probably mid-20th century, unrecorded Senufo artist, Côte d'Ivoire (Pl. 10). Photo: Tony Vaccaro/ Hulton Archive/Getty Images

Guggenheim Collection Director Karole P.B. Vail, the project's Curatorial Advisory Committee—comprising Christa Clarke, R. Tripp Evans, Ellen McBreen, and Fanny Wonu Veys—reconsidered this collection within contemporary revisionist approaches to the cultural production of countries in Africa, Oceania, and the indigenous Americas. By thus doing, they questioned enduring assumptions about this pocket of Guggenheim's holdings, and reframed these objects and what they signified in the past and may signify today.

Even the standard "tombstone" caption format used to describe works—which appears on the labels alongside objects in galleries and next to their illustrations in books—was recast, taking cues from decolonizing practices that Western museums are now adopting because the typical criteria for captions is premised on post-medieval Western art and traditions. For example, often it is impossible to ascertain who made a work given the absence of documentation about its author. This information might have been passed down orally. Or, since creators of ritual objects were believed to be from the spiritual realm, their terrestrial personae were not always recognized. When makers were known, those who brought the objects to Europe and the United States did not necessarily register their names. Consequently, with all but one of the Peggy Guggenheim Collection works, since those who fashioned them are unidentified, the designation "unrecorded artist" is utilized in the captions.[2] With a rearticulation as straightforward and seemingly minor as this, the fact that individual people created these objects is acknowledged.

Semantics also matter greatly.[3] Inadequate vocabulary—still mired in Western imperialist or, at the very least, paternalistic epistemological systems—prompted questions with which many institutions and scholars have been and are grappling. Can sacred ceremonial objects be referred to as art? Why are works from multiple continents often gathered under the single problematic heading of non-Western? How should the art and architecture of the ancient Americas be categorized to shift away from a lexicon marking time in accordance with Western colonial intervention, as with the appellation pre-Columbian? In addition to the thoughtful and thought-provoking essays in this book, which parse these issues and more, the editor's notes to the reader call out these types of dilemmas, admitting that current terminology is deficient and that the nomenclature in these fields is evolving. With the exhibition proper, parallel principles were employed. Guggenheim's African, Oceanic, and indigenous Americas objects are presented in dialogue with European works from Peggy Guggenheim's collection and, alternately, in groupings emphasizing their original contexts. These contrasting methodologies physically magnify the inherent downfalls of the affinities paradigm and purposely disrupt the flawed narratives that Western culture has historically imposed on objects of this kind. *Migrating Objects* endeavors to confront such fault lines—it is hoped that further correctives in this fraught field will ensue.

Vivien Greene

1   Until *Migrating Objects*, this collection had
been the subject of only one in-depth study,
the 2008 exhibition and catalogue overseen by
Francesco Paolo Campione, *Ethnopassion: Peggy
Guggenheim's Ethnic Art Collection*. This was a
collaboration between the Peggy Guggenheim
Collection, Venice, and the Museo delle Culture
and the Galleria Gottardo of the Banca del
Gottardo in Lugano. The show was presented at
the latter space and then toured to the Fondazione
Antonio Mazzotta in Milan (Edizioni Gabriele
Mazzotta published the catalogue).

2   The exception is the headdress (*Ago Egungun*)
by the workshop of Oniyide Adugbologe (ca.
1875–1949) from Abeokuta, Nigeria, which eminent
Yoruba scholar Henry John Drewal identified (Pl. 15).

3   For more on the question of language, see
*Words Matter: An Unfinished Guide to Word Choices
in the Cultural Sector* (Amsterdam, Berg en Dal,
Leiden, and Rotterdam: National Museum of World
Cultures, 2019).

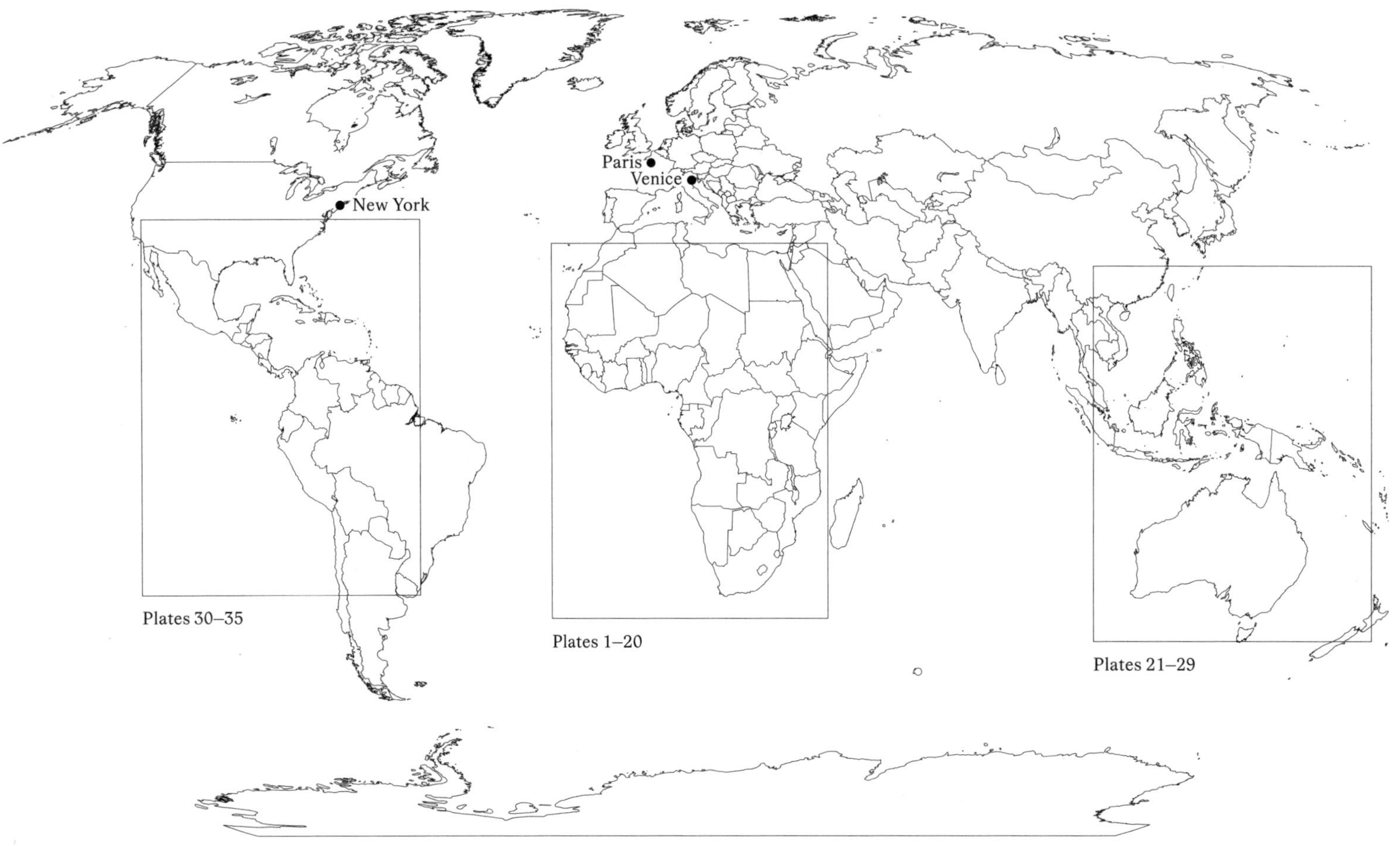

Paris
Venice
New York
Plates 30–35
Plates 1–20
Plates 21–29

Migrating Objects

From Maker
to Museum

Ellen McBreen

PLS. 13, 23

In 1959, Peggy Guggenheim purchased what she later recalled were "twelve fantastic artifacts, consisting of masks and sculptures from New Guinea, the Belgian Congo, the French Sudan, Peru, Brazil, Mexico, and New Ireland."[1] This was the origin of her African, Oceanic, and Americas art collection, with objects ranging from a Baga *D'mba* headdress from Guinea to a *malangan maramarua* funerary carving from New Ireland, Papua New Guinea. She made her first acquisition from the New York dealer Julius Carlebach:

> It reminded me, in reverse, of the days when Max [Ernst] had left our home...and removed his treasures one by one from the walls. Now they all seemed to be returning. I even succumbed to the dangerous little Mr. Carlebach, who had formerly sold so many things to Max in New York.... His prices had doubled, but at least they were still possible.[2]

This brief mention in Guggenheim's memoirs is full of ambivalence, and for good reason. Guggenheim knew Carlebach through her former husband, the Surrealist artist Max Ernst. A fellow German émigré, Carlebach had been Ernst's dealer at a time when both Surrealist and indigenous arts were conceived as complementary. Most Surrealists in New York went to Carlebach for his connections to the Heye Foundation collection of Native American art, where Guggenheim accompanied Ernst and fellow Surrealist André Breton in the early 1940s.[3] These Heye visits were typical of Guggenheim's orientations to non-Western art, consisting of experiences filtered by the sensibilities of the Surrealists she supported.[4]

Carlebach supplied Ernst with most of the removed "treasures" to which Guggenheim referred, many of these deaccessioned by Heye. The ambitious dealer was, as Guggenheim wrote, "perpetually...finding things with which to tempt Max," including objects Ernst obsessively accumulated in the early 1940s, such as a Kwakiutl mask from British Columbia and an army of so-called *kachina* dolls from the U.S. Southwest. Ernst's collection was installed alongside work made by the couple's artist friends in a townhouse they shared on Beekman Place in New York (fig. 1). Guggenheim's narrative about the first steps in her lesser-known collecting path is overdetermined by Ernst, to whom she assigned the role of originator, another in a line of advisors whose statures have since overshadowed a sense of her individual agency. She implied that her acquisition was both a corrective to their painful separation and a resurrection of the type of objects with which they had lived. Today, however, this modest collection in Venice warrants more than a facile consideration of it as a therapeutic compensation for loss.[5]

Guggenheim's story also focused on prices, but given how many other affordable areas she could have turned to in 1959, budget does not adequately address her selections either. In doing so she echoed an aspect of the more celebratory tales of earlier artist-collectors, who recalled low cost as an incentive for their early twentieth-century hunts in the flea markets and antique shops of France. Already by 1920, poet and art critic André Salmon waxed nostalgic about the "situation before 1905" when the "first statuettes, the first Dahomean, Nigerian, Senegalese, or Oceanic masks that were so fiercely competed for by Henri Matisse, Picasso, André Derain, Maurice de Vlaminck and M. de Goloubeff...were in fact fished out of the piles of shields, clubs, spears, arrows, and assegais thrown together haphazardly in old curiosity shops."[6] This image of happenstance acquisition at very low prices helped to convey purity of artistic intentions. Not coincidentally, it remained a central aspect in the subsequent discovery narratives of several artists, including Henri Matisse, who consistently recalled the exact amount (fifty francs) he paid in 1906 for his first African sculpture, a Vili figure from the Democratic Republic of the Congo.[7] Among other motivations, Matisse's insistence established his interest in Africa to a time well before fashion and a mainstream commercial market would take hold, a market with preferences and priorities that, decades later, shaped Guggenheim's collecting.

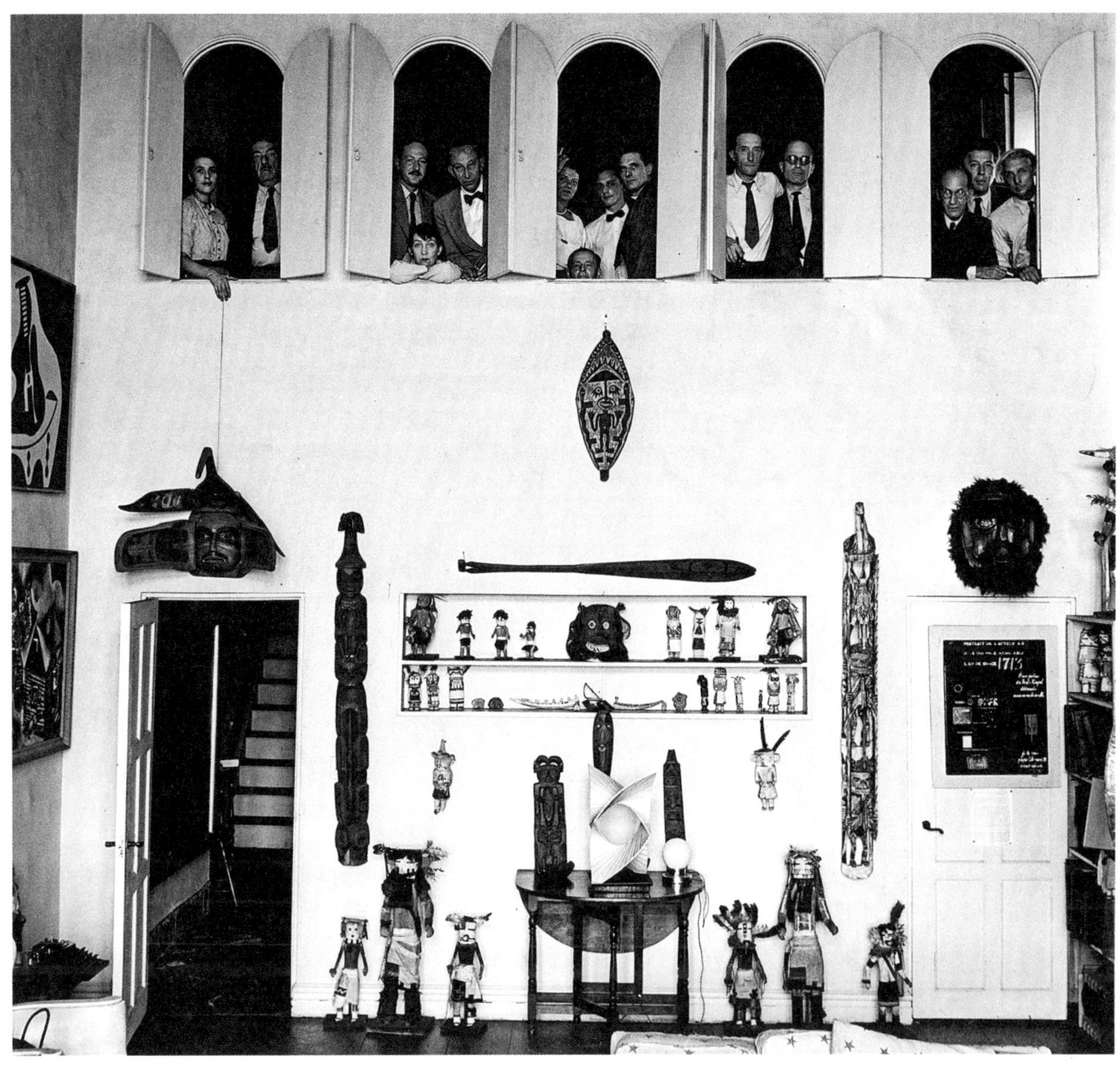

Fig. 1 Artists in Peggy Guggenheim's Beekman Place townhouse, New York, fall 1942. Left to right: Leonora Carrington, Fernand Léger, John Ferren, Berenice Abbott, Amédée Ozenfant, Peggy Guggenheim, Frederick Kiesler, Jimmy Ernst, Stanley William Hayter, Marcel Duchamp, Kurt Seligmann, Piet Mondrian, André Breton, Max Ernst. Photo: Herman Landshoff

But like these artists, Guggenheim collected for reasons that transcend the details of her love life or her pocketbook. The type of objects still possible for her to collect in New York and Italy (where she continued to acquire artworks during the 1960s) were determined by a web of political and commercial forces, institutional agendas, and the ideas of specialists and tastemakers who came before her.[8]

There would have been nothing for Guggenheim to acquire without the imperialist history of colonial trade and ethnographic expeditions that made the works available. The first generation of Westerners to conceive these objects as *art* in the early twentieth century could only admire what colonialism showed them. Paris-based art dealers Joseph Brummer and Paul Guillaume, who were instrumental in establishing a market for African art before World War I, promoted the material culture of traditions that arrived via shipments by commercial firms in the now-former French colonies of West and Central Africa. Brummer and Guillaume helped create a lasting preference for figurative sculpture and masks—often referred to as "classical" African art—made in places such as Côte d'Ivoire, the source of seven of the works in Guggenheim's collection.

The horizon of expectations for African and Oceanic objects in Europe and the United States was then shaped by how artists borrowed from select traditions for their work. Beginning in the first decade of the twentieth century, modern artists, including André Derain, Maurice de Vlaminck, Ernst Ludwig Kirchner, Matisse, and Pablo Picasso, began to collect, study, and appropriate concepts from African and Oceanic sculpture. Their primarily aesthetic engagement (few were concerned with the objects' original functions) built the foundations of a formalist language that Western specialists and collectors would continue to speak for decades, focusing on qualities such as spatial dynamics and authenticity of expression. This is now referred to as "modernist primitivism": a fascination with cultures and objects from parts of the world erroneously believed to be more "primitive."[9] One of the many simplifications of modernist primitivism was the idea that "untrained" creators worked with the elementary vocabulary of object-making, from which modernity had tragically distanced their European counterparts. By engaging more closely with materials from these cultures, a languishing tradition might locate the means to revitalize itself. Modernist primitivism was fueled by outdated racial clichés, which were also used as critical springboards to articulate new motivations for the making of art. Picasso visited the Musée d'Ethnographie du Trocadéro, Paris, in 1907, to study African objects while developing his icon of modernist primitivism, *Les Demoiselles d'Avignon*, but he was not there just to purloin a few scarification patterns from a mask. As he later recalled, it was not the appearance of African art, but its very function—imagined as an "intercessor" against the unknown—that prompted his realization: "I understood why I was a painter."[10]

As Picasso's self-serving narrative of heroic discovery suggests, the history of modernist primitivism reveals more about the observer than the observed, since it is ultimately about Western values and misperceptions.[11] It is the history of how, in each movement of a migrating object after reaching Europe or the United States, new audiences generated new meanings. Objects once shown in natural history or ethnographic museums—deployed with evolutionary bias as evidence of an "earlier" stage of civilization—gradually began to appear in art museums, with a shift in focus to highlight visual form divorced from contextual information. Many of Guggenheim's peers, in fact, argued for the deliberate ignorance of original uses or meanings as a prerequisite for aesthetic appreciation. Writing in the catalogue for the Museum of Modern Art's (MoMA) groundbreaking 1935 exhibition of African art, the curator James Johnson Sweeney, Guggenheim's close friend, claimed that "historical and ethnographic considerations have a tendency to blind us to [African art's] true worth."[12] This idea was echoed in the writings of artists whom Guggenheim supported and collected, such as the English sculptor Henry Moore: "Primitive Art is a mine of information...but to understand and appreciate it, it is more important to look at it than to learn the history of primitive peoples, their religions and social customs."[13] Guggenheim's own presentation of her collection favored this purely visual "just look and learn" decontextualization, which ultimately sought to elevate non-Western objects to the status of art over artifact.

Most fundamentally, the history of modernist primitivism is also a complex history of ideas about race, a series of evolving assumptions that generations of white people projected onto people of color. However those beliefs were articulated, they collectively helped to naturalize deep imbalances of power. In celebrating the "discovery" of African, Oceanic, and pre-Columbian art, a hazy, depoliticized fascination with universal affinities between modernism and its sources obscured a space from where more discomforting revelations could have emerged. The fact that twentieth-century art fed itself on the displaced spoils of cultures, whose local traditions were also eradicated in the name of other Western endeavors of "progress" and regeneration, is now an inescapable reality in the light of decolonization.[14]

Modernist artists and their supporters, including scholars and collectors, are unavoidably implicated. No matter how well intentioned, they collectively championed these objects from inside a Eurocentric worldview as commentaries that focused back on Western art. African, Oceanic, and pre-Columbian art was employed to provide a global justification for what detractors saw as abstract art's ahistorical aberrations. Moore, for example, saw in these objects "a common world-language of form" from which Greek naturalism was "only a digression from the main world tradition of sculpture."[15] To locate an alternative set of imaginary ancestors, modernists claimed to be studying centuries-old objects from Africa. Several of the objects in Guggenheim's collection, however, were just a few decades old when she acquired them. This complex mythmaking of modernist primitivism is the frame in which to understand her individual selections and how she moved the objects from room to room to create contrasts with her European and U.S. works. By 1959, this was commonplace curatorial practice and based on the model of what artists had done for decades in their own studios. The juxtapositions seemed so self-evident, in fact, that radical recontextualization (a process beginning as soon as these objects left the hands of their makers) was inevitable. But how, and on what terms, did it occur in Guggenheim's collection?

A 1966 photograph of objects in Guggenheim's Palazzo Venier dei Leoni foyer in Venice provides one way into this question. It depicts Picasso's *On the Beach* (*La Baignade*), 1937, with a Dogon seated male figure from central Mali placed just in front of the painting's pneumatic left-hand bather (fig. 2). While the contrast potentially evokes the incommensurability of cultural origins, its careful staging emphasizes visual overlaps: in the vivid delineation between the segments of abstract forms that both artists used to reorganize the motif of the body; in the sudden transitions between rounded and straightened volumes (breasts versus neck in both); and in the abruptly flattened planes of the faces, each with its own sign-system for eyes and nose. Even the gesture of the bather's handless arms, reaching out to her partner's toy boat, finds an enigmatic parallel in the Dogon figure's presentation of a rectangular object, likely a percussive instrument.[16] In neither work, however, do the protagonists' narrative actions account for overall impact or expressive power. The Dogon sculpture functions as a free-floating signifier that confers an additional layer of authenticity back onto Picasso and, by extension, to Guggenheim's choices. Soon after acquiring the painting, she described seeing its main characters as "the embodiment of all femininity of all time."[17] Such were the projections of timelessness made onto the Dogon people and their traditions, key to the founding of French ethnology in the 1930s, when Dogon beliefs became the cornerstone of the French anthropologist Marcel Griaule's research and writing.[18]

As photographs of her installations reveal, however, Guggenheim did not settle on static juxtapositions. In another, color, image, Picasso's *On the Beach* is placed alongside a pair of painted Nkanu panels from the Democratic Republic of the Congo, each carved with a sculpted mask (fig. 3). While details of the panels are partially hidden by the forms of Alexander Calder's *Arc of Petals*, 1941, fragments of the pair

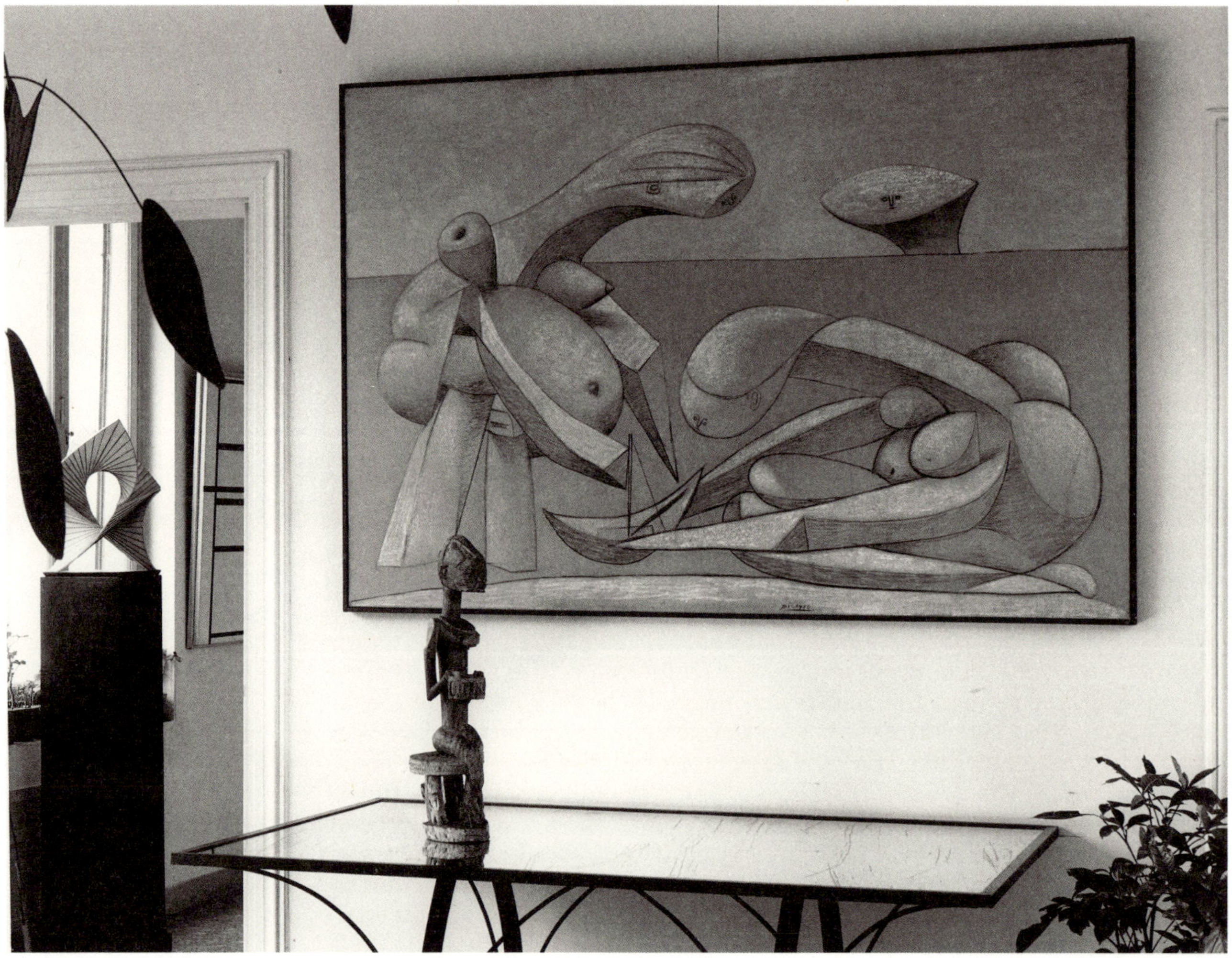

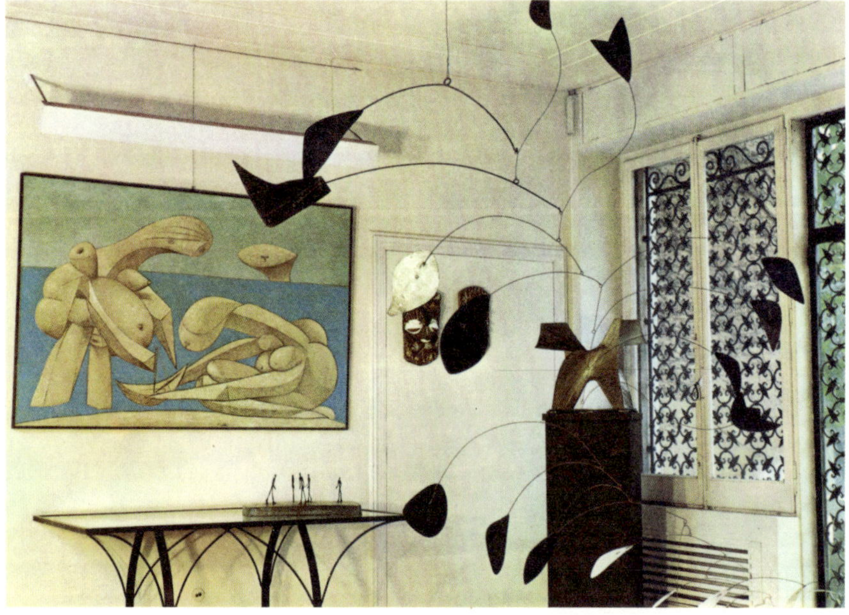

Fig. 2   The foyer, Palazzo Venier dei Leoni, Venice, 1966. Left to right: on pedestal, *Developable Surface (Surface développable)*, 1938–August 1939, Antoine Pevsner; on table, seated male figure, probably first half of 20th century, unrecorded Dogon artist, N'duleri region, Mali (Pl. 1); *On the Beach (La Baignade)*, February 12, 1937, Pablo Picasso. Photo: Gianni Berengo Gardin

Fig. 3   The foyer, Palazzo Venier dei Leoni, Venice, 1967. Back wall, left to right: *On the Beach (La Baignade)*, February 12, 1937, Pablo Picasso; two panels, probably first half of 20th century, unrecorded Nkanu artists, Democratic Republic of the Congo (Pls. 17, 18). On table: *Piazza*, 1947–48 (cast 1948–49), Alberto Giacometti. On pedestal: *Developable Surface (Surface développable)*, 1941, Antoine Pevsner. Suspended from ceiling: *Arc of Petals*, 1941, Alexander Calder emerge, strategically hung at a level so that their protruding white eyes mirror the third mask-face of Picasso's voyeur at the edge of the sea.

The majestic *D'mba* sculpture made by a Baga artist from Guinea that often dominated the palazzo foyer was another player in these Picasso ensembles. It appears at left in a photograph of Guggenheim reading in front of Picasso's *The Studio* (*L'Atelier*), 1928 (fig. 4). Calder is again the screen through which the group is visible, the wires of his mobile creating a sinuous road map connecting the two languages of abstraction. Picasso acquired a Baga shoulder dance mask of this type around the same time he painted *The Studio*. Baga motifs had already appeared in his work beginning in 1907, likely inspired by a *D'mba* sculpture then in the collection of the Trocadéro (fig. 5).[19] Baga *D'mba* is the kind of African object, which, having received this avant-garde imprimatur, became the predilection of collectors. This type of Baga mask was also in Nelson A. Rockefeller's ambitious collection for The Museum of Primitive Art (today, the core of The Metropolitan Museum of Art's collection of the Arts of Africa, Oceania, and the Americas), a historical capsule of taste with a vision that Guggenheim closely followed. Her preferences reflected the African traditions then being canonized in U.S. museums. In 1959, the very year Guggenheim started collecting African art, The Museum of Primitive Art featured *The Sculpture of Three Tribes: Senufo, Baga, Dogon*. This exhibition included several works with close ties to objects Guggenheim acquired, such as three Senufo zoomorphic helmet masks similar to the chimerical example now in Venice.[20]

By the time Guggenheim chose to install these African objects alongside Picasso's painting, the idea to do so was a half century old. As early as 1913 his works were shown alongside African sculpture in both Berlin and Dresden. In the following year, New York visitors to the exhibition *Statuary in Wood by African Savages: The Root of Modern Art* at Alfred Stieglitz's 291 gallery saw African sculpture presented as art, with its forms emphasizing a parallel language to modernism.[21] (Guggenheim later had her first interaction with modern art, an abstraction by Georgia O'Keeffe, in that same gallery.)[22] Photographs of the exhibition were subsequently published in the journal *Camera Work* in 1916, in which Stieglitz reproduced a now iconic photograph of what was for its time an innovative combination: a Kota reliquary figure between Cubist works on paper by Picasso and Georges Braque (fig. 6).[23] Picasso eventually acquired two of these types of Kota sculpture.[24] Known in the West since at least the 1870s, the "Kota" designation was used by Europeans to label the productions of several distinct populations, each with complex histories of migration in Gabon and neighboring areas. In the history of African collecting, preference was often given to what early interlocutors believed to be representative examples, based on their faith to connect a recognizable style to a monolithic culture or region. In art-world circles, Kota reliquaries were consistently associated with Picasso throughout the century. MoMA helped to canonize the Kota-Picasso link in its exhibition *Timeless Aspects of Modern Art*, 1948–49, by presenting his *Painter and Model* (*Le Peintre et son modèle*), 1928, a variation on the theme of Guggenheim's *The Studio*, in a dramatic quasi-religious pairing with a Kota reliquary (fig. 7). The plan published for the exhibition even featured an imaginary transcultural migration that stopped at a silhouette of the Kota before arriving at Picasso's masterpiece.

It is no small wonder, then, that Guggeheim chose a Kota figure from a reliquary ensemble to form the nucleus of her collection in 1959. By this time, the cult associated with these objects had been suppressed by colonial and missionary forces. The Kota figure is an especially instructive example of how extreme the recontextualization of objects was (and continued to be) once they migrated to the West. Kota reliquaries are very literally shown in fragmentary form: the Guggenheim Kota figure (*mbulu ngulu*) has a lozenge-shaped base designed to anchor it inside a basket holding either ancestral remains or diviner's substances. The lower portion of that base, unadorned by the brass and copper sheets that are found elsewhere, was not meant to be seen. Many European viewers, like Picasso, however, read the diamond as an abstract sign for the body, an understanding on display in his Kota-inspired paintings such as *Nude with Raised Arms, The*

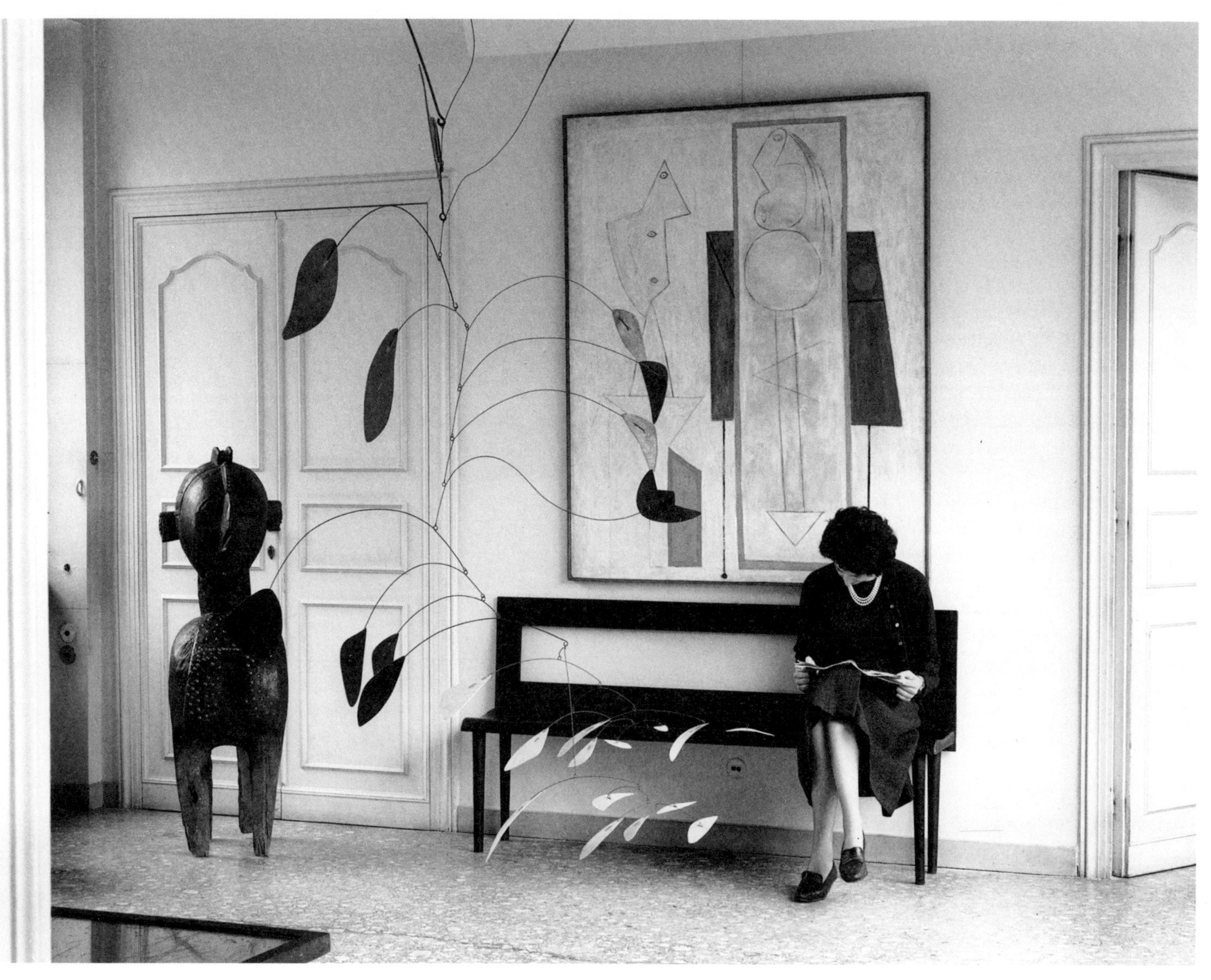

Fig. 4　Peggy Guggenheim in the foyer, Palazzo Venier dei Leoni, Venice, 1966. Left to right: *D'mba* headdress, probably first half of 20th century, unrecorded Baga artist, Guinea (Pl. 13); *The Studio* (*L'Atelier*), 1928, Pablo Picasso. Suspended from ceiling: *Arc of Petals*, 1941, Alexander Calder. Photo: Gianni Berengo Gardin

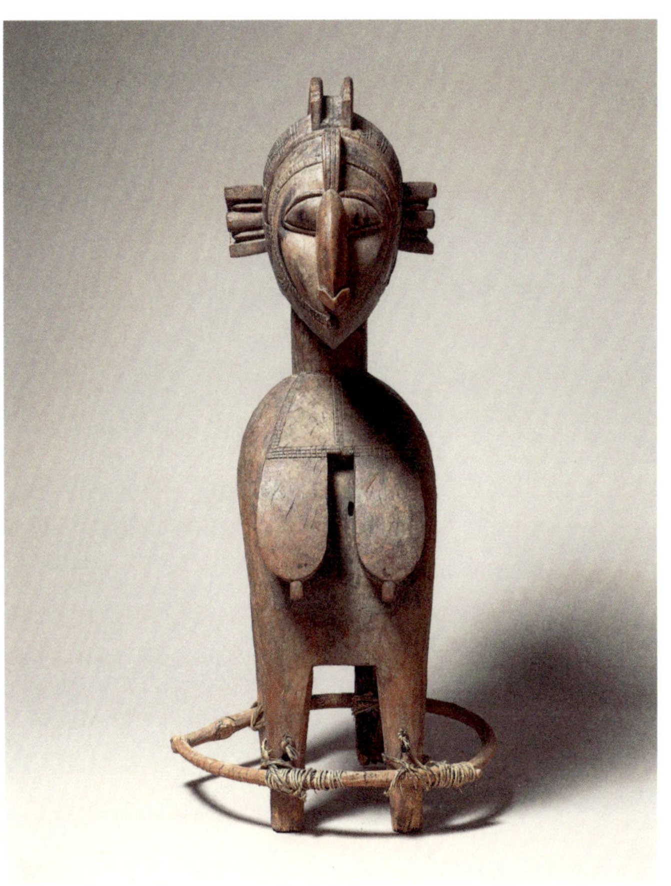

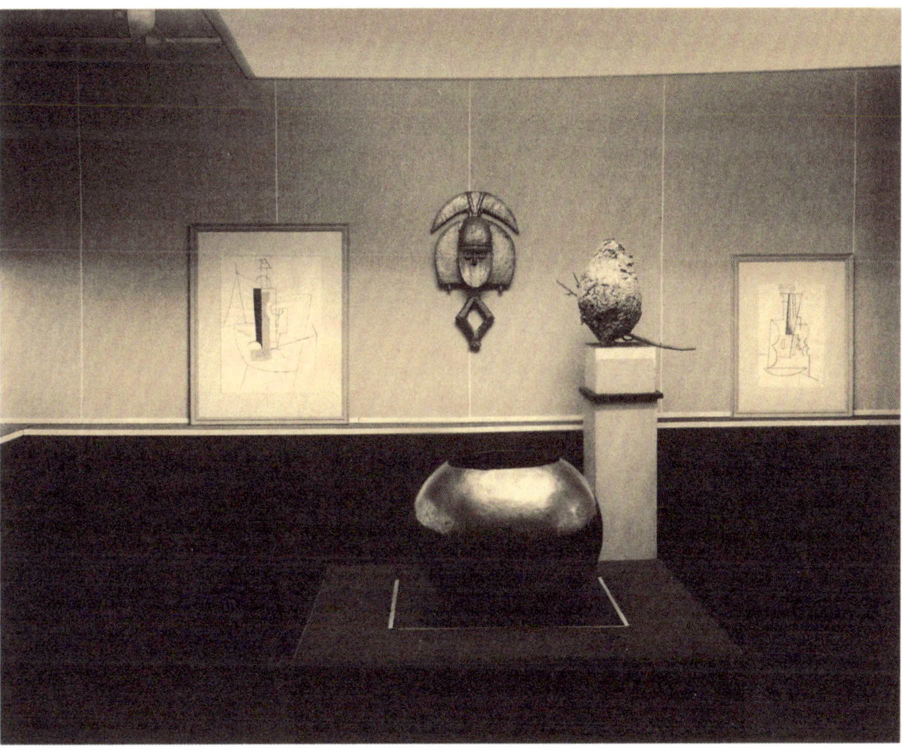

Fig. 5 *D'mba* headdress, late 19th to early
20th century, unrecorded Baga artist, Guinea
(ex-collection Pablo Picasso). Musée national
Picasso-Paris, dation Pablo Picasso, 1979

Fig. 6 Alfred Stieglitz, *Arrangement at 291*,
from gallery 291, New York, 1915. Reproduced in
*Camera Work, A Photographic Quarterly Edited
and Published by Alfred Stieglitz, New York* in
1916. Platinum print, The Metropolitan Museum
of Art, Alfred Steiglitz Collection, 1949

Avignon Dancer, 1907. In other words, by the time Guggenheim acquired her Kota sculpture, not only were the original meanings and functions of these reliquaries suppressed, but an entirely new layer of understanding was grafted onto them, in some sense conditioning the possibilities of how they are seen now.

In contrast to how African objects highlighted visual parallels with Picasso or the earlier Cubist-inspired paintings by Fernand Léger, Louis Marcoussis, or Jean Metzinger (fig. 8), the juxtapositions Guggenheim made with her Surrealist works were closer in spirit to that later movement's more open-ended primitivism. As *L'africanisme* was institutionally canonized, and increasingly commercialized, the Surrealists looked further afield for inspiration, and especially to Oceania. Breton later recalled: "From the beginning, the course of Surrealism is inseparable from the power of seduction, of fascination, that Oceanic objects exerted over us."[25] As an earlier generation had projected an instinctual form of proto-Cubism onto West and Central African statuary and masks, so now the Surrealists imagined their own anti-rationalist values in Oceanic art: seeing in its objects a resolution of the real and imaginary that they collectively pursued in their own work. Many Surrealists (like Ernst) were voracious Oceanic art collectors, including founders Breton and Paul Éluard, who considered it an extension of their creative practice; they saw no ideological contradiction between an "irresistible need to possess" and their anti-colonialist politics. The Surrealist counter-exhibition *Truth About the Colonies* (*La Verité sur les colonies*), 1931, was mounted as an anti-imperialist protest of the *International Colonial Exhibition* (*L'Exposition coloniale internationale*) in Paris, which took place the same year as a much-publicized and profitable auction of the Breton-Éluard collection.[26]

The nine Oceanic works at the Guggenheim are all from Melanesia, specifically from areas the Surrealists "claimed" as their own. But their primitivist worldview was not just *what* they collected, it was also embedded in the recontextualizations they performed on these objects. Breton advocated for a *détournement*: placing an object into a heterogeneous recombination to liberate meanings.[27] The May 1936 *Surrealist Exhibition of Objects* (*Exposition d'objets surréalistes*) at Galerie Charles Ratton in Paris proposed a "cabinet of curiosity" model, deliberately rejecting the visual primitivist affinities then in vogue for more incongruous encounters: Marcel Duchamp's readymades with mathematical objects and Alberto Giacometti's *Suspended Ball* (*Boule suspendue*), 1930–31, below a Torres Strait mask (fig. 9). Scrambling cultural codes was part of a larger Surrealist effort to rupture the ways knowledge and experience were classified.[28]

While some of the experimental exhibitions held in Guggenheim's museum/gallery, Art of This Century, in New York might have been closer to this spirit of *détournement*, her Surrealist galleries in Venice offered a more traditional take on their constellation of ideas.[29] A *malangan* carving from New Ireland in Papua New Guinea is one of those (metaphorically speaking) "returned" objects to which Guggenheim's memoir refers. Not surprisingly, it often found a place facing Ernst and other Surrealist painters (fig. 10). Guggenheim had lived with a similar *malangan* figure, belonging to Ernst, visible on the wall at right beneath the group photograph taken in their New York home (fig. 1).[30] The carving at the Peggy Guggenheim Collection, an effigy believed to host the spirit of a deceased clan member, is an overlapping frame of birds, snakes, and flying fish that cradles a male figure, whose seemingly animated sea-snail opercula eyes gaze across at the other fantastically hybrid figures in Ernst's painted bestiaries. In these installations, however, Guggenheim did not force the personal connections she highlighted in her writing. Another view of the gallery shows an Asmat soul canoe and a *Tatanua* mask (*malangan*)—both also Melanesian—in this Surrealist cluster, but it was, in fact, an African work of a standing male Senufo figure that was positioned next to Ernst's *Antipope*, 1941–42 (fig. 11). These changing arrangements reflect the more fluid ethnographic sensibilities of the Surrealists, many of whom insisted that it was not the forms of one tradition, per se, but the connections to visionary imagination, and ideas about ritual and myth (as mediated as they were), which drew them in. Using the now-discredited concept of "affinity" to describe Surrealist appropriations, Christian Zervos attempted to distinguish their complexity from the earlier,

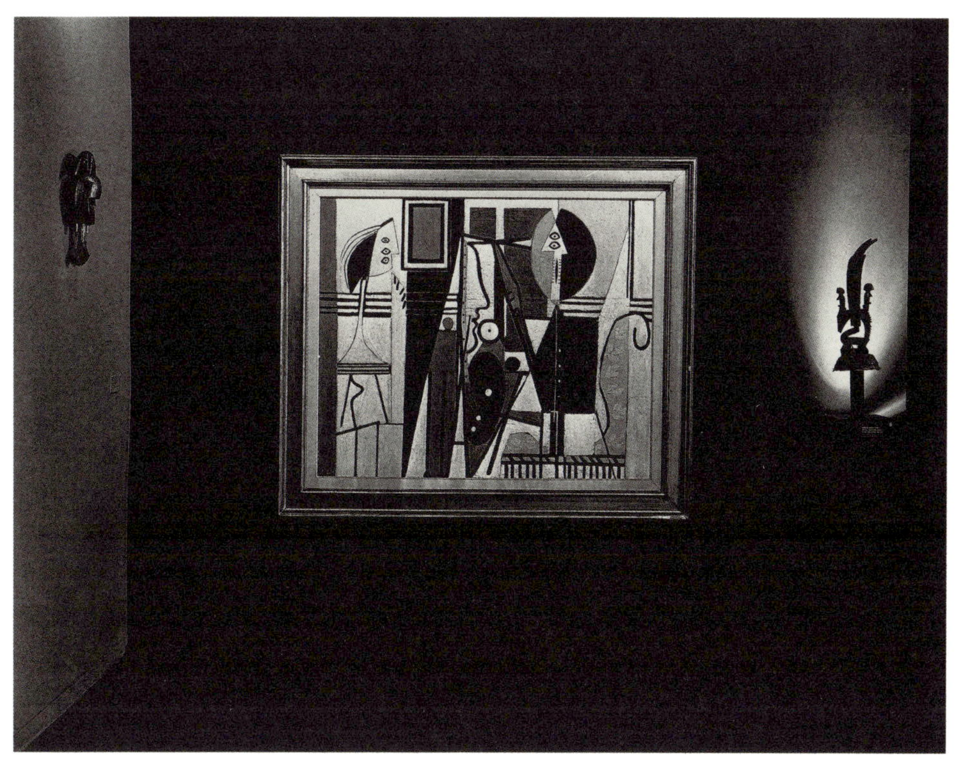

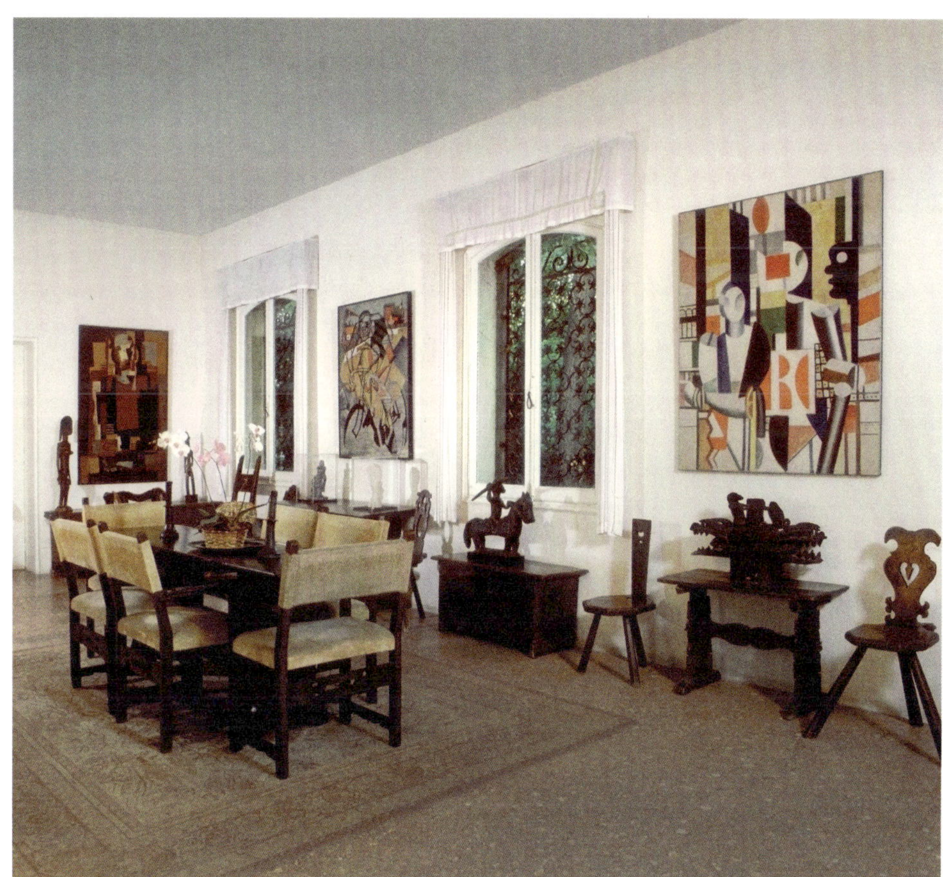

Fig. 7   Installation view of the MoMA exhibition
Timeless Aspects of Modern Art, November 16,
1948 – January 23, 1949. Center: *Painter and Model*
(*Le Peintre et son modèle*), 1928, Pablo Picasso, a
variation on the theme of *The Studio* (*L'Atelier*),
1928, Pablo Picasso, in the Peggy Guggenheim
Collection. Photographic Archive, The Museum of
Modern Art, New York. Photo: Soichi Sunami

Fig. 8   The dining room, Palazzo Venier dei Leoni,
Venice, 1960s. On wall, left to right: *The Regular*
(*L'Habitué*),1920, Louis Marcoussis; *At the
Velodrome* (*Au Vélodrome*), 1912, Jean Metzinger;
Men in the City (*Les Hommes dans la ville*), 1919,
Fernand Léger. On furniture, left to right: *Seated
Pierrot* (*Pierrot assis*), 1922, Jacques Lipchitz;
equestrian figure, probably first half of 20th century,
and two-faced helmet mask (*wanyugo*), probably
mid-20th century, both by unrecorded Senufo artists,
Côte d'Ivoire (Pls. 11, 10). Photo: Peter Vitale

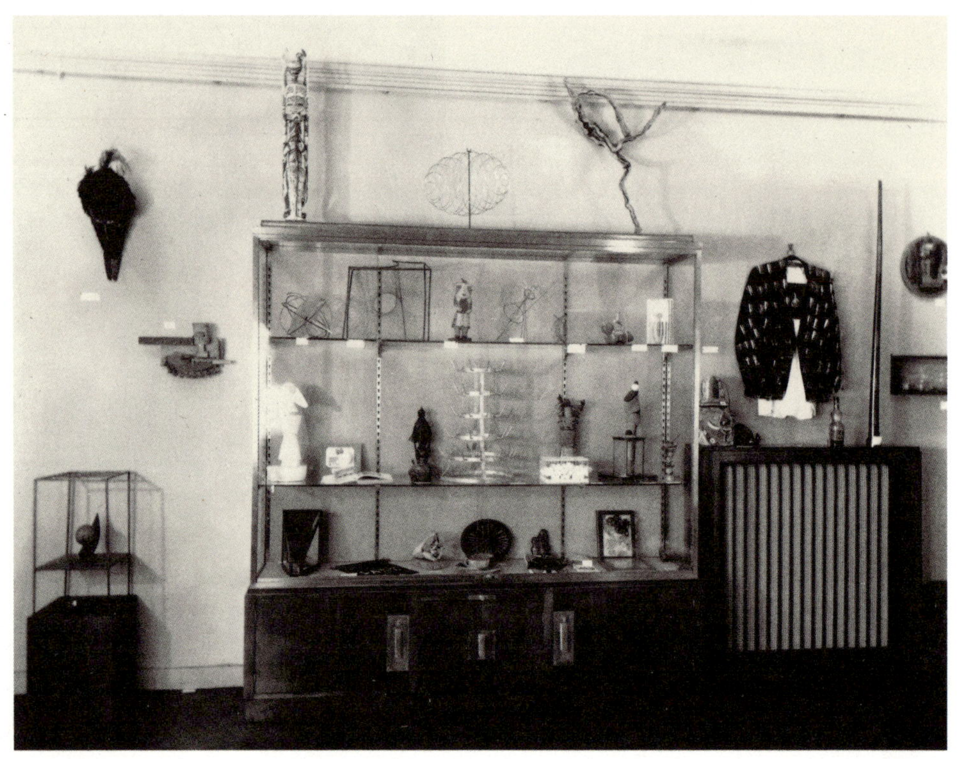

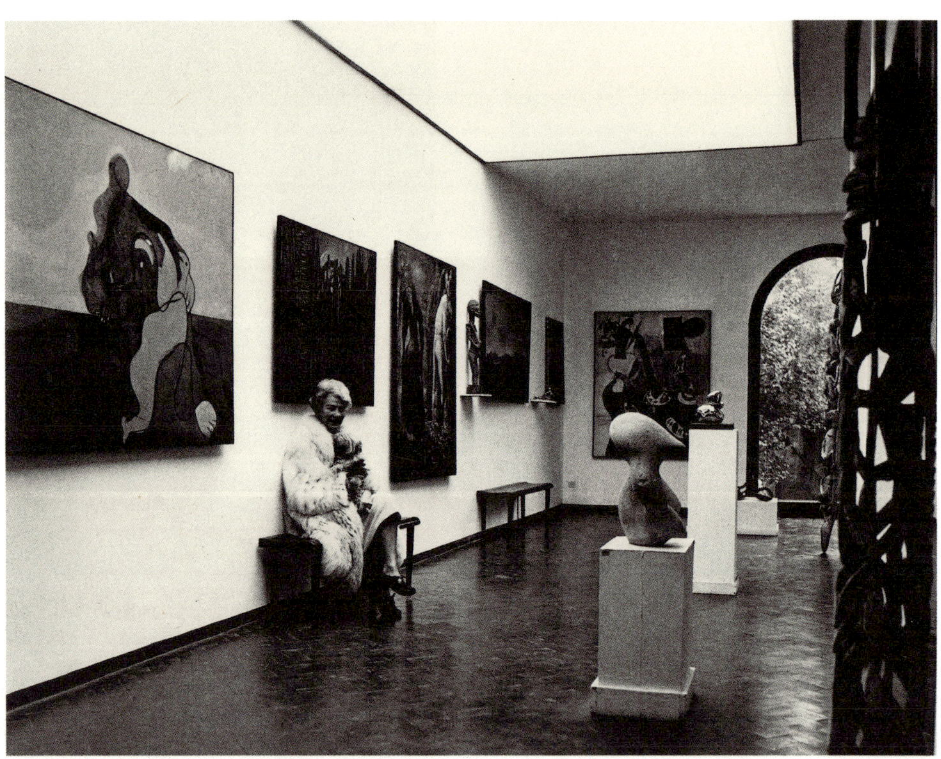

Fig. 9   Man Ray, *Surrealist Exhibition of Objects* (*Exposition d'objets surréalistes*), Galerie Ratton, Paris, 1936, including Oceanic objects. Left, on wall: Torres Strait mask. Left, on case: New Ireland standing figure

Fig. 10   Peggy Guggenheim in the *barchessa*, Palazzo Venier dei Leoni, Venice, mid-1960s. Left: *The Kiss* (*Le Baiser*), 1927; *The Forest* (*La Forêt*), 1927–28; *The Antipope*, December 1941–March 1942, all by Max Ernst; male figure (*pombia*), probably mid-20th century, unrecorded Senufo artist, Côte d'Ivoire (Pl. 8). Back wall: *Seated Woman II* (*Femme assise II*), February 27, 1939, Joan Miró. Foreground center: *Crown of Buds I* (*Couronne de bourgeons I*), 1936, Jean Arp. Right: funerary carving (*malangan maramarua*), early 20th century, unrecorded Mandara (or Tabar) artist, Tabar Island, Northern New Ireland, Papua New Guinea (Pl. 23)

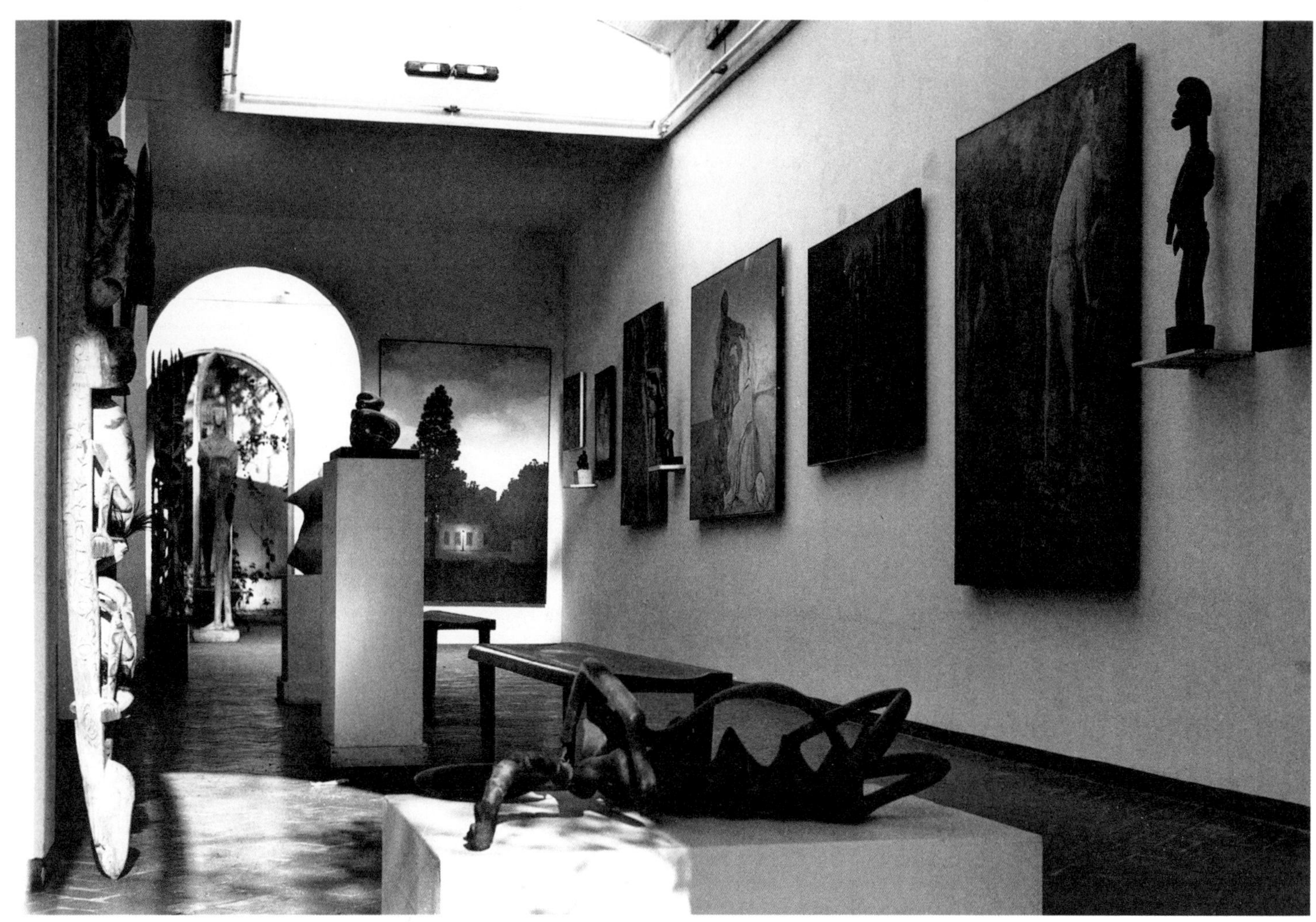

Fig. 11   The *barchessa*, Palazzo Venier dei
Leoni, Venice, 1966. Left: soul canoe (*wuramon*),
mid-20th century, unrecorded Asmat artists,
Papua (Western New Guinea), Indonesia (Pl. 22).
Center: background, on pedestal: *Head and Shell*
(*Tête et coquille*), ca. 1933, Jean Arp; foreground:
Woman with Her Throat Cut (*Femme égorgée*),
1932 (cast 1940), Alberto Giacometti. Back wall:
Empire of Light (*L'Empire des lumières*), 1953–54,
René Magritte. Right: *The Antipope*, December
1941 – March 1942, Max Ernst, next to male figure
(*pombia*), probably mid-20th century, unrecorded
Senufo artist, Côte d'Ivoire (Pl. 8). Photo: Gianni
Berengo Gardin

more materialist raid of African art by the Cubists: "What happened twenty years ago with Negro sculpture is what is happening at present with Melanesian and pre-Columbian art, from which we do not require direct inspiration but feelings of affinity."[31]

The concrete forms of the *malangan* carving, however, are linked to another late Surrealist artist in Guggenheim's stable: Matta (Roberto Sebastián Matta Echaurren), whose central *personnage* in *The Un-Nominator Renominated* (*Le Dénommeur renommé*), 1952–53, borrows from New Ireland carvings in his own vast Oceanic collection.[32] This Matta painting conjures the past: Guggenheim's earlier work at Art of This Century involved close collaborations with him. It also speaks to its present, and a post–World War II shift in modernist primitivism characterized by a pronounced mood of terror. Non-Western art, once the object of serious ethnographic inquiry and avant-garde tribute, had been relegated to the Hitlerian category of degenerate art. Artists inspired by those traditions were, for the Nazis, a clear symptom of modern art's moral weaknesses. At the infamous *Degenerate Art* (*Entartete Kunst*) exhibition in Munich in July 1937—with hundreds of works confiscated from German collections (including those by "her" artists Ernst, Paul Klee, Raoul Hausmann, and Léger)—primitivism, in particular, was a target of vitriol and racist condemnation. *Degenerate Art* argued that the fraud of modernist art had been carried out by dangerous outsiders, namely Jews and Bolsheviks. But the outsiders whom the cover of the exhibition guide explicitly targeted, via an image of Otto Freundlich's primitivist sculpture *The New Man* (*Der neue Mensch*), 1912 (fig. 12), were the non-Europeans who had invaded the minds of artists pursuing their dangerous "dissolution of all nations and all races."[33]

The dehumanizing concept of degenerate art appeared later in the frontispiece for Guggenheim's 1942 publication *Art of This Century*, which encompasses an excerpt from Adolf Hitler's Munich speech given five years prior at the opening of the *Great German Art Exhibition* (*Grosse Deutsche Kunstausstellung*), an event designed as the Aryan antithesis to the "primitives" mocked in the paranoid display of *Degenerate Art*.[34] Among other ideas, Hitler proposed that modern art was a fickle fashion; what the nation needed was a lasting art integrally rooted to a unified race. The text contains some especially harrowing lines in which Hitler relates non-realistic art to physical inferiority, suggesting that "unhappy" artists who see "green skies and purple seas" should be handed over to "the Ministry of the Interior where sterilization of the insane is dealt with" or to the criminal courts, so as to protect future generations from "their unfortunate inheritance." *Art of This Century* itself, published during the war, is also a chronicle of the conflict. Guggenheim began planning the publication in 1940 during a stay in Grenoble, where her own potentially "degenerate art" collection was sheltered from the Nazis by Pierre-André Farcy, the curator who directed the art museum there and was arrested by the Gestapo in 1943.

While the 1942 publication has seemingly little to do with Guggenheim's later interest in African, Oceanic, and pre-Columbian art, it is a reminder of the deeply political stakes in making transcultural connections and of leaving, even in one's imagination, the boundaries of the West. Among the many works featured in the catalogue was Léger's *Men in the City* (*Les Hommes dans la ville*), 1919, which would go on to play such a pivotal role in stories Guggenheim and others told about the origins of her European collection during the winter of 1939–1940 in Paris: "The day Hitler walked into Norway, I walked into Léger's studio and bought a wonderful 1919 painting from him for $1,000. He never got over the fact that I should be buying paintings on such a day...."[35] Her Léger story created a lasting image of Guggenheim as either blithely unaware of the catastrophe looming, or worse, taking advantage of artists in a desperate time.[36] Reading the Hitler passage today, however, makes it difficult to accept this idea of an apathetic Guggenheim disengaged from the menace of fascism, both as a Jew, and as a supporter of the internationalism of modernism, for whom the idea of a nation-state defined by race or religion was anathema.

With this history in mind, the recontextualization of non-Western objects in her home—seeing the sleek geometry of Léger's figures emerge from the

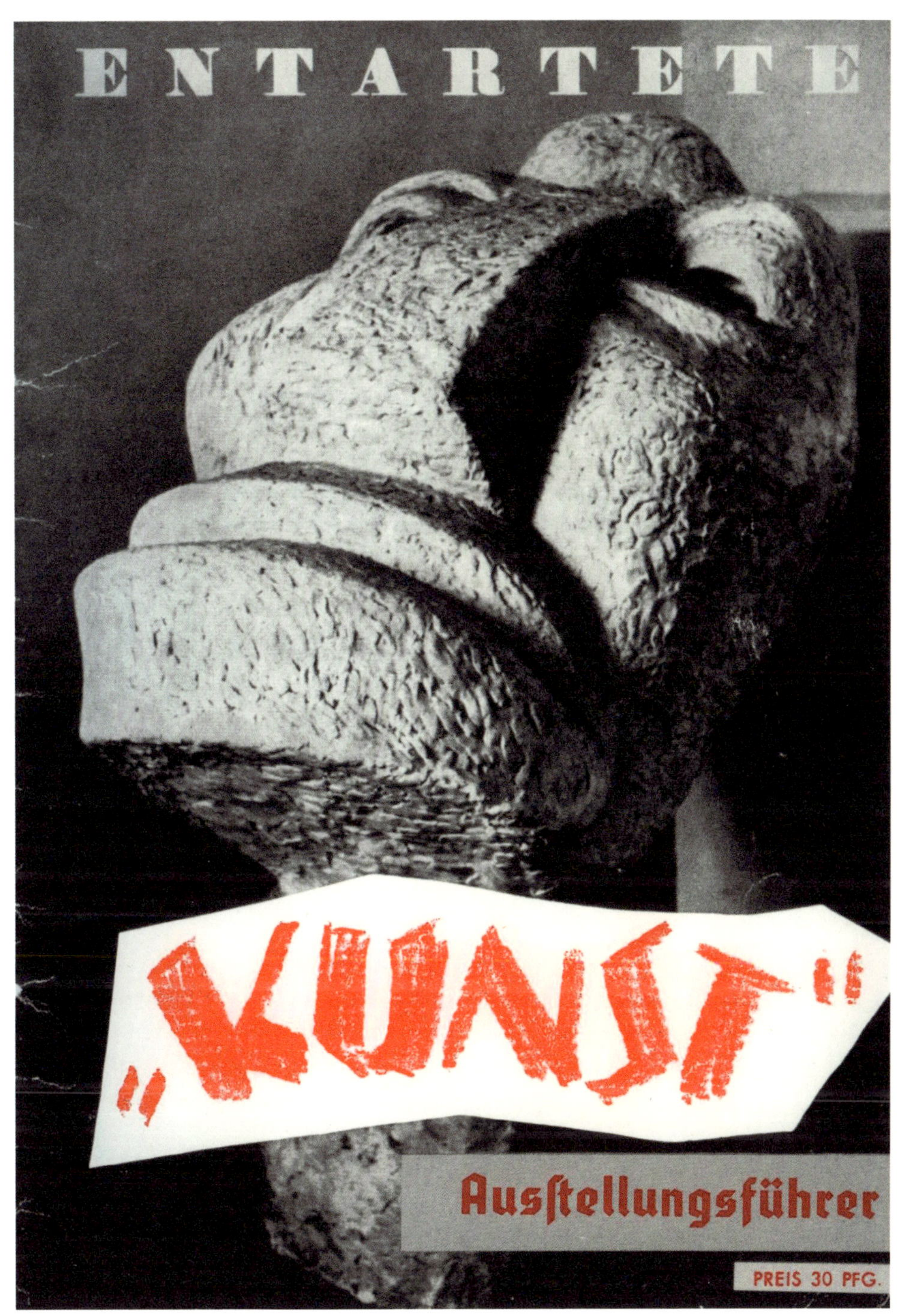

Fig. 12   Cover of the exhibition catalogue
for *Degenerate Art* (*Entartete Kunst
Ausstellungsführer*), Munich, 1937. Image: Otto
Freundlich, *The New Man* (*Der neue Mensch*),
1912. Plaster cast, location unknown

foundations of the Senufo helmet mask, for example—had a different, potentially antifascist, resonance in the post–World War II period (fig. 8). It is worth remembering that her collection had been deemed too "degenerate" by city officials in Turin, where an offer to show it was withdrawn in 1948.[37] Today, however, these African, Oceanic, and pre-Columbian objects will likely find viewers in Venice who will see them as appropriated emblems for Guggenheim's cosmopolitanism, and ultimately, a vestige of a colonialist era.[38] Her fascination with modernist primitivism was an expression of her elite worldview. Her freewheeling, experimental installations spoke uncritically about a dominant culture borrowing from another, an extension of her globe-trotting. It was one of her many socioeconomic privileges to migrate at will with an international cast of objects moving with her, except, of course, for at least one terrifying experience when she apparently escaped a roundup of Jews in Marseille. In some cases, however, these juxtapositions may still have the potential to stir twenty-first-century viewers, as the Surrealists had once hoped, to consider the relativity of their own cultural values. The language that Ernst, Matta, or Picasso used is just as coded and context-specific as the one used by a Guinean artist or a New Ireland carver and, depending on their viewers' life experiences, can be just as productively disorienting. In this framework the potential impact of these objects depends on the viewer's recognition of their radical independence from the works of modernists who appropriated from them. The histories written about modernist primitivism can no longer support false claims for universality that have made over the rest of the world in the self-image of the West. Viewers who see this collection as only a fashionable capsule of Guggenheim's taste are certain to remain within this Eurocentric hall of mirrors.

The following essay relies on the research of Peggy Guggenheim's collection, when it was catalogued by the Museo delle Culture Lugano, for a 2008 exhibition at the Galleria Gottardo, Lugano, and the Fondazione Antonio Mazzotta, Milan. This essay is a more expansive treatment of ideas from my "Africa and Oceania in Venice," in Karole P.B. Vail with Vivien Greene, eds., *Peggy Guggenheim: The Last Dogaressa* (Venice: Solomon R. Guggenheim Foundation, 2019), pp. 185–97. For one proposed list of the original nucleus of objects, see Alessia Borellini, "Peggy's Ethnopassion," in Francesco Paolo Campione, ed., *Ethnopassion: Peggy Guggenheim's Ethnic Art Collection*, exh. cat. (Milan: Mazzotta, 2008), p. 39.

1   Peggy Guggenheim, *Out of This Century: Confessions of an Art Addict* (New York: Universe Books; London: André Deutsch, 1979), p. 363. *Out of This Century: The Informal Memoirs of Peggy Guggenheim* was first published by The Dial Press, New York, in 1946.

2   Ibid., p. 363.

3   "Another museum Max adored was the Museum of the American Indian, the Heye Foundation, where Breton took us. It had the best collection of British Columbian, Alaskan, Pre-Columbian, South Sea, Indian and Mayan art." Ibid., p. 251. George Gustav Heye's collection, displayed at the Museum of the American Indian on West 155th Street and Broadway in Washington Heights, would later serve as the foundation for today's Smithsonian National Museum of the American Indian. Julius Carlebach's inventory was largely filled with objects deaccessioned by Heye.

4   Like my fellow contributors to this volume, I use the term "non-Western" elsewhere in this essay with hesitation, knowing that the category is deeply flawed, since it aggressively yokes vast areas of the world into opposition with others. The binary of West and non-West, however, created a series of other historical and conceptual oppositions that Peggy Guggenheim and the artists/thinkers in her circle used to map their own values onto the diverse array of objects we study in the present volume. Those values, as I hope our essays will suggest, are part of a much larger ongoing critical focus. See Christa Clarke, n. 2 in the present volume, p. 43. For a brief discussion of the distinction between "art" and "artifact" see Fanny Wonu Veys in the present volume, p. 46.

5   Philip Rylands, director emeritus of the Peggy Guggenheim Collection, referred to this collection in similar terms: "Peggy's activity as a dealer and collector waned in the 1960s ... [she] was incredulous of the inflated monetary values for art. To compensate, she assembled a small collection of African, Oceanic and Pre-Columbian art." Philip Rylands, "A Genesis of a Museum," *Peggy Guggenheim: A Collection in Venice*, exh. cat.(New York: Solomon R. Guggenheim Foundation; Perth: Art Gallery of Western Australia, 2010), p. 28.

6   André Salmon, "L'Art nègre" (1920), in *Propos d'atelier* (1922), pp. 115–33. This passage is cited in Jack Flam and Miriam Deutch, eds., *Primitivism and Twentieth-Century Art: A Documentary History* (Berkeley: University of California Press, 2003), p. 134.

7   Henri Matisse recounted the fifty francs price to Pierre Courthion in 1941. See Flam and Deutch, *Primitivism and Twentieth-Century Art*, p. 31.

8   In Italy, Guggenheim worked with the Milanese specialist and artist Franco Monti and the gallerist Paolo Barozzi. See Paolo Barozzi, *Con Peggy Guggenheim: Tra storia e memoria* (Milan: Christian Marinotti Edizioni, 2001), pp. 177–80.

9   While "primitive" is a pejorative, fundamentally flawed term—given the conceptual complexities of the objects to which that adjective was condescendingly attached—the term "modernist primitivism" is useful, since it refers to an episode within the history of Western culture.

10   Excerpt from André Malraux, *La Tête d'obsidienne* (Paris: Gallimard, 1974), pp. 17–19. The 1937 conversation between André Malraux and Pablo Picasso can be found in Flam and Deutch, *Primitivism and Twentieth-Century Art*, p. 33.

11   Writing in 1915, Carl Einstein recognized that "the earlier verdict on the Negro and his art applied more to the judge than the judged." Carl Einstein, *Negerplastik* [1915]. Translated as "Negro Sculpture" by Charles W. Haxthausen and Sebastian Zeidler, *October* 107 (Winter 2004), pp. 122–38.

12   James Johnson Sweeney, *African Negro Art*, exh. cat. (New York: Museum of Modern Art, 1935), pp. 11, 21. Cited by Kate Ezra, "Collecting African Art at New York's Museum of Primitive Art," in Kathleen Bickford Berzock and Christa Clarke, eds., *Representing Africa in American Art Museums: A Century of Collecting and Display* (Seattle: University of Washington Press, 2011), p. 125.

13   Henry Moore, "Primitive Art," *The Listener* (April 24, 1941). See Flam and Deutch, *Primitivism and Twentieth-Century Art*, p. 270.

14   A key text in the critical literature, inspired by the Museum of Modern Art exhibition *"Primitivism" in 20th Century Art: Affinity of the Tribal and the Modern*, remains Hal Foster's essay "'The Primitive' Unconscious of Modern Art," published in *October* 34 (Fall 1985), pp. 45–70. As Foster writes: "Primitivism, then, not only absorbs the potential disruption of the tribal objects into Western forms, ideas, and commodities, it also symptomatically managed the ideological nightmare of great art inspired by spoils," p. 61.

15   Moore, "Primitive Art," pp. 598–99, see Flam and Deutch, *Primitivism and Twentieth-Century Art*, p. 270.

16   See Alessandra Cardelli Antinore's entry on the Dogon sculpture (catalogue no. 9) in Campione, *Ethnopassion*, pp. 90–93. For more on Dogon figurative sculpture, see Kate Ezra, *Art of the Dogon: Selections from the Lester Wunderman Collection*, exh. cat. (New York: The Metropolitan Museum of Art), 1988.

17   Guggenheim's 1955 published remarks on the Picasso painting continue in this universalizing vein. She went on to describe her realization of the work's gendered themes: "Then the boat became only an excuse—it lost all its importance and the painting became changed completely in my eyes. This added to its fascination; I no longer saw it as a humoristic painting...but as a terrifically profound study of the weaker sex. These poor little girls pretending to enjoy their little boat were in reality merely making a gesture. What they were really preoccupied with was their future, their destiny as women...." "Peggy Guggenheim Chooses Picasso's 'Girls by the Seashore,'" 1955 press clipping, Peggy Guggenheim Scrapbook, 1951–1957, Peggy Guggenheim Foundation Papers, M0002. Solomon R. Guggenheim Foundation, New York. I am grateful to Gražina Subelytė for sharing this source with me.

18   It is doubtful that Guggenheim arranged these ensembles with an art-historical motivation, to approximate the sculpture from which Picasso had appropriated. Guggenheim's installations did not present Dogon art as a source for Picasso; the parallels she makes are retroactive. Although Dogon art was not especially well known in France until the Dakar-Djibouti mission of 1931–33, it was represented in the Musée d'Ethnographie du Trocadéro collections. One standing figure was photographed by the Czech Cubist Josef Čapek as early as 1909. See William Rubin, ed., *"Primitivism" in 20th Century Art: Affinity of the Tribal and the Modern*, exh. cat. (New York: Museum of Modern Art, 1984), p. 271.

19   Rubin, *"Primitivism" in 20th Century Art*, p. 326. The Baga *D'mba* mask now in the Musée Picasso is reproduced by Rubin, p. 327.

20   The Baga mask from Nelson A. Rockefeller's collection is illustrated as catalogue no. 305 in Robert Goldwater et al., *Arts of Oceania, Africa and the Americas from the Museum of Primitive Art* (New York: The Metropolitan Museum of Art, 1969), n.p. For the three Senufo zoomorphic helmet masks similar to the one in Guggenheim's collection, see Robert Goldwater, *The Sculpture of Three Tribes: Senufo, Baga, Dogon*, exh. cat. (New York: The Museum of Primitive Art, 1959), catalogue nos. 3, 4, and 6. For instructive comparisons with the motivations and strategies of other collectors of African art, see Berzock and Clarke, *Representing Africa in American Art Museums*.

21   The exhibition was held November 3–December 8, 1914, organized by Marius de Zayas, with an installation designed by Edward Steichen. It featured eighteen objects from the Côte d'Ivoire and Gabon. At the time, African, Oceanic, and pre-Columbian objects could be found in U.S. museums, but they were largely restricted to natural history or ethnographic displays.

22   Helen and Leon Fleischman took her to the gallery, apparently in the autumn of 1920, when Guggenheim was working at the Sunwise Turn Bookshop in New York. Guggenheim, *Out of This Century*, p. 24.

23   Alfred Stieglitz, *Detail: Picasso-Braque Exhibition*, January 1915. For a reproduction and discussion, see Wendy A. Grossman, *Man Ray, African Art and the Modernist Lens* (Minneapolis: University of Minnesota Press, 2010), p. 15. The photograph depicts Picasso's *Bottle and Wine Glass on a Table* (*Bouteille et verre sur un guéridon*), 1912, and a wasp's nest belonging to the artist Emil Zoler.

24   Peter Stepan, *Picasso's Collection of African & Oceanic Art: Masters of Metamorphosis* (Munich: Prestel, 2006).

25   André Breton, "Océanie" (1948) in *La Clé des Champs*, Paris 1970. pp. 275–81. Cited by Elizabeth Cowling, "'L'Oeil Sauvage': Oceanic Art and the Surrealists," in Suzanne Greub, ed., *Art of Northwest New Guinea: From Geelvink Bay, Humboldt Bay, and Lake Sentani* (New York: Rizzoli, 1992), p. 177.

26   Ibid. For more on the *Truth About the Colonies* protest of the 1931 *Colonial Exhibition* in Paris, see Janine Mileaf, "Body to Politics: Surrealist Exhibition of the Tribal and the Modern at the Anti-Imperialist Exhibition and the Galerie Charles Ratton," *RES: Anthropology and Aesthetics*, no. 40 (Autumn 2001), pp. 239–55. André Breton and Paul Éluard were obliged to sell their non-Western collections (almost half of which were Oceanic) during the financial crisis; the Breton-Éluard sale at Drouot in July 1931 effectively provided a commercial association between Surrealism and this market.

27   The concept of *détournement* is treated in Breton's 1936 essay "Crisis of the Object." See André Breton, "Crise de l'objet," *Cahiers d'art* (May 1936), *Le Surréalisme et la peinture* (Paris: Gallimard, 1965).

28   Philippe Peltier gives a more complete list of Oceanic works displayed in the 1936 Charles Ratton exhibition. Philippe Peltier, "From Oceania," in Rubin, *"Primitivism" in 20th Century Art*, p. 122, n. 81. That the exhibition focused on Oceania and the Americas, rather than on African art, is a revealing sign of a shift in the 1930s.

29   Guggenheim's Art of This Century museum/gallery featured *Natural, Insane, Surrealist Art* (Dec. 1–31, 1943), which combined work by Alexander Calder, Max Ernst, Paul Klee, and André Masson alongside driftwood, petrified tree roots, bones, skeletons, and drawings by people with mental illnesses.

30   The *malangan* funerary carving from New Ireland, an island in Papua New Guinea, also appears in a photograph of Guggenheim and Ernst, taken by Herman Landshoff in their New York home in 1942, depicting the couple on either side of Ernst's *Attirement of the Bride* (*La Toilette de la mariée*), 1940, which Ernst would gift to Guggenheim. The *malangan* figure is visible just over Ernst's shoulder. That sculpture is also reproduced in color in Rubin, *"Primitivism" in 20th Century Art*, pp. 516–17, where it is identified as "Collection Dorothea Tanning, New York. Formerly Collection Max Ernst." While the geographical origins of Ernst's collection were diverse, Papua New Guinea was a major reference for his highly personal primitivist mythmaking. The character "Papou," the archetype of a tribal man with whom Ernst identified himself in *Beyond Painting*, first published in 1938, comes from the first part of the French designation Papouasie Nouvelle Guinée. See Evan Maurer, "Dada and Surrealism," in Rubin, *"Primitivism" in 20th Century Art*, p. 553.

31   Christian Zervos, "Introduction," in *Cahiers d'art* 7–8 (1927), p. 229. Cited by Peltier, "From Oceania," p. 111. Zervos devoted an entire issue of *Cahiers d'art* (March–April 1929) to Oceanic art, where he promoted the connections between its visionary imagination and the theme of modern European art.

32   Guggenheim purchased the Matta (Roberto Sebastián Matta Echaurren) from a Venice gallery in 1953, so it provides an even more recent coordinate to understand her predilection for the *malangan* figure. Writing in the 1960s, Nicolas and Elena Calas recognized the Oceanic connection to this painting early on, noting how *The Un-Nominator Renominated* "belongs to a series of works in which he reinterprets Futurism in terms of imagistic concretions that have their origin in the sculpture of the South Pacific." Nicolas and Elena Calas, *The Peggy Guggenheim Collection of Modern Art* (New York: H.N. Abrams, 1966), p. 109. Rubin reports seeing several New Ireland carvings in Matta's house. Rubin, "Preface," *"Primitivism" in 20th Century Art*, p. ix. His introduction to the catalogue notably opens with reproductions of Matta's *A Grave Situation*, 1946, and a *malangan* figure from New Ireland, pp. 2–3.

33   From an Adolf Hitler speech given at the sixth NSDAP conference, Nuremberg, September 5, 1934. Cited in Stephanie Barron, ed., *"Degenerate Art": The Fate of the Avant-Garde in Nazi Germany*, exh. cat. (Los Angeles: Los Angeles County Museum of Art, 1991), p. 57.

34   Peggy Guggenheim, ed., *Art of This Century: Objects, Drawings, Photographs, Paintings, Sculpture, Collages 1910–1942* (New York: Art Aid Corporation, 1942), p. 7. Hitler's text comes in the middle of two excerpts from Guggenheim's mentor Herbert Read, who attributed the failure of fascist and Nazi regimes to "inspire a great art" to an absence of freedom. Hitler's speech was originally published as "Der Führer eröffnet die Grosse Deutsche Kunstausstellung 1937" in *Die Kunst im Dritten Reich I* (nos. 7–8), Munich (July–August 1937), pp. 47–61. Excerpts in English can be found in Charles Harrison and Paul Wood, eds. *Art in Theory, 1900–2000: An Anthology of Changing Ideas* (Malden, Mass.: Blackwell Publishing, 2003), pp. 439–41. Guggenheim may have been encouraged to add the Hitler text by one of the people she named in her signed foreword. For more on Breton's input, for example, see Guggenheim, *Out of This Century*, pp. 262–63.

35   Guggenheim, *Out of This Century*, p. 218. Guggenheim was describing her April 9, 1940, purchase from Léger.

36   This perception may have to do with Guggenheim's tone. Earlier when Guggenheim was contemplating a modern art museum in London, she laconically wrote to her friend, "I hope you will come back and see it all before Mr. Hitler drops bombs on it." The April 1939 letter to Emily Coleman is cited by Susan Davidson, "Focusing an Instinct: The Collecting of Peggy Guggenheim," in Susan Davidson and Philip Rylands, eds., *Peggy Guggenheim & Frederick Kiesler: The Story of Art of This Century* (New York: Solomon R. Guggenheim Foundation, 2004), p. 57.

37   The 1948 Turin episode is recounted in Mary V. Dearborn, *Mistress of Modernism* (New York: Houghton Mifflin, 2004), p. 269. In Guggenheim's own telling, she characterized the rescinded invitation less politically; it was that officials in Turin found her collection too "modern." Guggenheim, *Out of This Century*, p. 330.

38   Francesco Paolo Campione sees the decontextualization of these objects in Venice as "idealizing the worldview of the values of an élite...as time passes, they set a trend and become the fashion." Campione, "The Paradigm of Complexity: An Introduction to the Values of The Peggy Guggenheim Collection of Ethnic Art" in Campione, *Ethnopassion*, p. 23.

"Fantastic Artifacts"

Peggy Guggenheim
and
African Art at
Mid-Century

Christa Clarke

In April 1959, Peggy Guggenheim returned to New York for the first time in more than a decade since the close of her 57th Street museum/gallery, Art of This Century, and subsequent relocation to Venice. After the long absence, she recalled being "thunderstruck" by the changes in the contemporary art world, which she saw now as "an enormous business venture" with collectors buying more for investment than appreciation. Frustrated by the economically driven art market and finding prices for paintings prohibitively expensive, Guggenheim shifted her attentions to a new arena of collecting:

> I could not afford to buy anything that I wanted, so I turned to another field...I began buying pre-Columbian and primitive art. In the next few weeks I found myself the proud possessor of 12 fantastic artifacts, consisting of masks and sculptures from New Guinea, the Belgian Congo, the French Sudan, Peru, Brazil, Mexico and New Ireland.[1]

The "fantastic artifacts" that Guggenheim purchased in 1959 became the nucleus of her non-Western art collection, which she continued to build upon throughout the 1960s.[2] The collection eventually numbered some fifty works, a disparate group of objects from varied cultures throughout the world, spanning more than a millennium in their creation. Sculpture from Africa, however, constitutes the majority, an emphasis that reflects both its increasing popularity and greater availability in the West beginning in the 1950s. Guggenheim's selections were broadly informed by her modernist sensibilities and represent genres belonging to the early canon of African art established in the West as well as those newly introduced to the market. Acquired during an era of rapid decolonization, their migratory journeys from Africa to Venice were fueled by both Western taste and desire as well as social and political changes on the continent at mid-century.[3]

Guggenheim's later-in-life collecting of art from Africa, along with that of Oceania and the indigenous Americas, is not entirely surprising given her longtime patronage of European and U.S. modernism. As is generally known, beginning in the first decades of the twentieth century, many proponents of modern art found interest and inspiration in works from diverse non-Western cultures—collectively, and erroneously, labeled as "primitive" art.[4] Guggenheim moved in the same circles as these early artists and patrons and had ample opportunity to become acquainted with such objects in the decades preceding her decision to collect. Indeed, in her memoir, she offered a description of what may be her earliest encounter with African art in 1938—one indicative of not only modernism's fashionable (not to say deviant) appropriation of African art but also Guggenheim's turbulent love life. Recalling an affair with Roland Penrose, the English promoter and collector of Surrealism, Guggenheim observed:

> He had one eccentricity: when he slept with women he tied up their wrists with anything that was handy. Once he used my belt but another time in his house he brought out a pair of ivory bracelets from the Sudan. They were attached with the chain and Penrose had a key to lock them. It was extremely uncomfortable to spend the night this way, but if you spent it with Penrose it was the only way.[5]

From Guggenheim's memoir, we also know that she was well-acquainted with Nancy Cunard, whose book *Negro Anthology*, published in 1934, was amply illustrated with examples of African art from private and public collections (including Cunard's own trademark African ivory bracelets). And that, by the early 1940s, she was familiar with the collections of Walter and Louise Arensberg and of Helena Rubinstein, who collected African art as an extension of their focus on Western modernism. Guggenheim was famously an early patron and promoter of Jackson Pollock, whose fascination with myth and ritual was stimulated by African art.[6] And she considered James Johnson Sweeney, organizer of the Museum of Modern Art's highly influential 1935 exhibition *African Negro Sculpture*, a mentor. Despite these connections, non-Western art hardly merits a mention until Guggenheim's relationship with the Surrealist artist Max Ernst, who began actively acquiring pre-Columbian, Oceanic, and especially Native American works during their brief marriage in the early 1940s. Even at that time, Guggenheim was less taken with Ernst's collection than she was concerned about his spending all his income— and then some—surrendering to the near-daily temptations offered by his New York dealer Julius Carlebach.

It would be almost two decades before Guggenheim shifted her own attentions to this arena of collecting during her New York visit, turning then to "the dangerous little Mr. Carlebach, who…now had a magnificent gallery on Madison Avenue. His prices had doubled but at least they were still possible."[7] Carlebach was originally from Lübeck, Germany, where he grew up frequenting the ethnology galleries of a local museum.[8] Arriving in New York in 1937, he opened his first gallery two years later with his wife, Josefa, after purchasing a group of Pacific Islands works from a diamond merchant for eight dollars, the sale of which he used to launch his fledgling business. Fast-forward twenty years and Carlebach was a well-established dealer, with a recent move from a Third Avenue shop to a stylish new gallery that warranted the attention of *The New York Times* art critic Rita Reif. "Primitive art is moving up in the world," Reif observed in a profile on the gallery that appeared in April 1959. "Now becoming well entrenched in fashionable decorating schemes, it recently made a formidable appearance on Madison Avenue."[9] Reif went on to describe the gallery—designed by Ladislav Rado, a protégé of Bauhaus architect Walter Gropius—as "one of the most sophisticated backdrops in the city," so much so that it was often mistaken for a museum. Inset shelves with recessed lighting showcased striking silhouettes of African sculpture (and other non-Western works) and, in the center, a gravel pool presented larger freestanding works to theatrical effect. It is certainly tempting to speculate that this article—published the same month as Guggenheim's first purchases—prompted her visit to the gallery.

Regardless, if Guggenheim was a pioneer in her patronage of European and American contemporary art and artists, her turn to African art was squarely in the mainstream. By the 1950s, New York had become the epicenter of the African art market, with several galleries specializing in "primitive" art established by Jewish émigrés who had relocated to New York with the advent of World War II.[10] Carlebach was among those dealers who played an instrumental role in the formation of major private collections in the United States, which increasingly focused on African art, and also supplied works to U.S. art museums, where African art was gaining entrée at mid-century, though typically as part of a larger department of "primitive" art.[11] In 1957, non-Western art gained a kind of institutional validation with the opening of the Museum of Primitive Art on West 54th Street, just across from the Museum of Modern Art (MoMA). The museum was founded by collector Nelson A. Rockefeller and René d'Harnoncourt, then director of MoMA. Its director, Robert Goldwater, was one of the first American art historians to turn his attention to African art, helping establish it as a subject of serious study and mounting an influential series of exhibitions that sought to define artistic styles of individual African cultures (fig. 13).[12]

African art was also gaining popular attention throughout the 1950s. As Carlebach observed in 1959, "interest in primitive art has gone beyond a mere handful of collectors to embrace the rich and poor alike," adding that it was both fashionable in interior décor and available at affordable prices.[13] Indeed, just six months prior, a *New York Times* magazine feature, "Living with Sculpture," showcased the non-Western collection of *Life* photographer Eliot Elisofon on display in his New York apartment. Taking special note of the current fascination with African art, the article highlighted the home decorating potential of masks and figural sculptures while accompanying photographs offered "many ideas for dramatic display" on pedestals and wall shelves and as table accessories. "Today, good sculpture is available at very reasonable prices," readers were advised, a point illustrated with examples of "typical inexpensive pieces" of non-Western art available for sale, all under one-hundred dollars; many were African sculpture from Carlebach's gallery.[14] Carlebach's inventory reached an even wider public through its prominent positioning in the 1958 romantic comedy *Bell, Book and*

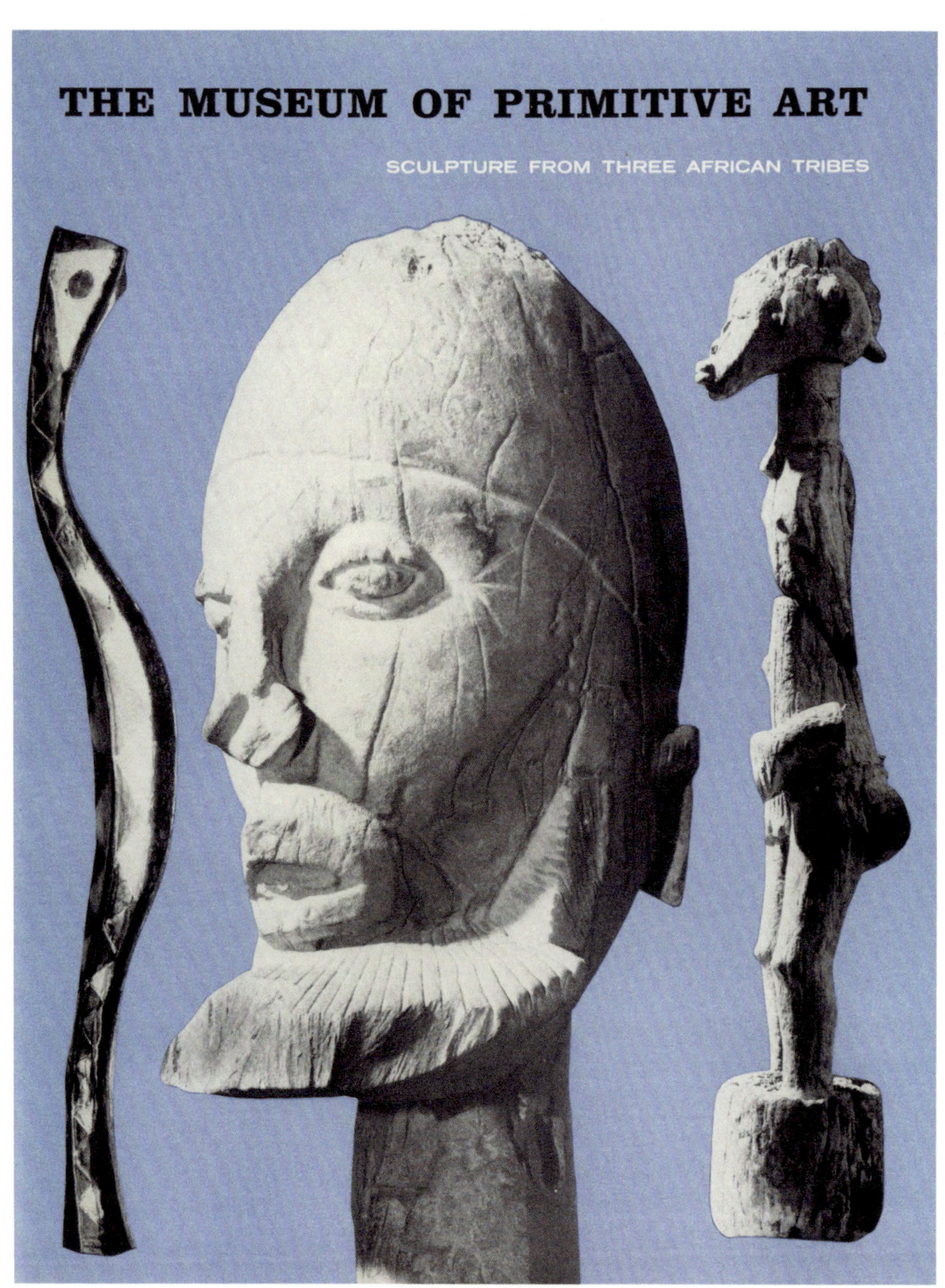

Fig. 13   Cover of the exhibition catalogue for
*Sculpture from Three African Tribes: Senufo, Baga,
Dogon*, New York, Museum of Primitive Art, 1959

Candle, starring James Stewart and Kim Novak (and for which Elisofon served as color consultant). The masks and figures that Carlebach provided were not merely set dressing but integral to Novak's character, a modern-day witch who owns a "primitive" art gallery in bohemian Greenwich Village (fig. 14).[15] Art historian Susan Vogel has commented on how the movie expressed "mid-century pop-culture associations of African art with sex, magic, bongo drums and radical avant gardes"—a sensibility that the adventurous Guggenheim surely embraced in seeking a new and more affordable category of collecting.[16]

Guggenheim continued to build her collection after her return to Venice, acquiring works throughout the 1960s, mostly in Italy. She patronized Franco Monti, a sculptor with a gallery in Milan, who was among a new wave of exploratory dealers. Monti traveled extensively in West Africa from the mid-1950s onward, spending several months of each year collecting works for his gallery.[17] Monti built his reputation as an expert by mounting exhibitions and authoring publications on African art and selling works to both private collectors and museums. His field research seems to have fostered a more sensitive cultural understanding than typical of the era: in a published interview, for example, he rejected the term "primitive" and recommended referencing specific cultures rather than using the all-encompassing label of "African."[18] Guggenheim also bought from Paolo Barozzi, who showed "primitive" art in Venice thanks to Guggenheim's connections and encouragement. Assisted by Monti, Barozzi described how, in the early 1960s, he turned an empty office owned by his father "into a magnificent gallery where I could show Dogon, Baule and Bamana sculptures...the night of the opening there was a great crowd, anyone who counted in Venice was there."[19] Among them was Guggenheim, who became one of Barozzi's first patrons, purchasing a few works that evening.

The African art collection that Guggenheim formed is a window onto Western taste and the art market in the 1950s and '60s. The twenty extant works reflect prevailing aesthetic preferences for sculpture from West and Central Africa, spanning the present-day countries of Guinea, Mali, Côte d'Ivoire, Nigeria, Gabon, the Democratic Republic of the Congo, and Angola. They include types of objects celebrated (and collected) early on by Western modernist artists, such as the striking Baga *D'mba* headdress from Guinea and the Kota reliquary guardian PLS. 13, 16 figure from Gabon. These iconic works were likely among Guggenheim's first purchases and, in fact, both genres feature prominently among the works of African art from Carlebach's gallery in *Bell, Book and Candle*. There are a few examples of Dogon sculpture from Mali, which were the focus of French ethnographic mis- PLS. 1–3 sions in the 1930s and had captured the attention of Surrealist writers and artists.[20] Guggenheim's collection has a particular concentration of objects attributed to Senufo artists from the area where Burkina Faso, Côte d'Ivoire, and Mali meet; works PLS. 6–12 from this region, plentiful on the market beginning in the 1950s, gained prominence through the influential exhibition *Senufo Sculpture from West Africa* at the Museum of Primitive Art in 1963 (fig. 15).[21] Other works, like the Salampasu mask and the PLS. 20, 17–18 pair of Nkanu painted panels, both from the Democratic Republic of the Congo, are types of objects not commonly seen in Western collections until the second half of the century.

Nearly all of the works in Guggenheim's collection were created during the first half of the twentieth century, making them roughly contemporaneous with her Western modern art. This period also coincided with the cultural ruptures of the colonial era, which impacted their creation, use, and, ultimately, their path to market. Some of them embody traditions that had fallen out of use earlier in the twentieth century, such as the metal-sheathed figure used by Kota PL. 16 families in Gabon to guard the relics of their ancestors, a religious practice abandoned as a result of both conversions to Christianity and efforts of the French colonial government.[22] Others may have been commissioned for local use but then deemed unacceptable by the patron on artistic, technical, or even spiritual grounds, as may have been the case with the *Egungun* headdress attributed to the atelier of Oniyide Adugbologe. This family-based workshop of Yoruba sculptors in Abeokuta, Nigeria, began selling such rejected works to local traders by

39

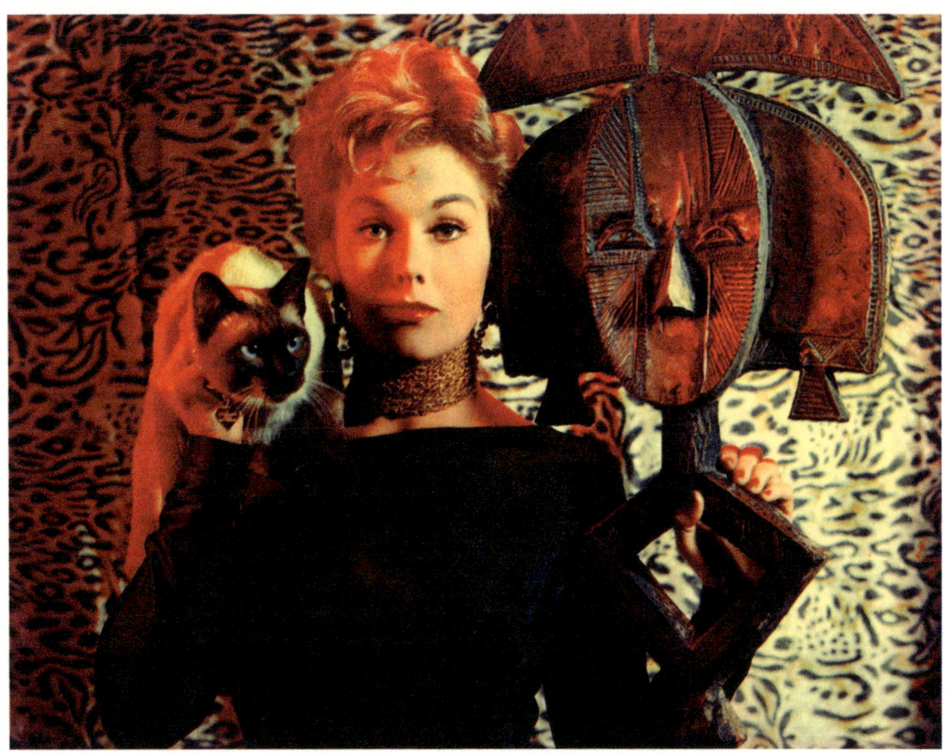

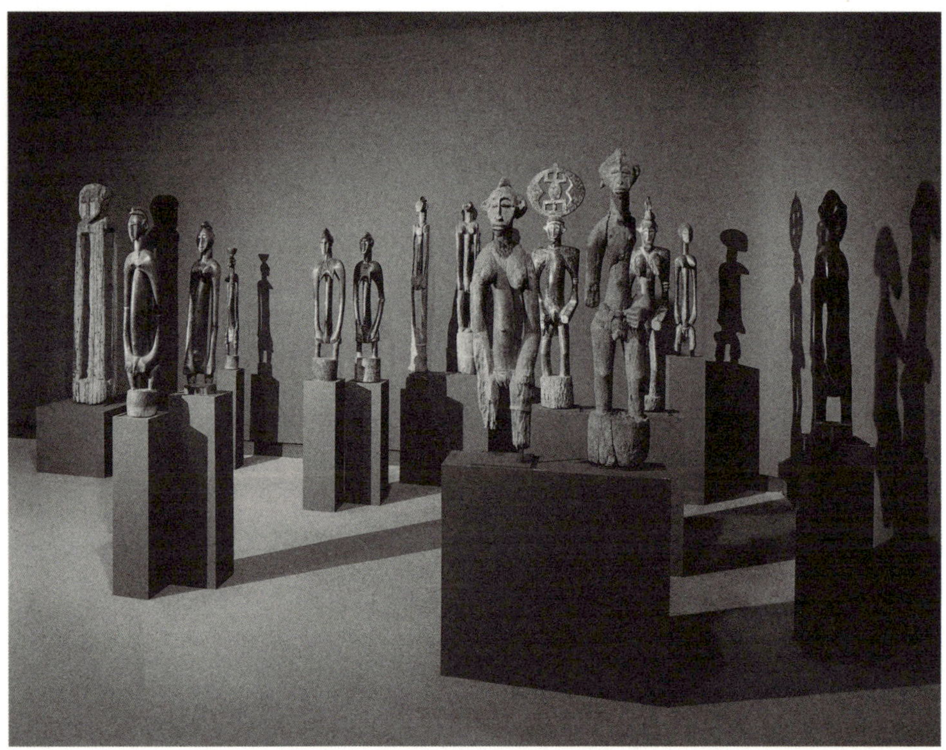

Fig. 14   Kim Novak with a reliquary guardian figure by an unrecorded Kota artist, Gabon, in a publicity photograph for *Bell, Book and Candle*, 1958

Fig. 15   Installation view, Museum of Primitive Art, *Senufo Sculpture from West Africa*, February 20 – May 5, 1963. The gallery here features numerous examples of a sculptural genre known as *poro piibele*, used in funerary rituals. Guggenheim acquired at least three such works. Photo: The Museum of Primitive Art Records, The Department of the Arts of Africa, Oceania, and the Americas, The Metropolitan Museum of Art, New York the first decades of the twentieth century, eventually shifting from indigenous production to commodity carving for outside markets at mid-century.[23] Many more works in Guggenheim's collection, however, were likely casualties of recent iconoclastic movements. Among Senufo communities in northern and central Côte d'Ivoire, for example, masks and figurative sculpture were abandoned or destroyed by followers of Massa, a movement intended to restore social order after the French ended forced labor in 1946.[24] In Baga communities in Guinea, where the French colonial government had already restricted the performance of masquerades earlier in the twentieth century, conversion efforts on the part of two Muslim missionaries in the mid-1950s led to the near depletion of ritual objects like the majestic *D'mba* headdresses.[25]

Such social changes set in motion an exodus of art from certain regions of Africa, as an international network of dealers and collectors capitalized on the opportunities they created. Paris-based dealer Hélène Leloup described collecting visits to Côte d'Ivoire, Mali, and Guinea during this period, where she amassed large quantities of sculpture either being discarded or offered for sale, often under conditions characterized by unequal power dynamics (fig. 16).[26] The rapidly transforming political landscape further expanded the market for African art. Mid-century ushered in the era of decolonization, with Ghana becoming the first African nation to declare independence, in 1957. In 1960 alone—heralded as the "Year of Africa"—seventeen African territories gained freedom from their European colonizers, bringing the total to twenty-six independent nations. In turn, new commercial networks and the loosening of colonial export controls increased the supply of African art to Europe and the United States.[27] Thousands of objects are believed to have left Africa from the late 1950s through the '60s, through a combination of circumstances, including discarded cultural traditions, but also economic opportunity and, of course, outright theft.[28]

Human interactions were at the heart of the art trade in Africa. In the wake of independence movements, African dealers emerged as a market force, alongside the foreigners who were already traveling to the continent to collect, supplying objects to gallery owners and private collectors in Europe and the United States. These dealers established expanded channels of distribution from rural villages to new urban centers in Africa—especially Dakar (Senegal), Bamako (Mali), Abidjan (Côte d'Ivoire), Lagos (Nigeria), and Kinshasa (Democratic Republic of the Congo)—then on to international buyers, such as Carlebach.[29] Many European dealers, like Monti, built their reputations in the art world through field collecting in this era. In contrast, their African counterparts were dismissively termed "runners" and their names typically dissociated from the objects they supplied.[30] Whatever the source, most Western collectors remained distant from, and ignorant of, not only the meanings and contexts of the works they acquired, but also the circumstances and motivating factors underlying their circulation. As a collector, Guggenheim was no different: the African sculpture she placed in dialogue with Western modernist works remained far removed geographically as well as conceptually from its origins.[31]

Walking through the Palazzo Venier dei Leoni today, one could easily assume that the African sculpture on display was acquired alongside Guggenheim's pioneering collection of Western modernism—and in the same spirit of those artists, who sought inspiration in art from Africa and elsewhere in the first decades of the twentieth century. Instead, Guggenheim's African collection reveals a lesser known, and perhaps more interesting, chapter in the history of African art collecting, one involving the complex history of decolonization, evolving commercial networks, and the emergence of an expanded taste for the "primitive" manifested in new museums, mid-century interior décor, and even in Hollywood.

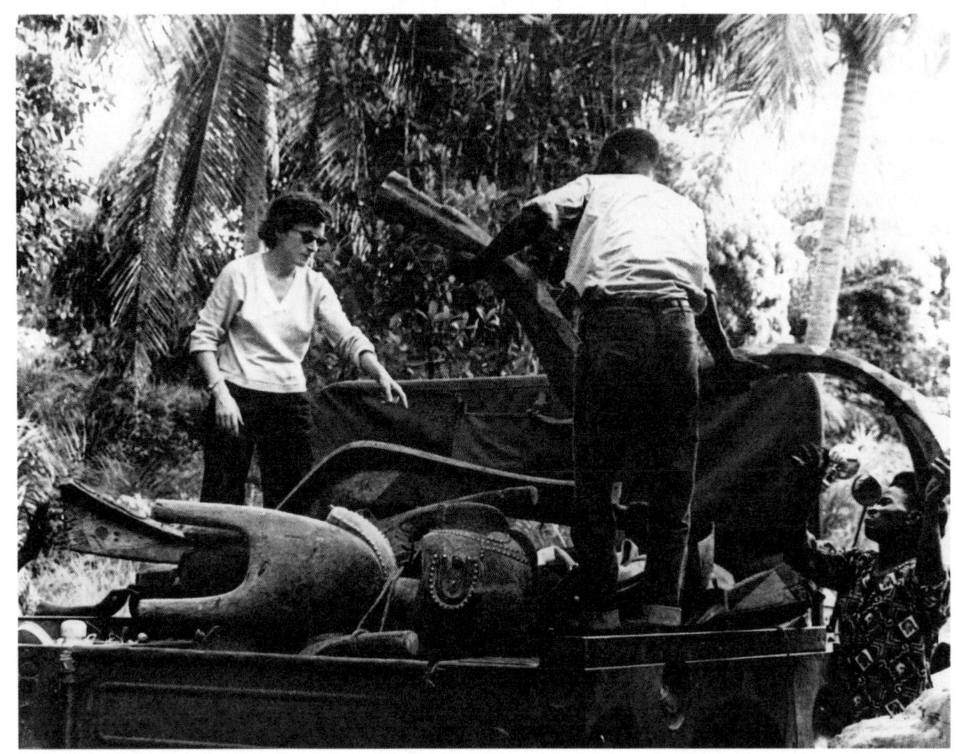

Fig. 16   Dealer Hélène Leloup in Guinea loading
Baga sculptures, including a *D'mba* headdress,
onto the back of a truck, ca. 1956

1   Peggy Guggenheim, *Out of This Century: Confessions of an Art Addict* (New York: Universe Books; London: André Deutsch, 1979), pp. 362–63. Peggy Guggenheim's non-Western art collection was the focus of a 2008 exhibition at the Galleria Gottardo, Lugano, and the Fondazione Antonio Mazzotta, Milan, and an accompanying publication. See Francesco Paolo Campione, ed., *Ethnopassion: Peggy Guggenheim's Ethnic Art Collection*, exh. cat. (Milan: Mazzotta, 2008). This essay draws upon research in that publication by the essayists and the authors of the individual object entries.

2   The term "non-Western" art is a problematic one, uniting works from unrelated cultures that are geographically and chronologically far-flung. As Cecelia Klein notes, it is also one that is tied to and reinforces "a conceptual dichotomy between the civilized and the primitive and a host of other oppositions that rank peoples within a hierarchy of values privileging one category over the others." See Cecelia F. Klein, "Not Like Us and All the Same: Pre-Columbian Art History and the Construction of the Nonwest," *RES: Anthropology and Aesthetics*, no. 42 (Autumn, 2002), p. 131. Although I employ the term "non-Western" art on occasion throughout this essay, I do so as imperfect shorthand and with full understanding of its fictive nature and prejudicial associations.

3   Christraud Geary and Stephanie Xatart, eds., *Material Journeys: Collecting African and Oceanic Art, 1945–2000* (Boston: Museum of Fine Arts, 2007), which focuses on the physical and conceptual voyages of works in the Genevieve McMillan collection (now part of Boston's Museum of Fine Arts), offers an important model for this essay.

4   I include quotations for the term "primitive" art in this essay to indicate its use as a historical concept, one built on prejudicial assumptions and that is both inaccurate and outdated.

5   Guggenheim, *Out of This Century*, p. 191.

6   Jackson Pollock was greatly influenced by the writings of artist John Graham on the relationship between African sculpture and Western modernism, especially his 1937 "System and Dialectics of Art." See Christa Clarke, "John Graham and the Crowninshield Collection of African Art," *Winterthur Portfolio* 30, no. 1 (Spring 1995), p. 38.

7   Guggenheim, *Out of This Century*, p. 363.

8   The biographical details here are provided by Rita Reif, "Gallery Here Will Offer Talks on Primitive Art," *New York Times*, April 7, 1959, p. 37. The "Lübeck Museum" that Reif mentions in this profile of Julius Carlebach is most certainly the Museum am Dom (Museum at the Cathedral), which housed the Museum für Völkerkunde (Museum of Ethnology) from 1893 until 1942, when it was bombed during the war.

9   Ibid.

10   In addition to Julius Carlebach, they included John Klejman, from Warsaw, and Ladislas Segy and Mattias Komor, both originally from Hungary.

11   For an overview of institutional reception of objects from Africa in the United States, see Kathleen Bickford Berzock and Christa Clarke, eds., *Representing Africa in American Art Museums: A Century of Collecting and Display* (Seattle: University of Washington Press, 2011). Kate Ezra's essay in this volume specifically focuses on the formation of the Museum of Primitive Art in New York.

12   The catalogues accompanying Robert Goldwater's exhibitions, all published by the Museum of Primitive Art, include: *Sculpture from Three African Tribes: Senufo, Baga, Dogon* (1959), *Bambara Sculpture from the Western Sudan* (1960), and *Senufo Sculpture from West Africa* (1963). The underlying assumptions of "ethnic style" and "culture area" have since been challenged by many scholars over the past decades.

13   Reif, "Gallery Here Will Offer Talks on Primitive Art," p. 37.

14   Cynthia Kellogg. "Living with Sculpture," *New York Times*, October 5, 1958, p. SM48. For a discussion of the use of non-Western art in home decoration in France around the same time, see Daniel J. Sherman, "Post-Colonial Chic: Fantasies of the French Interior, 1957–1962," *Art History* 27, no. 5 (November 2004), pp. 770–81, and also the chapter on "Primitive Accumulation" in his more recent publication, *French Primitivism and the Ends of Empire, 1945–1975* (Chicago: University of Chicago Press, 2011).

15   See Katherine E. Flach, "Eliot Elisofon: Bringing African Art to *Life*," Ph.D. dissertation, Case Western Reserve University, 2015, pp. 203–12.

16   Susan Vogel, "Whither African Art? Emerging Scholarship at the End of an Age," *African Arts* 38, no. 4 (Winter 2005), p. 17.

17   *Tribal Elements: The Franco Monti Collection and Others*. Auction catalogue (Vienna: Palais Dorotheum, 2018), p. 6. The objects Guggenheim acquired from Monti include the Dogon lidded container from Mali (Pl. 3), the Toma mask from Guinea (Pl. 14), and likely the Senufo male figure from the Côte d'Ivoire (Pl. 8). Correspondence from Jacopo T. Monti, December 15, 2019. I am grateful him for this information.

18   "I Misteri dell'arte nera," *Bolaffiarte* 4, no. 28 (1973), pp. 8–17. I am grateful to Vivien Greene for her excellent summary of this interview.

19   Paolo Barozzi, *Con Peggy Guggenheim: Tra storia e memoria* (Milan: Christian Marinotti Edizioni, 2001), pp. 177–80, as quoted by Alessia Borellini, "Peggy's Ethnopassion," in Campione, *Ethnopassion*, p. 39.

20   The visual culture of the Dogon and its twentieth-century history is examined from multiple perspectives in the online publication *ReCollecting Dogon*, Paul R. Davis, ed. Accessed November 18, 2019, https://www.menil.org/read/online-features/recollecting-dogon.

21   For more on this landmark exhibition and its legacy, see Susan Elizabeth Gagliardi, *Senufo Unbound: Dynamics of Art and Identity in West Africa*, exh. cat. (Cleveland: Cleveland Museum of Art/5 Continents, 2014). Gagliardi, and other scholars, have also noted that "Senufo" identity was a creation of the French colonial administration in the late nineteenth century.

22   See Ivan Leopoldo Bargna's entry on *mbulu ngulo* (catalogue no. 20) in Campione, *Ethnopassion*, p. 133.

23   Norma H. Wolff, "'A Matter of Must': Continuities and Change in the Adugbologe Woodcarving Workshop in Abeokuta, Nigeria," in Sidney Littlefield Kasfir and Till Förster, eds., *African Art and Agency in the Workshop* (Bloomington: Indiana University Press, 2013). I am grateful to Henry John Drewal for his attribution of this work to the Adugbologe workshop (personal communication, August 26, 2019).

24   See Boureima T. Diamatani, "The Insider and the Ethnography of Secrecy: Challenges of Collecting Data on the Fearful Komo of the Tagwa-Senufo," *The African Archaeological Review* 28, no. 1 (2011), p. 67; and also Till Förster, "New Markets, New Patrons: Work-Trade Relationships in a West African Art Market," in Silvia Forni and Christopher B. Steiner, eds., *Africa in the Market: Twentieth Century Art from the Amrad African Art Collection* (Toronto: Royal Ontario Museum, 2015), p. 82.

25   Frederick Lamp, *Art of the Baga: A Drama of Cultural Reinvention*, exh. cat. (New York: Museum for African Art, 1996), p. 227.

26   Hélène Leloup offered a personal account of acquiring objects in Guinea, Mali, and Côte d'Ivoire in the 1950s in an article published in the French periodical *Le Point* on November 19, 2018. Accessed November 20, 2019, see https://www.lepoint.fr/culture/oeuvres-culturelles-helene-leloup-les-restitutions-annoncees-ne-doivent-pas-etre-detournees-de-leur-sens-19-11-2018-2272548_3.php.

27   Sherman, "Post-Colonial Chic," p. 777.

28   Vogel suggests that the number of objects leaving Africa during this period far exceeded that of the colonial era. Vogel, "Whither African Art?," p. 14.

29   Geary and Xatart, *Material Journeys*, p. 19. See also Sherman, "Post-Colonial Chic," p. 777.

30   Geary and Xatart, *Material Journeys*, pp. 19, 69. See also Silvia Forni and Christopher B. Steiner, "The African Art Market as Ego-System," *Critical Interventions* 12, no. 1 (2018), pp. 1–7.

31   Though Guggenheim recalls an evening spent in 1941 with a young Hubert Maga, the future first president of Dahomey (now the Republic of Benin), while vacationing on the shores of Lake Annecy in France, Africa merits nary a mention in her memoirs.

Peggy Guggenheim and the Pacific

Fanny Wonu Veys

Peggy Guggenheim's ethnographic collection comprises nine objects from the Pacific, the vast region that covers one third of the earth's surface. Remarkably, except for the Asmat soul canoe from the current Indonesian province of Papua, formerly colonized by the Dutch, all of the works come from the part of New Guinea that was occupied by Germany. Annexed in 1884, German New Guinea encompassed the northeastern corner of the island of New Guinea, as well as the Bismarck Archipelago (New Britain and New Ireland) and northern Solomon Islands.[1]

Art and artifact

Since the beginning of the twentieth century, objects originating from the Pacific—and objects of the cultural 'Other,' for that matter[2]—have been categorized into two groups: "art" and "artifact," respectively corresponding to "art history" and "anthropology," academic disciplines formally developed in the late nineteenth century. This binary division has always revealed some tension, which, according to the art historians and anthropologists Ruth Phillips and Christopher Steiner,[3] has led to the dualistic art/artifact distinction being seen as a given in academic literature. Because the canon of art history, a product of eighteenth-century Enlightenment ideas, "has operated as 'self-evidently universal,'"[4] specific histories of the non-West have been overlooked or even silenced. There was no place for the functional artifact in the realm of the aesthetically pleasing art. Instead of questioning this dualism, the focus has been placed on the ambiguities and inadequacies linked to the division.[5]

Guggenheim's collection as a whole, thus both the modern art and ethnographic collection, demonstrates how it can be extremely challenging to distinguish between an aesthetically pleasing art object and a functional artifact. It presupposes that there are some qualities inherent in the groups of objects that enable us to differentiate easily art from artifact.[6] This leads to the obvious question of how to identify those qualities (fig. 17).

In considering this conundrum, it will be demonstrated that individual objects are in fact polysemic, thus having multiple meanings and capable of being placed in many different groupings.[7] Art objects—ethnographic objects or things, to use a more inclusive and neutral term[8]—are influenced by their makers, users, and spectators. As the Pacific historian and anthropologist Nicholas Thomas argues: "objects are not what they were made to be, but what they have become."[9] The inseparability of art and artifact is also stressed by the anthropologist Steven Hooper when he asserts that although so-called "ethnographic objects" are made to do a job, they are at the same time art.[10] Depending on their temporal and geographical contexts, objects offer, through their materiality, access and are witness to a world of emotions, thoughts, and sensory experiences. Objects may evoke knowledge, power, wealth, curiosity, awe, fear, and admiration or a combination of these. In short, this follows the anthropologist Alfred Gell's idea that art in its widest sense—it does not necessarily need to be aesthetically pleasing, or symbolize something—is intended to have an effect on its social milieu.[11]

Looking at Guggenheim's Pacific collection is an exercise in teasing out the enmeshment of these different ways of experiencing things, works of art if you will. Because the subject is a collection that originated from a Pacific context, the notion of "wayfinding"—as opposed to navigating—is particularly relevant. This means not relying so much on the application of scientific instruments or specific mechanical systems in an attempt to understand Guggenheim's collection, but trying to establish what things are exactly and will always be. The interpretative craft that is "wayfinding" will be used in the sense explained by the Pacific historian Greg Dening:

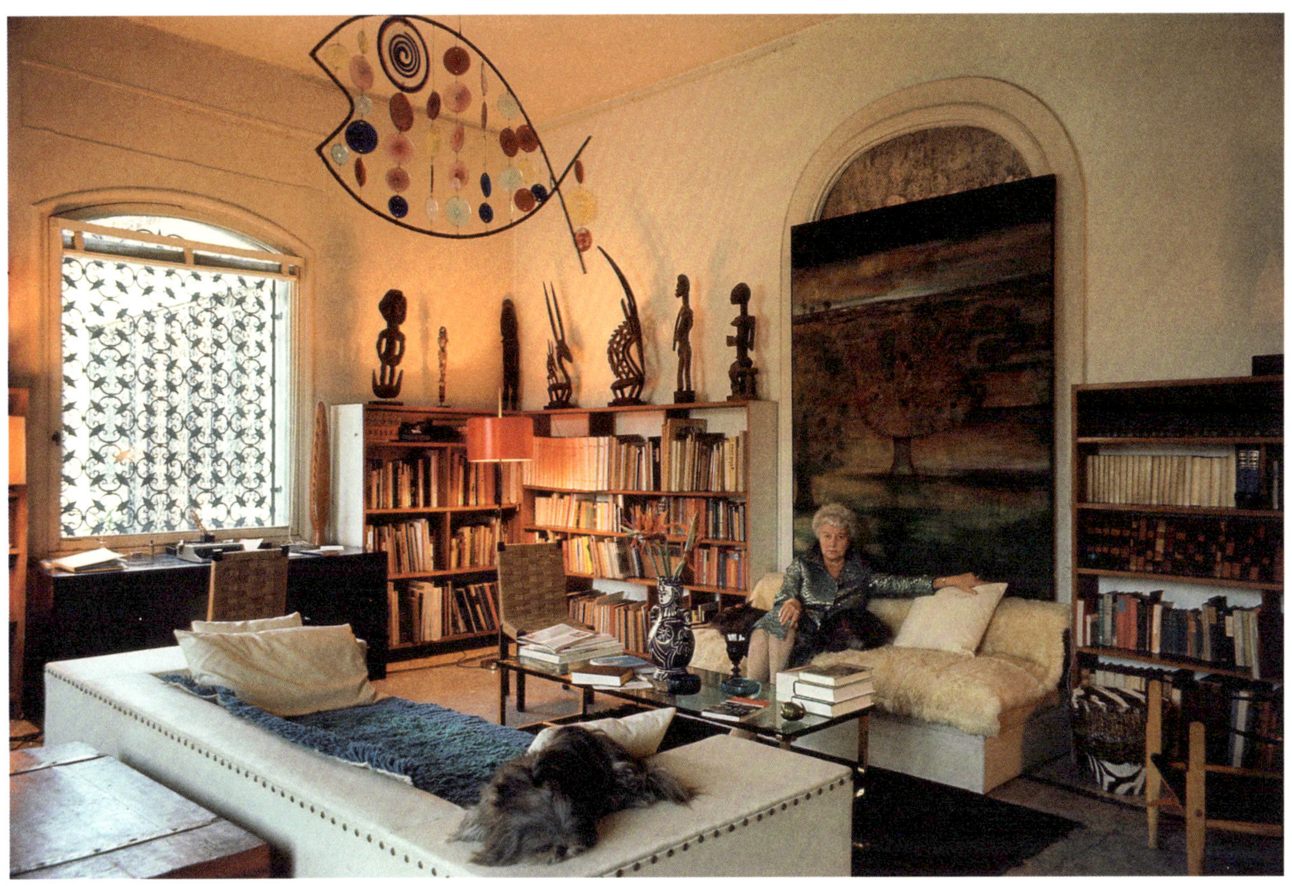

Fig. 17   Peggy Guggenheim in the library, Palazzo Venier dei Leoni, Venice, 1975. On back shelf, left to right: suspension hook, unrecorded Western Iatmul artist, early 20th century, Papua New Guinea (Pl. 24); flute figure, unrecorded Chambri artist, late 19th – early 20th century, Papua New Guinea (Pl. 26); male figure, unrecorded artist, early 20th century, Papua New Guinea (Pl. 29). On wall: *Autumn at Courgeron* (*L'Automne à Courgeron*), 1960, René Brô. Photo: Ray Wilson

'Way-finding' is the word that modern islanders use to describe their craft and the craft of their ancestors in piloting their voyaging canoes around the Great Ocean, the Pacific.[12]

Wayfinding implies a reliance on what happened before while at the same time dealing with relevant contemporary issues; it involves negotiating and accepting the ever-changing nature of things.

Makers of objects, makers of a collection: creativity and memory

When in the 1960s the Dutch anthropologist Adrian Gerbrands researched the carvers of Asmat objects, he stressed their individuality and artistry.[13] All of a sudden names of carvers (*wowipits*) such as Bapmes, Bifarji, Bishur, Initjajai, Itjembi, Matjemos, Ndojokor, and Tarras from the village of Amanamkai (southwest New Guinea) came to the fore, leaving the realm of static anonymous artists repeating movements to create designs that have been passed down by the generations that had preceded them (fig. 18). The Asmat soul canoe or *wuramon*, which Guggenheim most probably collected in the 1960s, exemplifies the creativity of the Joerat Asmat carver who made it. The *wowipits* portrayed supernatural creatures, each of which is named for a specific recently deceased ancestor, whose spirit it embodies. In the center is an *okom*, a dangerous Z-shaped water spirit. The other figures, gazing down through the bottomless hull, represent menacing water spirits (*ambirak*) or humanlike spirits (*etsjo*). A hornbill bird is probably depicted on one end. Even though referring fully to the formal Asmat art language, the Asmat carver reduced the length of the supernatural vessel—they could be up to 12.5 meters long[14]—in order to make this object carved for a one-time occasion amenable for collecting.

PL. 22

The creative developments started by Asmat artists, including the distortion of proportions—this *wuramon* is considerably smaller than many of the older ones—and the more dynamic figurative carvings, sparked the interest of Western collectors and museums from the 1950s onward. Even though Guggenheim had permanently settled in Venice by 1948, she was certainly aware of the exhibition *The Art of the Asmat, New Guinea*, featuring objects collected by Michael C. Rockefeller, which opened at the Museum of Primitive Art[15] in 1962.[16] While it has proved difficult to identify Guggenheim's motivations for collecting, the acquisition of the soul canoe may have been inspired by this New York exhibition.[17]

It has however generally been accepted that the main instigation for the making of a Pacific art collection stemmed from Guggenheim's relationship with the German Surrealist artist Max Ernst, with whom she lived in New York between 1941 and 1943.[18] Within Ernst's group of fellow Surrealist artists, art from the Pacific featured prominently as a source of inspiration. The Surrealist concern with all things Pacific was captured in the "Surrealist Map of the World" published in 1929 in the Belgian journal *Variétés*, where New Guinea, the Bismarck Archipelago, and Easter Island appear enlarged as well as Russia, Alaska, Mexico, and Greenland.[19] Indeed, Ernst was not only an avid collector of—and according to Guggenheim annoyingly attached to[20]—sculpture from New Guinea and New Ireland, but also, in the true Surrealist tradition, he acquired Inuit masks and *kachina* dolls from New Mexico.[21]

One of Ernst's trusted dealers was Julius Carlebach, a German Jew from Lübeck who had fled his home in Berlin and arrived in New York before World War II. Carlebach had a major art gallery in New York, buying and selling much Surrealist art as well as ethnographic art objects. His wife and business associate, Josefa Silberstein, was particularly keen on African and Oceanic art.[22] Guggenheim describes in her autobiography that she did not "succumb" to the tricks Carlebach performed on her to make her buy ethnographic art. However, a few years later she did give in and became the proud owner of her

48

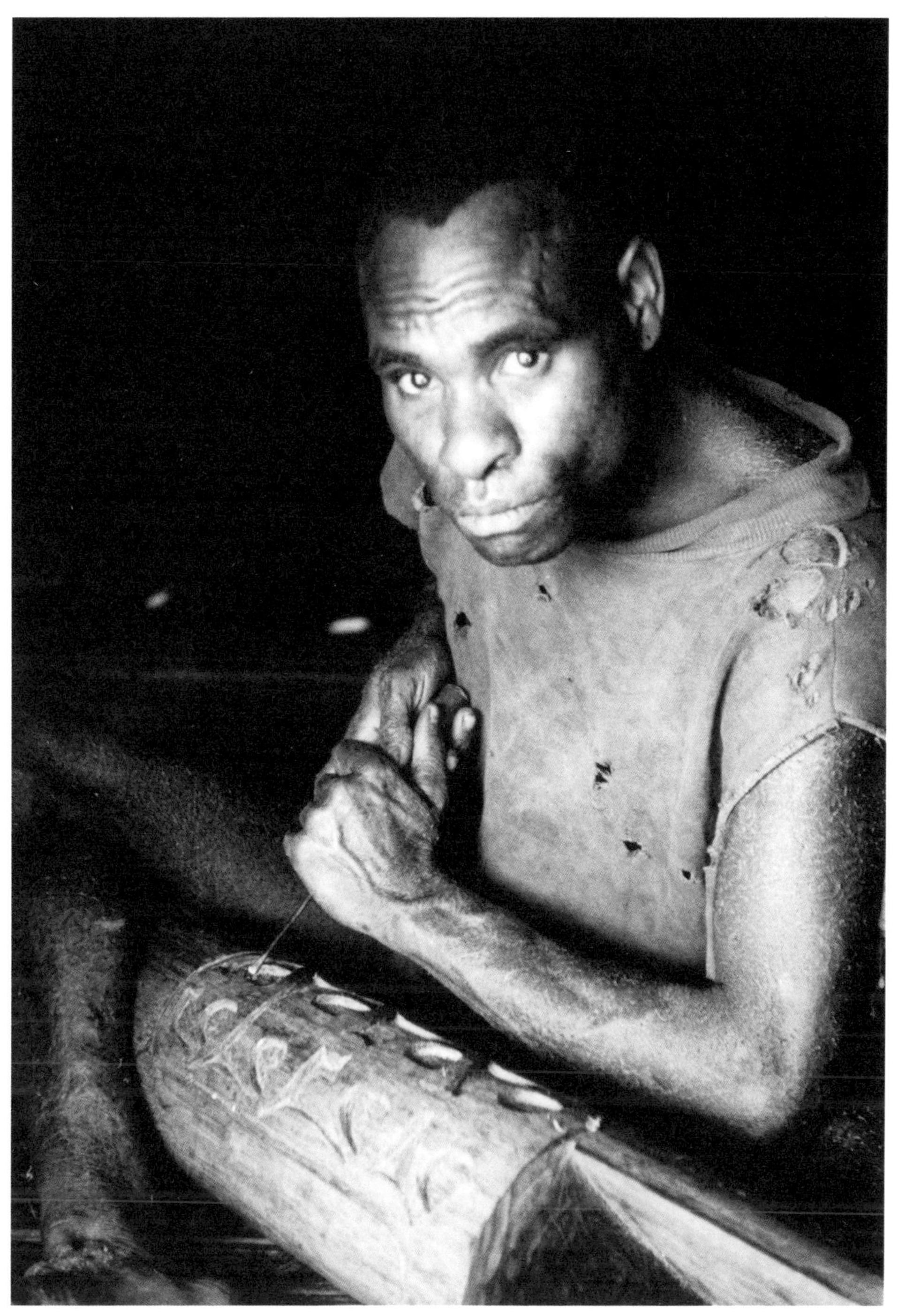

Fig. 18 Itjembi carving an ironwood cylinder in Nemengai, southwest New Guinea, December 28, 1960. Photo: Adrian Gerbrands. Nationaal Museum van Wereldculturen

PLS. 21, 23
PL. 26

first ethnographic collection, including two *malangan* objects—one mask and one sculpture—from New Ireland and one Chambri flute stopper from the Sepik River area in New Guinea. She felt that the works that Ernst had collected and removed from her apartment one by one, upon terminating their relationship, had now returned.[23] It reminded her in a sense of their relationship. The making of her ethnographic collection was connected to memory.

Unknowingly—nothing points to the fact that she was aware of the intellectual worlds encapsulated in her newly acquired works—Guggenheim bought objects, specifically the *malangan* sculpture, of which the manufacture is intimately connected to the production of memory. *Malangan* is a collective term referring to sculpture, dances, the mortuary ceremony, and the ceremonial exchange of people living in the northern part of New Ireland. *Malangan* art was meant to be ephemeral, left to rot, or burned. Starting in the 1840s sculpture was sold to European visitors in order to remove it from the northern New Ireland context. The designs for the art are not transmitted from one generation to the other through the presence of objects as examples from which to work. On the contrary, for each *malangan* ceremony, carvers recall from memory the imagery appropriate for objects. Therefore, both the *malangan* mask and the sculpture are re-embodiments of memorized imagery.[24] The making of *malangan* art and Guggenheim's ethnographic collection necessitate the conjuring up of memories.

Using objects, using a collection: mobility and transition

Guggenheim appears in a number of black and white, and a few color, photographs taken in the 1960s. She posed with her works of art—both modernist and ethnographic—in the library, foyer, living room, and dining room of the Palazzo Venier dei Leoni. Her use of the collection, with its ever-changing constellation, shows her intimate relationship with the works, as the anthropologist and collecting historian Alessia Borellini argues.[25] Parallels can be drawn with Ernst, who was known to pose in Guggenheim's New York apartment with his *kachina* dolls as if they were his children.[26] But Guggenheim's shifting presentation of her collection also stresses the mobility of the objects. Furthermore in its originating contexts, the art was being used in active and transitional ways; the pieces were transported to Europe or the United States and were now moving throughout Guggenheim's Venice palazzo. An example of a transitional object is the suspension hook that resembles the style of objects carved by the Iatmul people of the area of the Cambri Lake, the only remnant of what was once the interior sea of the Sepik River Valley.[27] Suspension hooks such as this were used to keep food out of reach of rodents and other animals. Attached from the rafters of the house with a rope or string pulled through the lug at the top, bags containing food were hung from the hook's crescent shape. Other valuable objects such as musical instruments could also be secured this way. The boldly carved male figure probably refers to an ancestor, but remarkably, does not show any traces of scarification. Sometimes, branches from the betel palm were attached to these objects by way of offering in order to attract the favor of the ancestor who is represented. Suspension hooks were placed and used in the houses of clan elders and thus belong to the sphere of the family houses. However, the depiction of specific ancestors—sacred beings—makes these suspension hooks objects of transition between the secular family house and the sacred men's house.[28] This is one of the main characteristics of Sepik art: it is always in flux in the same way as the movements of the longest river of New Guinea.

Guggenheim captured in her constantly changing placement of artworks some of the essence of Sepik art. She thus challenged the Western methodological logic that constantly searches for "the singular and true nature of things." This quest for certainty is summarized in the question "What is it?"[29] Is it possible to provide an answer to the latter issue when looking at Guggenheim's ancestor figure, the double-sided Sepik carving? Was it carved in the tradition of the village

PL. 24

PL. 25

of Yamok, north of the Sepik River, where Sawos men carved larger-than-life figures? Those figures usually represented a male ancestor, presumably more mythological than real, and each had a name. These monumental sculptures once dominated the interior space of the men's ceremonial house, where they were probably tied to the supporting architectural posts. As the posts supported the house, so the founding ancestors and their descendant clan members supported the village (fig. 19).[30] However, the figure looks male when observed from one perspective, female from the other. Could the fusion of the feminine and masculine be testament to the reproductive forces of both sexes that together can have agency on the social worlds that surround them?[31] Or is it rather, as the anthropologist Günther Giovannoni suggests, part of a rare type of giant suspension hook, moving between secular and sacred realms?[32]

Sepik art not only moves between the secular and the sacred, the feminine and the masculine, but also between the living and the dead, often conflating worlds. The carved male figure with scarification on its back and chest exemplifies this idea. The Chambri flute stopper was originally destined to be mounted at the end of a long bamboo flute and would only have been used during rituals in the village. The sound produced by the musical instrument is considered the PL. 26 voice of the ancestors. Only initiated men are allowed to play music. Each step of the initiation process involves learning to play specific instruments such as flutes, (slit) drums, and bull roarers. Usually hidden or stored in the men's house, these objects can only be seen by initiated people, for only they understand the true meaning of the instruments as the ancestors' vicinity. Returning to a more profane level: the figure shows a label at the back. Since Guggenheim bought this object from Carlebach, it could be the latter's label. However, it might also show that the artwork moved through other hands before reaching Carlebach's New York gallery, thus materializing the trajectory of the object and its link between past and present.

Spectators: looking and seeing
hidden and visible worlds

Gell famously proposed in his article "The Technology of Enchantment and the Enchantment of Technology" that art is a special kind of technology that has an effect on those individuals—its spectators—who are enmeshed with the intentionality of the art.[33] From spring until fall, Guggenheim opened her home to the public three afternoons a week, so visitors could also experience the enchantment of her newly found collection pursuit (fig. 20). In 1966, moreover, twenty of her ethnographic art objects were presented in a catalogue of the Venetian collection.[34] They fit the "primitivist" framework with which Guggenheim had grown familiar. In the early 1900s the so-called discovery of "non-Western" art by twentieth-century modernist artists was seen as central in the shaping of Western art. They started collecting these objects and drew inspiration from them.[35] Because of this, ethnographic art is often presented to a well-informed public as a way to better understand Western modernist art. The exhibition held in 1984 at the Museum of Modern Art (MoMA) in New York entitled *"Primitivism" in 20th Century Art: Affinity of the Tribal and the Modern* probably epitomized this approach. Even though the audience for the Guggenheim collection broadened considerably, it remained a restricted public, traveling from metropolitan areas and fascinated by the developments of art—spectators who knew how to approach art, how to look. Could viewers see all the worlds contained in the artworks?

Looking at the original Pacific contexts, the audiences were carefully chosen. Young men passing through initiation would be asked to look at—to become the first-time spectators of—the ancestor figure, *miamba maira*, a large sculpture PL. 27 characterized by openwork carving representing a stylized female being surrounded by birds. It was through observation rather than through verbal communication that the young initiates would have acquired the knowledge necessary to the cult

51

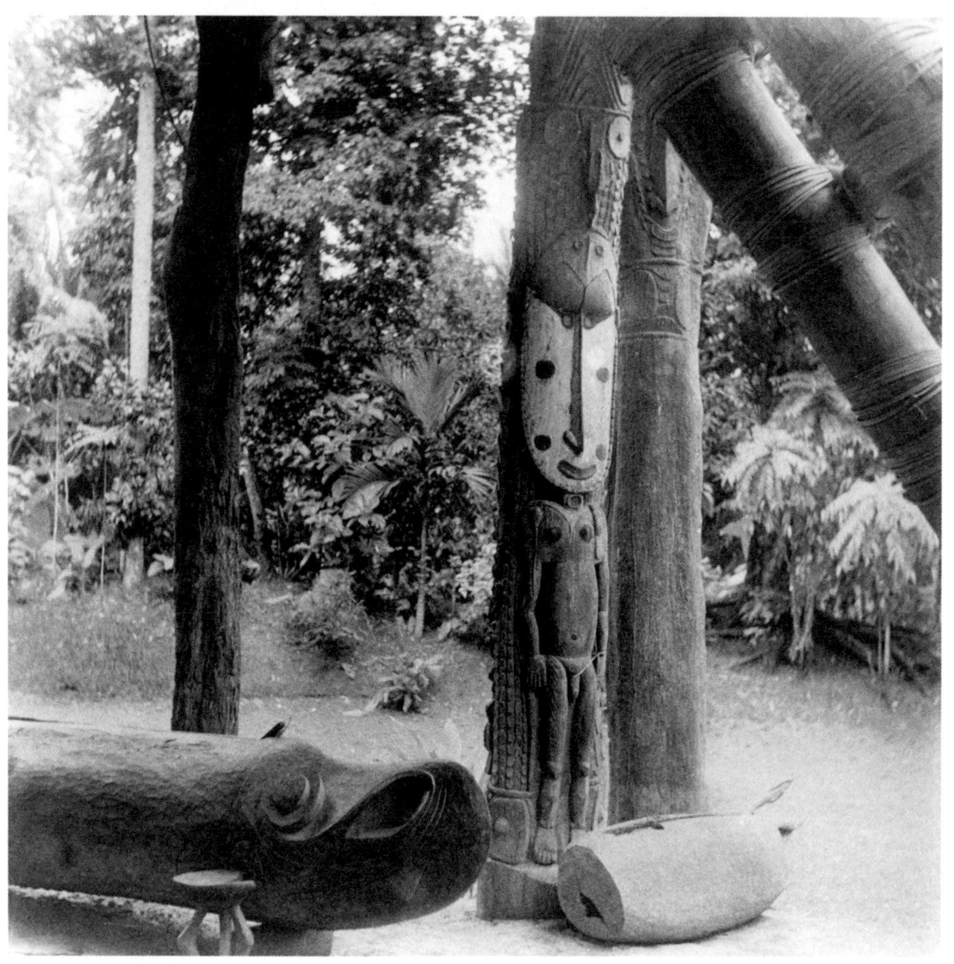

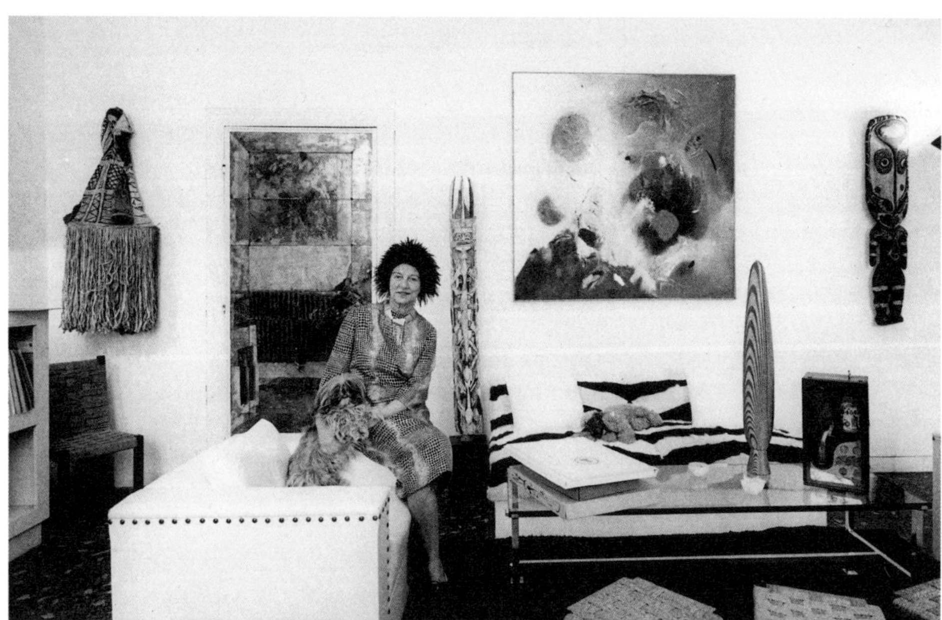

Fig. 19   Carved objects in the men's house of Kanganaman, Sepik area, New Guinea. Photographer and date unknown, Nationaal Museum van Wereldculturen

Fig. 20   Peggy Guggenheim in the living room, Palazzo Venier dei Leoni, Venice, early 1960s. Left to right: bark mask, unrecorded Cubeo artist, first half of the 20th century, Northern Amazon (Pl. 35); funerary carving (*malangan*), unrecorded Mandara (or Tabar) artist, early 20th century, Northern New Ireland (Pl. 23); *Event #247* (*Avvenimento #247*), 1956, Edmondo Bacci; ancestor figure, unrecorded Sawos artist, Yamok Village, East Sepik Province, Papua, New Guinea (Pl. 25). On table: *Untitled* (*Fortune-Telling Parrot for Carmen Miranda*), ca. 1939, Joseph Cornell of the short yam. Cultivating both edible as well as ceremonial yams was a role of fundamental importance to the Wosera Abelam society of New Guinea. While this sculpture helped men in transforming spiritually and thus achieving the highest level of initiation, initiated men—the only spectators—were reluctant to divulge the deeper levels of knowledge, which were essential in feeling the full impact of the forms and colors of the artwork. Hidden and visible worlds were palpable to the art lover.

Most people will be dazzled when looking at the colors of carved elements of a ceremonial house of the Arapesh or Boiken peoples, living in the northern fringes of the Abelam area. By contrasting the color pairs, black and white, and red and yellow, a visual vibrancy is created (fig. 21). To Abelam viewers, this is the essential power of the image; the brightness and vivacity can have an effect on its audience.[36] As very little is known about the placement of this winged structure within the ceremonial men's house, it is difficult to establish who its audience would have been. Similarly, one will probably never really understand all the layers of meaning connected to the *kadibon* or *kandimbog* male figure from the Murik Lagoon on the Sepik River. With its elongated projection emanating from the chest and tapering downward to the height of the knees, this figure most probably represents an ancestral being or spirit and was possibly only shown to young men during their process of initiation.

Presenting the ethnographic collection in its own right without needing to educate the public about its role within the meanderings of Western art history opens up possibilities of glimpsing different worlds. Through the perceived bedazzlement, the spectator oscillates between looking, seeing, and understanding the abundance of visual and hidden worlds.

Capturing the essence

Guggenheim was guided by instinct and resolve when assembling art of the avant-garde movements of the first half of the twentieth century.[37] The same can be said for her ethnographic collection, in which she instinctively seemed to have captured some of the essence of these carvings. The collection demonstrates entanglements of creative makers and collectors with memory. It reflects upon the fact that objects—like people—have always come from one place to go somewhere else, in an always mobile, perpetual transition. And it presents, to those who are wanting or allowed to look, the possibility to experience different parts of hidden and visible realms.

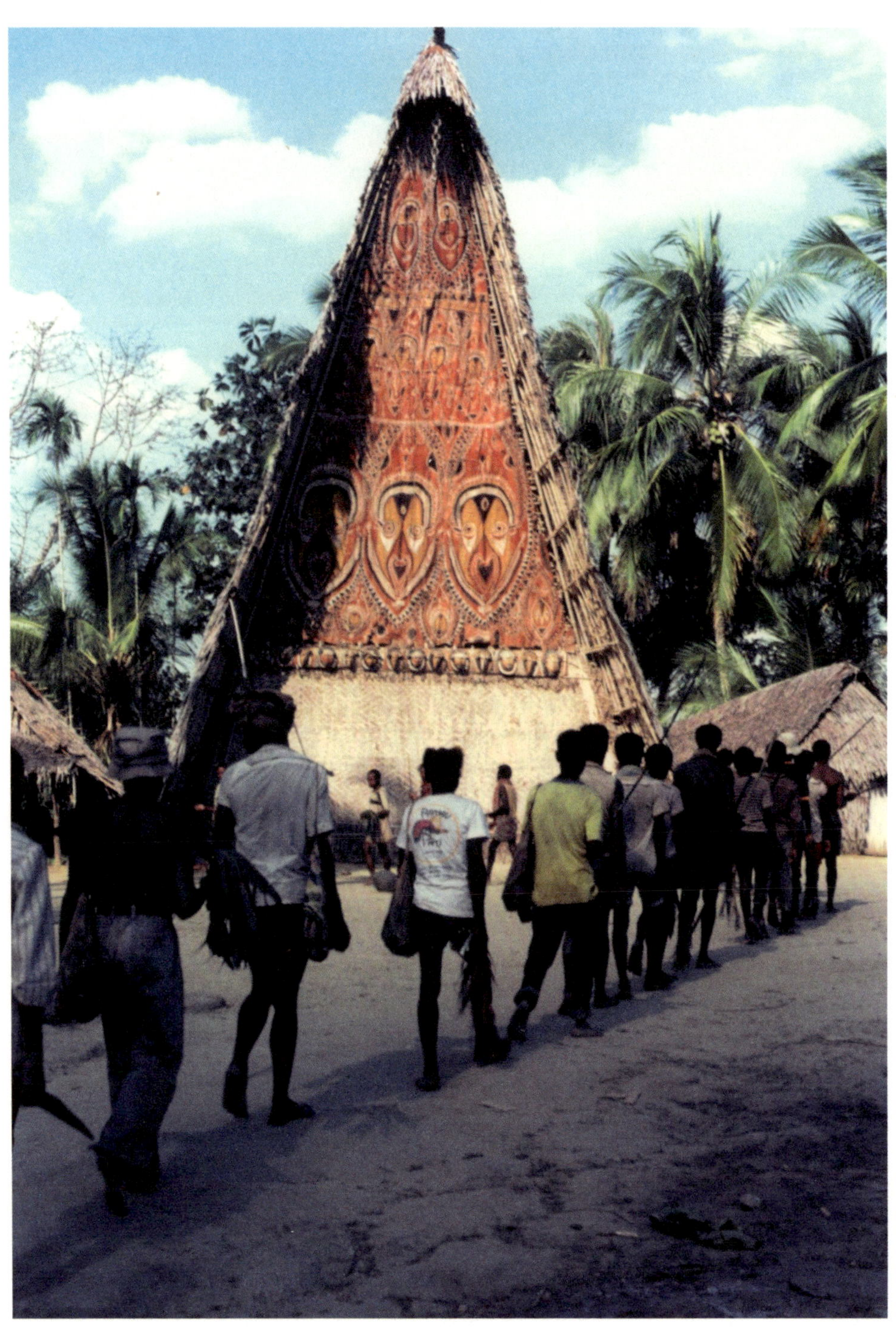

Fig. 21   Abelam men's house photographed
during a collecting trip of Dirk Smidt and Noel
McGuigan, 1987. Photo: Dirk Smidt, Nationaal
Museum van Wereldculturen

1   Rainer F. Buschmann, "Oceanic Collections in German Museums: Collections, Contexts, and Exhibits," in Lucie Carreau et al., eds., *Pacific Presences: Oceanic Art and European Museums* (Leiden: Sidestone Press, 2018), vol. 1, p. 203.

2   Ruth B. Phillips and Christopher B. Steiner, eds., *Unpacking Culture: Art and Commodity in Colonial and Postcolonial Worlds* (Berkeley and Los Angeles: University of California Press, 1999), p. 3.

3   Ibid.

4   Elizabeth Harney and Ruth B. Phillips, "Inside Modernity: Indigeneity, Coloniality, Modernisms," in Elizabeth Harney and Ruth B. Phillips, eds., *Mapping Modernisms: Art, Indigeneity, Colonialism* (Durham, N.C.: Duke University Press, 2018), p. 2.

5   Phillips and Steiner, *Unpacking Culture*, p. 5.

6   Jean-Marie Schaeffer, "Objets esthétiques?," *L'Homme* 170 (2004), pp. 25–26.

7   Eilean Hooper-Greenhill, *Museums and the Interpretation of Visual Culture* (New York: Routledge, 2000), p. 77.

8   Amiria Henare, Martin Holbraad, and Sari Wastell, eds., *Thinking Through Things: Theorising Artefacts Ethnographically* (London: Routledge, 2007).

9   Nicholas Thomas, *Entangled Objects: Exchange, Material Culture, and Colonialism in the Pacific* (Cambridge, Mass.: Harvard University Press, 1991), p. 4.

10   Steven Hooper, *Pacific Encounters: Art and Divinity in Polynesia 1760–1860*, exh. cat. (London: British Museum Press, 2006), p. 28.

11   Alfred Gell, *Art and Agency: An Anthropological Theory* (Oxford: Clarendon Press, 1998).

12   Greg Dening, *Beach Crossings: Voyaging Across Times, Cultures, and Self* (Philadelphia: University of Pennsylvania Press, 2004), p. 167.

13   Adrian A. Gerbrands, *Wow-ipits: Eight Asmat Woodcarvers of New Guinea* 3, *Art in Its Context, Field Reports* (The Hague: Mouton & Co., 1967).

14   Tobias Schneebaum, *Embodied Spirits: Ritual Carvings of the Asmat*, exh. cat. (Salem, Mass.: Peabody Museum of Salem, 1990), p. 45.

15   The Museum of Primitive Art in New York was founded in 1954 by Nelson A. Rockefeller in association with René d'Harnoncourt. It opened to the public in 1957. In 1978 the collection from the Museum of Primitive Art in New York, which had closed its doors in 1975, was legally transferred to The Metropolitan Museum of Art. Fanny Wonu Veys, "Art or Artefact: Is that the question? 'Pasifika Styles' at the University of Cambridge Museum of Archaeology and Anthropology, and the Refurbishment of the Michael Rockefeller Wing at the Metropolitan Museum of Art," *Paideuma* 56 (2010), p. 268.

16   Michael Clark Rockefeller and Adrian Alexander Gerbrands, *The Art of the Asmat, New Guinea, Collected by Michael C. Rockefeller*, exh. cat. (New York: The Museum of Primitive Art, 1962).

17   Susan Davidson, "Focusing an Instinct: The Collecting of Peggy Guggenheim," in Susan Davidson and Philip Rylands, eds., *Peggy Guggenheim & Frederick Kiesler: The Story of Art of This Century* (New York: Solomon R. Guggenheim Foundation, 2004), p. 51.

18   Alessia Borellini, "Peggy's Ethnopassion," in Francesco Paolo Campione, ed., *Ethnopassion: Peggy Guggenheim's Ethnic Art Collection*, exh. cat. (Milan: Mazzotta, 2008), pp. 31–35.

19   Eric Kjellgren, *Oceania: Art of the Pacific Islands in The Metropolitan Museum of Art* (New York: The Metropolitan Museum of Art; New Haven: Yale University Press, 2007), p. 18; Christine Dixon, "Max Ernst, Artist and Collector," in Max Quanchi and Susan Cochrane, eds., *Hunting the Collectors: Pacific Collections in Australian Museums, Art Galleries and Archives* (Newcastle-upon-Tyne: Cambridge Scholars Publishing, 2007), pp. 276–77; Evan Maurer, "Dada and Surrealism," in William Rubin, ed., *"Primitivism" in 20th Century Art: Affinity of the Tribal and the Modern*, exh. cat. (New York: Museum of Modern Art, 1984), p. 555.

20   Peggy Guggenheim, *Out of This Century: Confessions of an Art Addict* (New York: Universe Books; London: André Deutsch, 1979), p. 263.

21   *Kachina* or *katsina* dolls—in Hopi spelling—are the carved representations of the *Katsinam*, the spirit messengers of the universe who come to the Hopi in the form of life-giving rain clouds. Zena Pearlstone and Barbara A. Babcock, *Katsina: Commodified and Appropriated Images of Hopi Supernaturals* (Los Angeles: UCLA Fowler Museum of Cultural History, 2001); Samantha Kavky, "Max Ernst in Arizona: Myth, Mimesis, and the Hysterical Landscape," *RES: Anthropology and Aesthetics*, nos. 57/58, Spring/Autumn (2010), pp. 209–28.

22   Borellini, "Peggy's Ethnopassion," in Campione, *Ethnopassion*, p. 31; Martica Sawin, *Surrealism in Exile and the Beginning of the New York School* (Cambridge, Mass.: MIT Press, 1995), p. 185; Bernard de Grunne, "Statuette en ivoire, Lega, République Démocratique du Congo," *Sotheby's: Arts d'Afrique et d'Océanie* (2011).

23   Guggenheim, *Out of This Century*, p. 363.

24   Susanne Küchler, "Malangan: Art and Memory in a Melanesian Society," *Man* 22, no. 2 (1987), pp. 238–40.

25   Borellini, "Peggy's Ethnopassion," in Campione, *Ethnopassion*, p. 29.

26   Dixon, "Max Ernst, Artist and Collector," pp. 276–77; Kavky, "Max Ernst in Arizona," pp. 210–11.

27   Philippe Peltier and Markus Schindlbeck, "Introduction," in Philippe Peltier, Markus Schindlbeck, and Christian Kaufmann, eds., *Sepik: Arts de Papouasie-Nouvelle-Guinée*, exh. cat. (Paris: Skira, Musée du quai Branly, 2015), p. 16.

28   Philippe Peltier, Markus Schindlbeck, and Christian Kaufmann, "Les objets au long du fleuve," in Peltier, Schindlbeck, and Kaufmann, *Sepik*, p. 143.

29   Peltier, Schindlbeck, and Kaufmann, "Une image n'est jamais fixe," in Peltier, Schindlbeck, and Kaufmann, *Sepik*, pp. 114–15.

30   Peltier, Schindlbeck, and Kaufmann, "Les objets au long du fleuve," in Peltier, Schindlbeck, and Kaufmann, *Sepik*, p. 202.

31   Kathleen Barlow, "Enchantement et séduction. Pirogues à balancier et idéologie de genre sur la côte nord de la Papouasie-Nouvelle-Guinée," in Peltier, Schindlbeck, and Kaufmann, *Sepik*, p. 25.

32   See Günther Giovannoni's entry on the ancestor figure (catalogue no. 28) in Campione, *Ethnopassion*, pp. 158–61. As the figure is rather large (about 135 cm high), it is unlikely that it was produced for tourists, who would have had great difficulty in taking it home. Nonetheless it is impossible to confirm whether this figure was aged by a local Sepik artist.

33   Alfred Gell, "The Technology of Enchantment and the Enchantment of Technology," in Jeremy Coote and Anthony Shelton, eds., *Anthropology, Art and Aesthetics* (Oxford: Clarendon, 1992), p. 43.

34   Nicolas Calas and Elena Calas, *The Peggy Guggenheim Collection of Modern Art* (New York: H. N. Abrams, 1966).

35   James Clifford, *The Predicament of Culture: Twentieth-Century Ethnography, Literature, and Art* (Cambridge, Mass.: Harvard University Press, 1988), p. 190; Harney and Phillips, "Inside Modernity," p. 11; Modernist artists who acquired or used Pacific objects in their artwork include Pablo Picasso, Emil Nolde, Erich Heckel, Ernst Ludwig Kirchner, Karl Schmidt-Rotluff, André Breton, Wolfgang Paalen, Max Ernst, and Matta (Roberto Sebastián Matta Echaurren). Most of them believed they were also rescuing Pacific art from neglect. Elizabeth Cowling, "'L'Oeil sauvage': Oceanic Art and the Surrealists," in Suzanne Greub, ed., *Art of Northwest New Guinea. From Geelvink Bay, Humboldt Bay, and Lake Sentani* (New York: Rizzoli, 1992), p. 181; Kjellgren, *Oceania*, p. 18.

36   Ludovic Coupaye, "The Abelam," in Philippe Peltier and Floriane Morin, eds., *Shadows of New Guinea: Art of the Great Island of Oceania in the Barbier-Mueller Collections*, exh. cat. (Paris: Somogy éditions d'art, The Mona Bismarck Foundation; Geneva: Musée Barbier-Mueller, 2006), p. 80.

37   Davidson, "Focusing an Instinct," in Davidson and Rylands, *Peggy Guggenheim & Frederick Kiesler*, p. 51.

Guises of Commemoration

Peggy Guggenheim
and the
Funerary Arts
of the Americas

R. Tripp Evans

In contrast to her modernist collecting, Peggy Guggenheim's acquisition of the arts of Africa, Oceania, and the Americas has led even sympathetic critics to characterize this activity, unjustly, as a form of interior decoration. In 2008, Francesco Paolo Campione wrote that Guggenheim "did not derive aesthetic nourishment or intellectual and artistic suggestions from [these objects]: rather, she put them on show...according to a refined idea of décor."[1] Closer examination reveals that, in assembling her pre-Columbian and Amazonian works, Guggenheim demonstrated more than a decorative impulse; moreover, with this small but resonant collection of objects, she subliminally reinforced the commemorative nature of her collection as a whole.

Of the six works in this group, three derive from ancient West Mexico, produced between 300 BCE and 400 CE; two belong to the Andean Kingdom of Chimor (Peru), which flourished from 900 to 1470 CE; and one hails from the Cubeo people of Rio Uaupés in the Northern Amazon, made in the first half of the twentieth century.[2] Though divergent in culture, time, and geography, these works all share an association with funerary practice. Intended for an audience both singular and non-living, they participate in an economy of goods-as-memory.

PLS. 30–32 Guggenheim's terracotta figures from Nayarit—two freestanding figures and one marriage pair with infant—typify the small-scale, hollow sculpture of ancient West Mexico. Characteristic of Nayarit's Ixtlán del Río culture, they feature expressive gestures, slip-painted patterning, and anatomies that combine naturalism with stylization.[3] In the multichambered shaft tombs of West Mexico, these figures functioned as companions or guides for the dead and may have represented the deceased at important stages of life, up to and including death.[4]

To understand the journey from a West Mexican tomb to the Manhattan gallery of Guggenheim's dealer, Julius Carlebach, the "New World's" colonial past must be considered.[5] Whereas African and Oceanic material in Western collections reflects colonial extraction beginning in the late nineteenth century, Spain's American colonies had all gained independence by the 1820s. Antiquities from these new nations were virtually unknown beyond their borders, yet by the close of the nineteenth century, casual tourism had mushroomed in Mexico along with a brisk market in looted ancient works.[6] As an American travel writer wrote in 1890:

> The shape of Mexico is that of a cornucopia...The big end is towards the United States, and there is naught for us to do but pour out its treasures...for our delectation.[7]

When Guggenheim purchased her first pre-Columbian works in 1959, Mexico's "cornucopia" had considerably emptied. So widespread was the looting of shaft tombs between the 1930s and '50s, in fact, that it would be 1993 before the discovery of an intact site.[8] Among the first to collect these works were Mexican artists Frida Kahlo and Diego Rivera, whose interest in pre-colonial culture intensified following Mexico's 1910–17 revolution.[9] Critical to the works' appeal, particularly for leftists like Kahlo and Rivera, was the erroneous belief that these figures embodied secular and anecdotal subjects, devoid of the complex iconographies associated with the courtly Aztecs or Maya. By mid-century U.S. collectors had begun to acquire these works in turn, spurred in part by President Franklin Delano Roosevelt's wide-ranging "Good Neighbor Policy" with Central and South America.[10] These collectors, too, valued the sculpture as an ancient form of contemporary Mexican folk art, examples of which Guggenheim had first admired in the 1930s.[11]

Guggenheim's then husband, Max Ernst, introduced her to pre-Columbian art in the following decade, yet the immediate catalyst for her acquisition of these works appears to have been her month-long stay in Mexico at the end of 1959. On this trip Guggenheim enthusiastically toured the new Frida Kahlo Museum, whose presentation of pre-Columbian, colonial, and contemporary Mexican art was later mirrored in the house-museum that her friend, Robert Brady, created in Cuernavaca.[12] Inspired perhaps by the wide-ranging exploration of ancient Mesoamerican monuments in the 1930s by artists Josef and Anni Albers, moreover, Guggenheim even ventured as far as the remote Maya site of Palenque, whose ruins were "more beautiful than any I have seen anywhere."[13]

Guggenheim had less firsthand knowledge of ancient Andean and Amazonian forms, yet her selection of South American works nevertheless reveals engagement beyond that of a decorator. Her two Chimú works, a three-panel mummy mask and feather *poncho*, both derived from elite burials, a context Guggenheim and her dealer likely understood ("Chimú" is the ethnic descriptor for the Kingdom of Chimor).[14] Originally hinged, the panels of the mummy mask would have folded over a *fardo*, or "mummy bundle," its central icon substituting for the features of the deceased.[15] The schematic character of this mask is not unusual for the Chimú, whose economy often valued the quantity of grave goods over their quality. Prior to the death of a ruler, royal Chimú burial sites consisted of residential, storage, and administrative zones collectively known as a *ciudadela*, or "citadel." Upon a ruler's death the storage zone of the *ciudadela* was sealed, thus requiring the subsequent heir to amass his own burial goods—a cycle that enmeshed an enormous swath of the population in producing artworks for the dead.[16]

In contrast to the more hastily conceived mummy mask, which likely surrounded the sacrificial body of a commoner, Guggenheim's Chimú feather *poncho* was a luxury item.[17] Costly Amazonian imports, tropical feathers such as these were imbued with considerable talismanic powers and valued nearly as much as gold; in the *poncho*'s stepped-triangle patterning and stylized camelid motifs, moreover, the piece recalls the earlier, greatly admired, Nazca culture. In both materials and execution, then, the article would have constituted an elegant asset within its *ciudadela*.

Like the Chimú *poncho*, Guggenheim's Amazonian bark mask is a funeral costume, yet its contemporary manufacture and tribal affiliation distinguish it from the pre-Columbian works in Guggenheim's collection. Representing an animal spirit, it was worn in a dance performance as a full-body mask during part of the elaborate mourning ceremonies of the Cubeo that honored a deceased kinsperson; the mask was destroyed at the end of the ceremony.[18] Within the context of Guggenheim's residence the mask invokes, instead, the formal language of the modernist works it accompanies, epitomizing the modernist-primitive juxtaposition so important to this generation of collectors.[19] Indeed, in several photographs depicting Guggenheim in her house-museum, the mask appears to have inspired a kind of visual homage from its owner. In one such image (fig. 22), Guggenheim wears a heavily textured dress that mimics the mask's bark and fiber textures, a pairing that locates the collector herself within this modernist-primitive paradigm.

Guggenheim's installation of her ancient West Mexican pieces encouraged similar visual exchanges. Whether flanking Pablo Picasso's *The Poet* (*Le Poète*), 1911 (fig. 23), or migrating to bracket Vasily Kandinsky's *Landscape with Red Spots No. 2* (*Landschaft mit roten Flecken, Nr. 2*), 1913 (fig. 24), Guggenheim's standing figures mediate between viewer and painting, just as they once served as emissaries between the living and the dead. In her placement of the marriage pair with infant, moreover, she formed a sculptural suite with Max Ernst's *Young Woman in the Form of a Flower* (*Jeune femme en forme de fleur*), 1944, and Jacques Lipchitz's *Seated Pierrot* (*Pierrot assis*), 1922 (fig. 25). Not only do the three share a plastic affinity, but the Nayarit-Ernst grouping also suggests, however intuitively, a paired theme of transformation (scholar Peter Furst has proposed that conjoined ancient West Mexican figures represented hallucinogen-induced shamanic visions).[20]

Beyond Guggenheim's visual union of ancient, tribal, and modern works, the funerary role of her pre-Columbian and Amazonian objects acts as a metaphor of sorts for the broader goals of her collection. For what are the Palazzo Venier dei Leoni and the *barchessa*, if not a spectacular memorial preserving Guggenheim's precious worldly goods (though in her case, to be shared

PLS. 33, 34

PL. 35

PL. 32

59

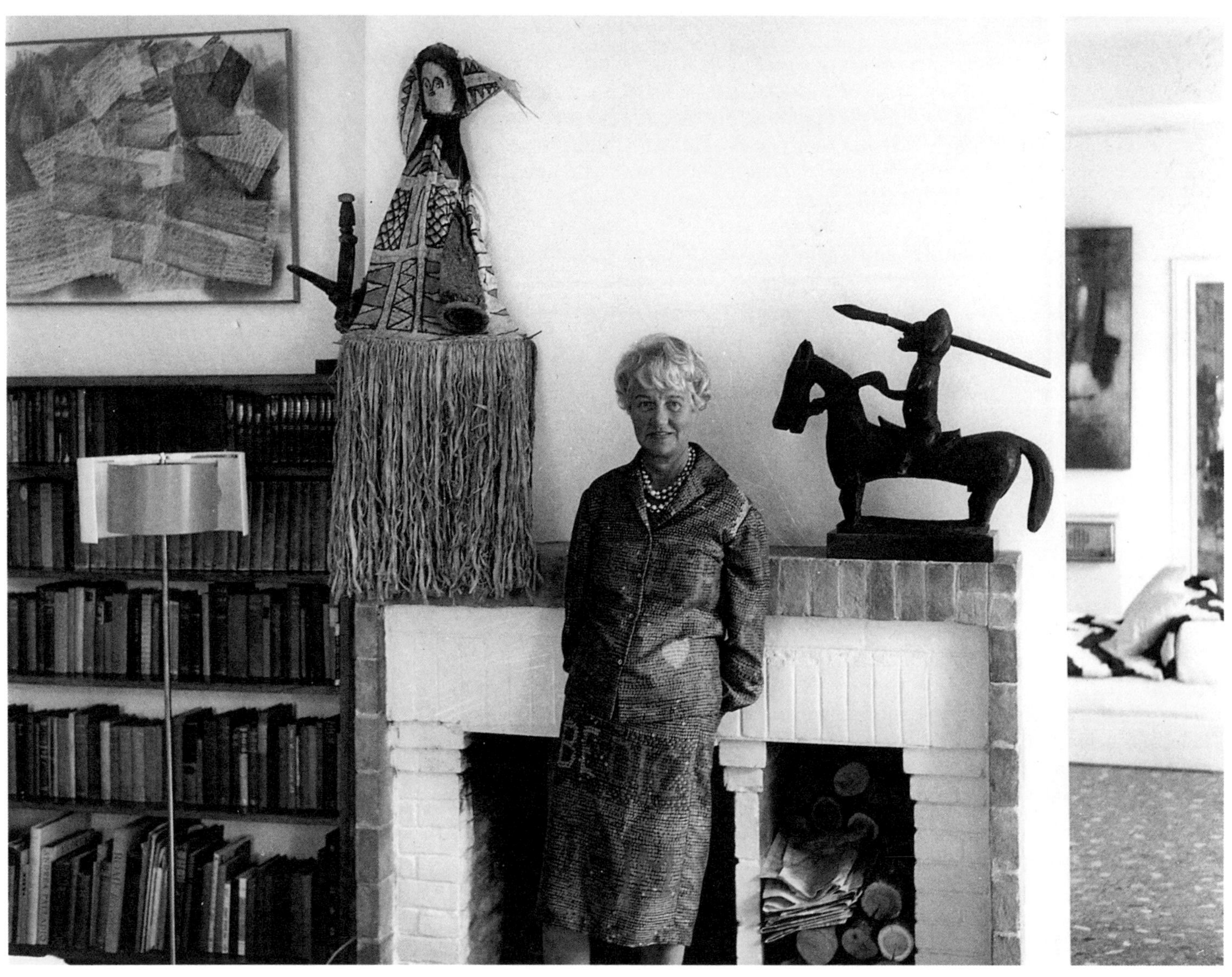

Fig. 22   Peggy Guggenheim in the library, Palazzo
Venier dei Leoni, Venice, 1960s. Left: bark mask,
first half of the 20th century, unrecorded Cubeo
artist, Northern Amazon (Pl. 35). Right: equestrian
figure, probably first half of 20th century,
unrecorded Senufo artist, Côte d'Ivoire (Pl. 11)

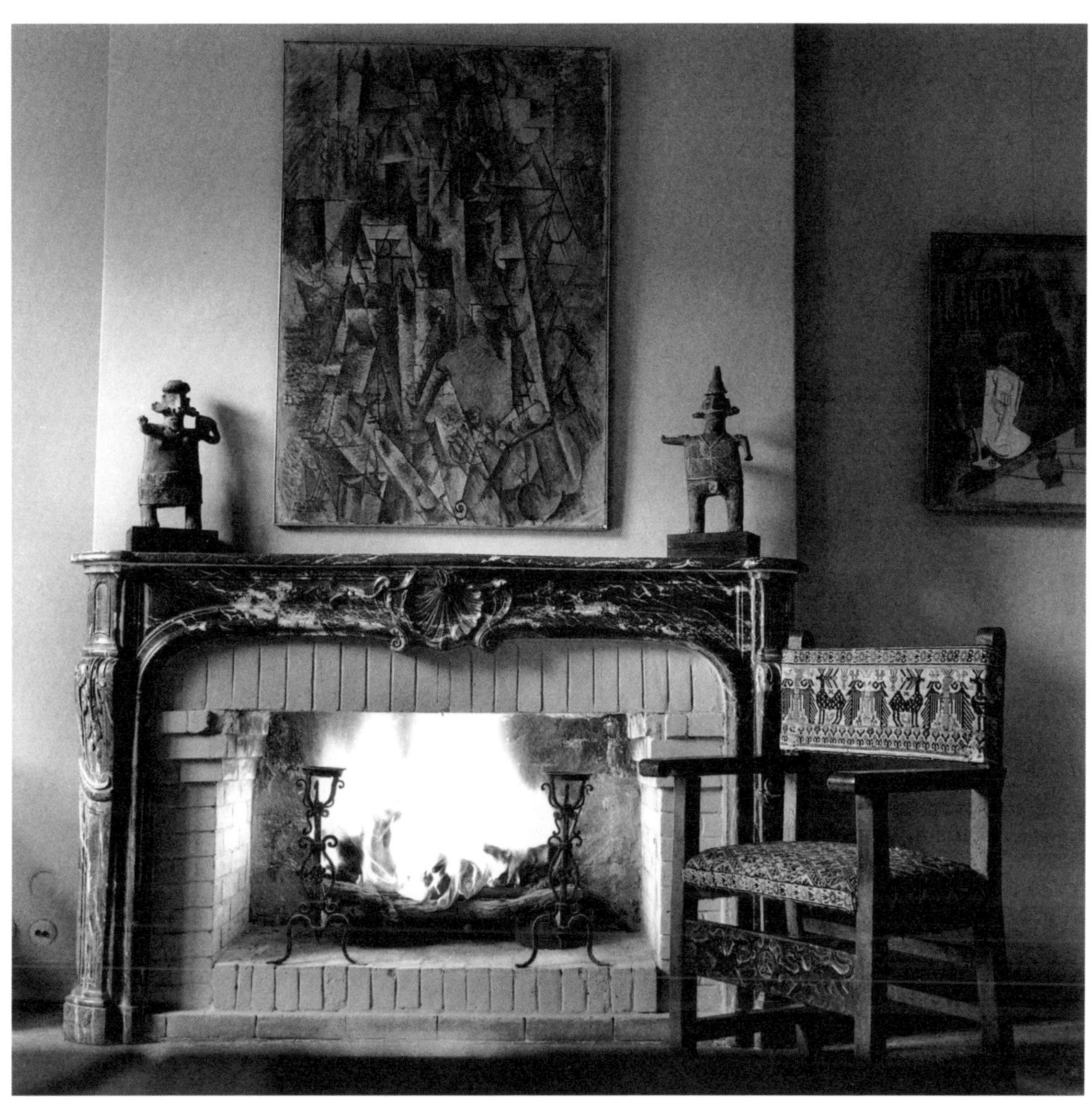

Fig. 23 Dining room, Palazzo Venier dei
Leoni, Venice, 1966. Center: *The Poet* (*Le Poète*),
August 1911, Pablo Picasso; flanked by female
and male figures, 300 BCE – 400 CE, unrecorded
Nayarit artist(s) (Ixtlán del Río culture), ancient
West Mexico (Pls. 30, 31). Photo: Gianni
Berengo Gardin

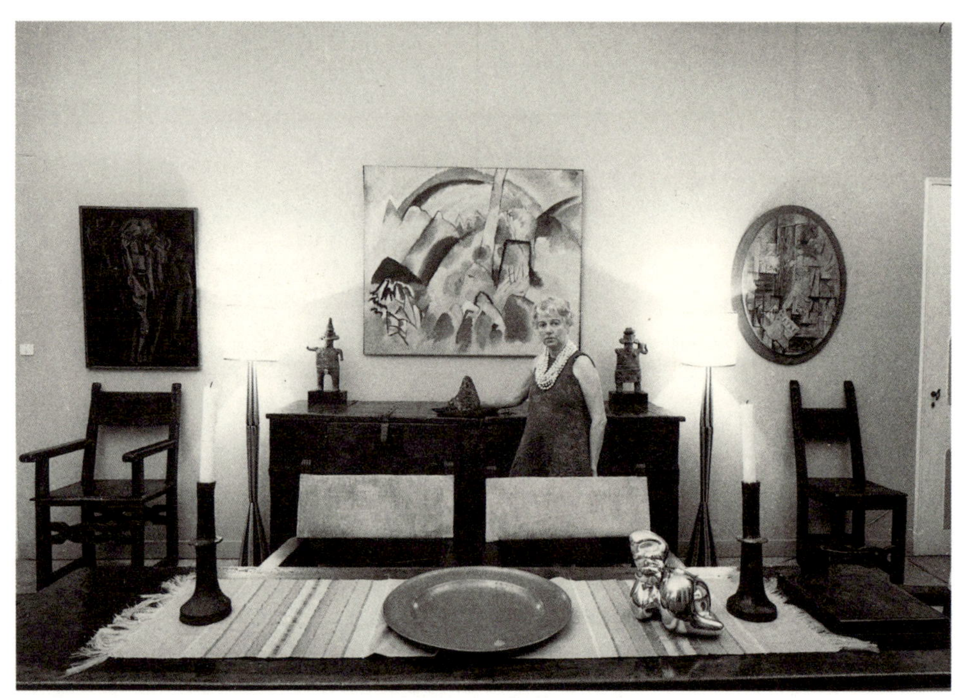

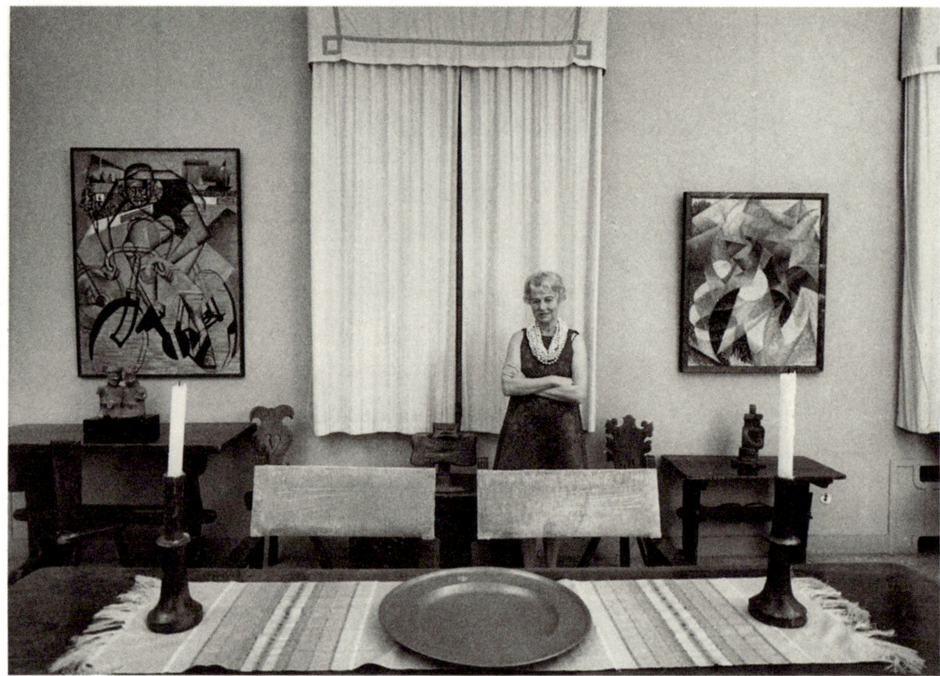

Fig. 24   Peggy Guggenheim in the dining room, Palazzo Venier dei Leoni, Venice, 1960s. Center: *Landscape with Red Spots No. 2 (Landschaft mit roten Flecken, Nr. 2)*, 1913, Vasily Kandinsky; flanked by female and male figures, 300 BCE – 400 CE, unrecorded Nayarit artist(s) (Ixtlán del Río culture), ancient West Mexico (Pls. 30, 31)

Fig. 25   Peggy Guggenheim in the dining room, Palazzo Venier dei Leoni, Venice, 1960s. Behind her, left: conjoined couple with infant, 300 BCE – 400 CE, unrecorded Nayarit artist (Ixtlán del Río culture), ancient West Mexico (Pl. 32), beneath *At the Velodrome (Au Vélodrome)*, 1912, Jean Metzinger. Center: *Young Woman in the Form of a Flower (Jeune femme en forme de fleur)*, 1944 (cast 1957), Max Ernst. Right: *Seated Pierrot (Pierrot assis)*, 1922, Jacques Lipchitz, beneath *Sea=Dancer (Mare=Ballerina)*, January 1914, Gino Severini with the world)? Guggenheim hinted at this function, herself, in describing the room she dedicated to her daughter, Pegeen Vail. Following Pegeen's death in 1967, Guggenheim explained, "I consecrated one room to Pegeen... To me this was [her] tomb."[21] However consciously or not, Guggenheim surely knew that every room in the Palazzo Venier dei Leoni and *barchessa* would eventually commemorate her and her own prescient collecting—rivaling, in their own way, the dazzling abundance of a Chimú *ciudadela*.

1   Francesco Paolo Campione, "The Paradigm of Complexity: An Introduction to the Values of the Peggy Guggenheim Collection of Ethnic Art," in Francesco Paolo Campione, ed., *Ethnopassion: Peggy Guggenheim's Ethnic Art Collection*, exh. cat. (Milan: Mazzotta, 2008), pp. 21 and 23.

2   The term "pre-Columbian," along with its numerous substitutes ("pre-contact," "pre-colonial," "pre-Cortesian," "pre-Conquest," and "pre-Hispanic"), has rightly been faulted for its paternalism and lack of clarity. Not only does this label define a multitude of ancient American cultures through the lens of Western contact, but it also collapses them within a single category. I use the term here in its traditional, if admittedly problematic, sense, both because "pre-Columbian" is the term Peggy Guggenheim's generation would have recognized, and because it remains in use by many Mesoamericanists. Increasingly, however, the term "ancient American" has emerged as a less charged (if still problematically vague) substitute. It should be noted that, of the six works under discussion here, the Amazonian bark mask is the only one that may not be described as "pre-Columbian."

3   The three primary types of ancient West Mexican sculpture are named for the Mexican states from which they derive: Nayarit, Jalisco, and Colima. This tripartite classification system, established by the 1940s, depends upon a range of subtle differences in surface finish, gesture, and anatomical distribution. See R. Tripp Evans, "Navigating the Afterlife: Two Shaft Tomb Figures from Ancient West Mexico," *Yale University Art Gallery Bulletin* (New Haven: Yale University Art Gallery, 1995–96), p. 30.

4   Ibid., p. 29.

5   Guggenheim's ancient West Mexican figures are undoubtedly the "sculptures...from Mexico" that she acquired from Julius Carlebach in 1959, part of the suite of twelve works that formed the genesis of her collection of African, Oceanic, and ancient American art. See Peggy Guggenheim, *Out of This Century: Confessions of an Art Addict* (New York: Universe Books; London: André Deutsch, 1979), p. 363. For more on Carlebach and his gallery, see Christa Clarke's excellent treatment in the present volume, p. 37.

6   While conducting research in this region in the 1890s, archaeologist Carl Lumholz encountered, to his alarm, a thriving market in ancient West Mexican figures in Guadalajara. See Richard F. Townsend, "Renewing the Inquiry in Ancient West Mexico," in Richard F. Townsend, ed., *Ancient West Mexico: Art and Archaeology of the Unknown Past*, exh. cat. (Chicago: Art Institute of Chicago, 1998), p. 16.

7   George C. Crawford, *A Tourist's Guide to Points in and near the City of Mexico* (New York: G.G. Crawford, 1890), p. 3; as cited in R. Tripp Evans, *Romancing the Maya: Mexican Antiquity in the American Imagination, 1820–1915* (Austin: University of Texas Press, 2004), p. 162.

8   For a full treatment of this revealing excavation, see Lorenza López Mestas Cambreros and Jorge Ramos de la Vega, "Excavating the Tomb at Huitzalapa," in Townsend, *Ancient West Mexico*, pp. 53–70.

9   Frida Kahlo and Diego Rivera's collection, first published in Rivera's *Art in Ancient Mexico*, 1941, formed the core of the first major exhibition to present the works of ancient West Mexico, organized at Mexico City's Palacio de Bellas Artes in 1946.

10   Beginning in the 1930s, Franklin Delano Roosevelt's "Good Neighbor Policy" aimed at greater cooperation between the United States, Central America, and South America, largely due to fears that Communism might gain a foothold in these regions. The policy, which shaped everything from trade to Hollywood filmmaking, had a profound impact on the U.S. perception of Latin America. See James Oles, *South of the Border: Mexico in the American Imagination 1914–1947*, exh. cat. (Washington: Smithsonian Institution Press, 1993), p. 5.

11   André Breton introduced Guggenheim to his personal collection of Mexican folk art at his apartment in Montmartre in 1937. See Guggenheim, *Out of This Century*, pp. 188–89.

12   The artist and collector Robert Brady moved from Venice to Mexico City in 1959, thus Guggenheim may have seen him on her trip. In 1961 he settled in Cuernavaca, and his residence eventually became a house-museum to showcase his collection of ancient and contemporary Mexican art, along with objects from Africa, Asia, and Oceania, and his own work. (An earlier model for his approach was The Barnes Collection, where he studied as a young man.) Guggenheim visited Brady in Cuernavaca on multiple occasions. For details of Guggenheim's Mexico trip, see Guggenheim, *Out of This Century*, pp. 358–60 (her visit to the Frida Kahlo Museum, which had opened the year before her trip, appears on p. 359). Further details on Brady were provided by the Museo Robert Brady, including correspondence with Andrea Díaz Vargas on December 11, 2019; Howard Scott, in a telephone interview on December 13, 2019; and Barbara Anne Beaucar, The Barnes Foundation. I am grateful to all three.

13   Considering Guggenheim's admiration for the work of Josef Albers, Paul Klee, and their Bauhaus circle, she may well have known of Josef and Anni Albers's numerous explorations of ancient Mesoamerican ruins, beginning in 1934 and continuing throughout the 1940s and '50s. See Barbara Braun, *Pre-Columbian Art and the Post-Columbian World: Ancient American Sources of Modern Art* (New York: Harry N. Abrams, 1993), pp. 303–4. For Guggenheim's visit to Palenque, see Guggenheim, *Out of This Century*, p. 359.

14   Given its remarkable state of preservation, this *poncho* almost surely derived from a tomb (the arid Andean desert climate has preserved feather and textile work as early as 500 BCE).

15   The carving of this panel set shares stylistic traits with two of the cultures absorbed by the Kingdom of Chimor—the Nazca and Chancay—yet its identification as Chimú seems far more likely given its minimalist style and the greater preponderance of Chimú works available to collectors at mid-century. Although Guggenheim's mummy mask is unusual, it is not without precedent. The Brooklyn Museum owns a similarly hinged, three-panel mummy mask of painted wood, ca. 1100–1400 CE.

16   Rebecca Stone-Miller estimates that, at its height, the Kingdom of Chimor employed thousands of state-supported artists who primarily produced goods for funeral use. See Rebecca Stone-Miller, *Art of the Andes from Chavín to Inca* (London: Thames and Hudson, 1995), p. 168.

17   The hypothesis that this mask might have covered the *fardo* of a commoner is my own, based on two factors: first, the work's rudimentary execution and humble material (mummy masks for the elite were typically made from beaten gold); and second, the widespread practice of placing sacrificial servants and wives within royal Chimú burials.

18   See Maria Camilla De Palma's entry on the *Ya'ko-ko su'ti-ro* (catalogue no. 4) in Campione, *Ethnopassion*, p. 73.

19   For more on this display strategy and its sources, see Ellen McBreen's thorough investigation of the practice in the present volume, pp. 17–34.

20   Peter Furst introduced his theory concerning the ritualistic use of hallucinogens in ancient West Mexico in 1965; see Peter Furst, "West Mexican Tomb Sculpture as Evidence for Shamanism in Prehispanic America," *Antropología* 14 (1965), pp. 1–37. Once considered controversial, Furst's theories concerning shamanic transformation are now generally accepted within the scholarship on ancient West Mexican sculpture. Furst's fullest and most recent treatment of his theories appears in Furst, "Shamanic Symbolism, Transformation, and Deities in West Mexican Funerary Art," in Townsend, *Ancient West Mexico*, pp. 169–90.

21   Guggenheim, *Out of This Century*, pp. 370–71.

Africa

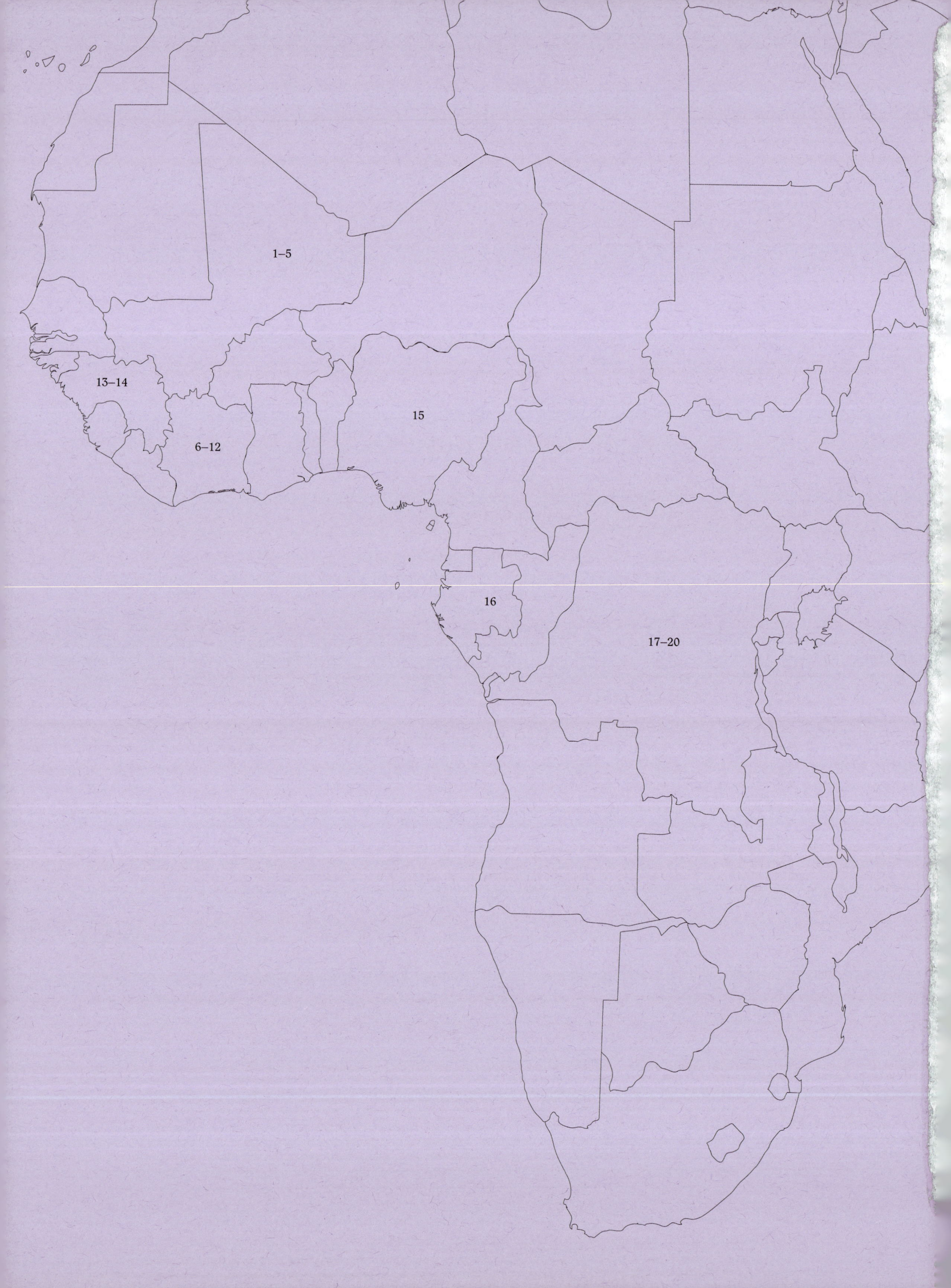

1–5
13–14
6–12
15
16
17–20

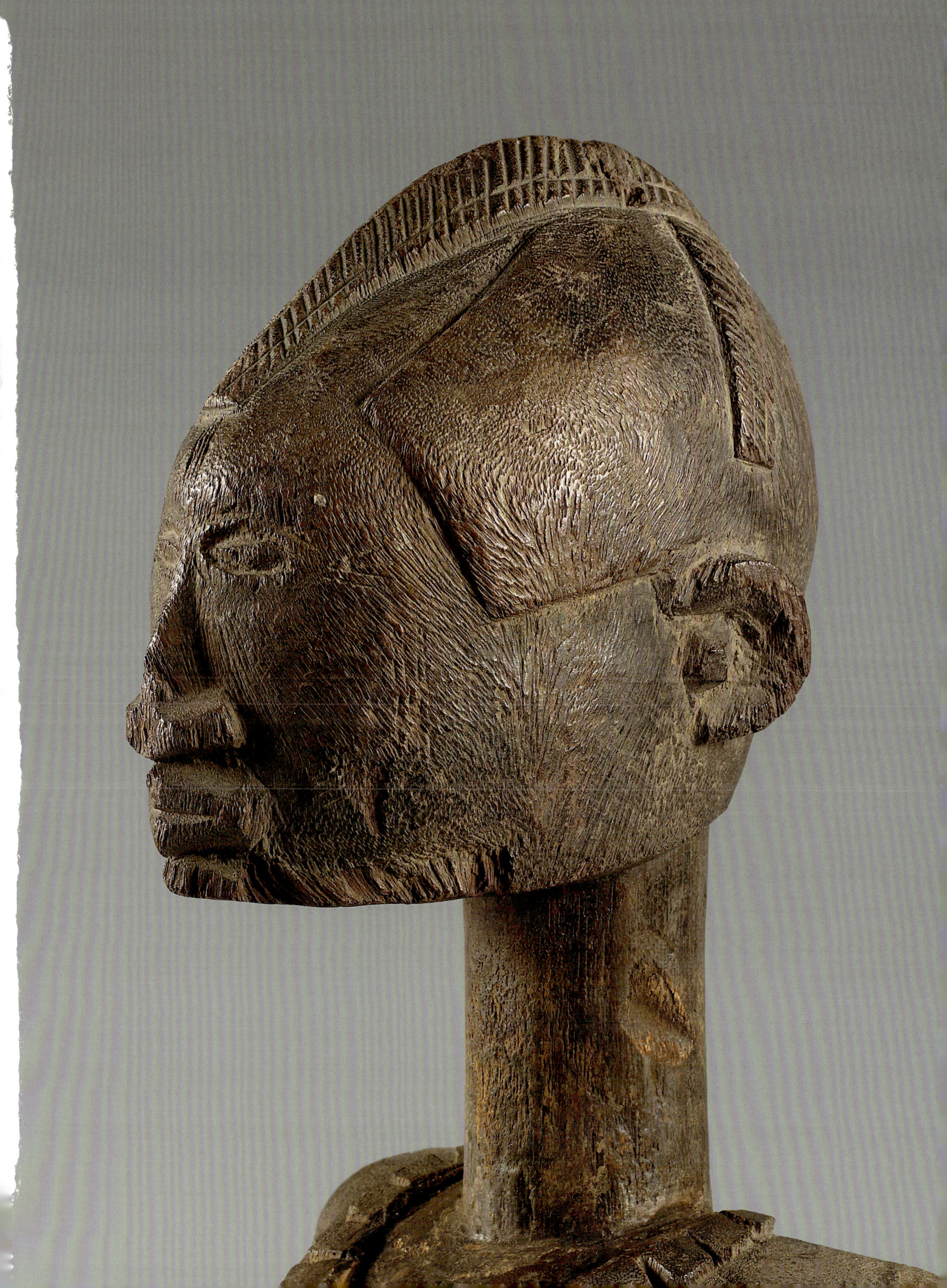

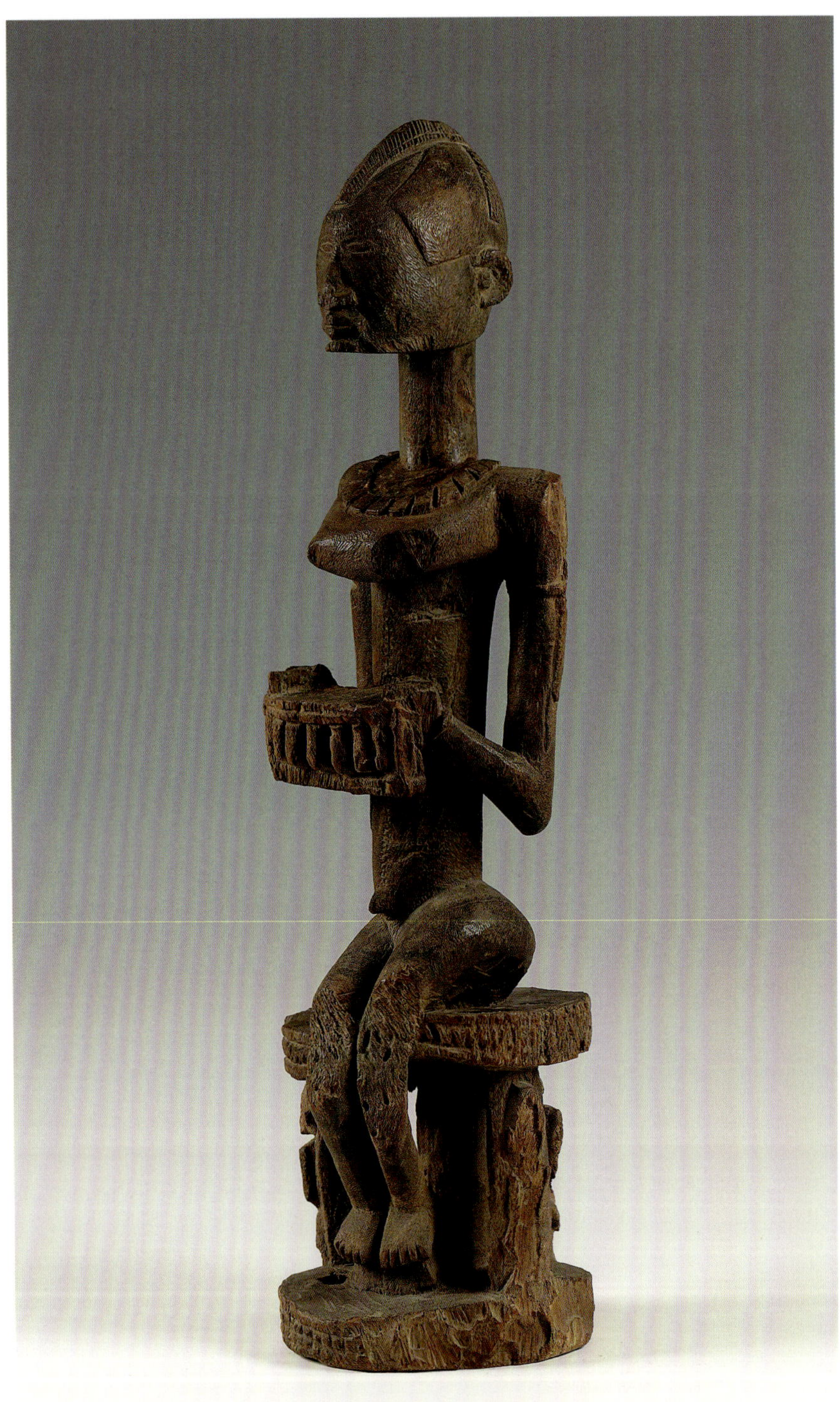

1   Seated male figure, probably first half of 20th century
Unrecorded Dogon artist, N'duleri region, Mali
Wood and natural pigment, 68 × 20 × 20 cm

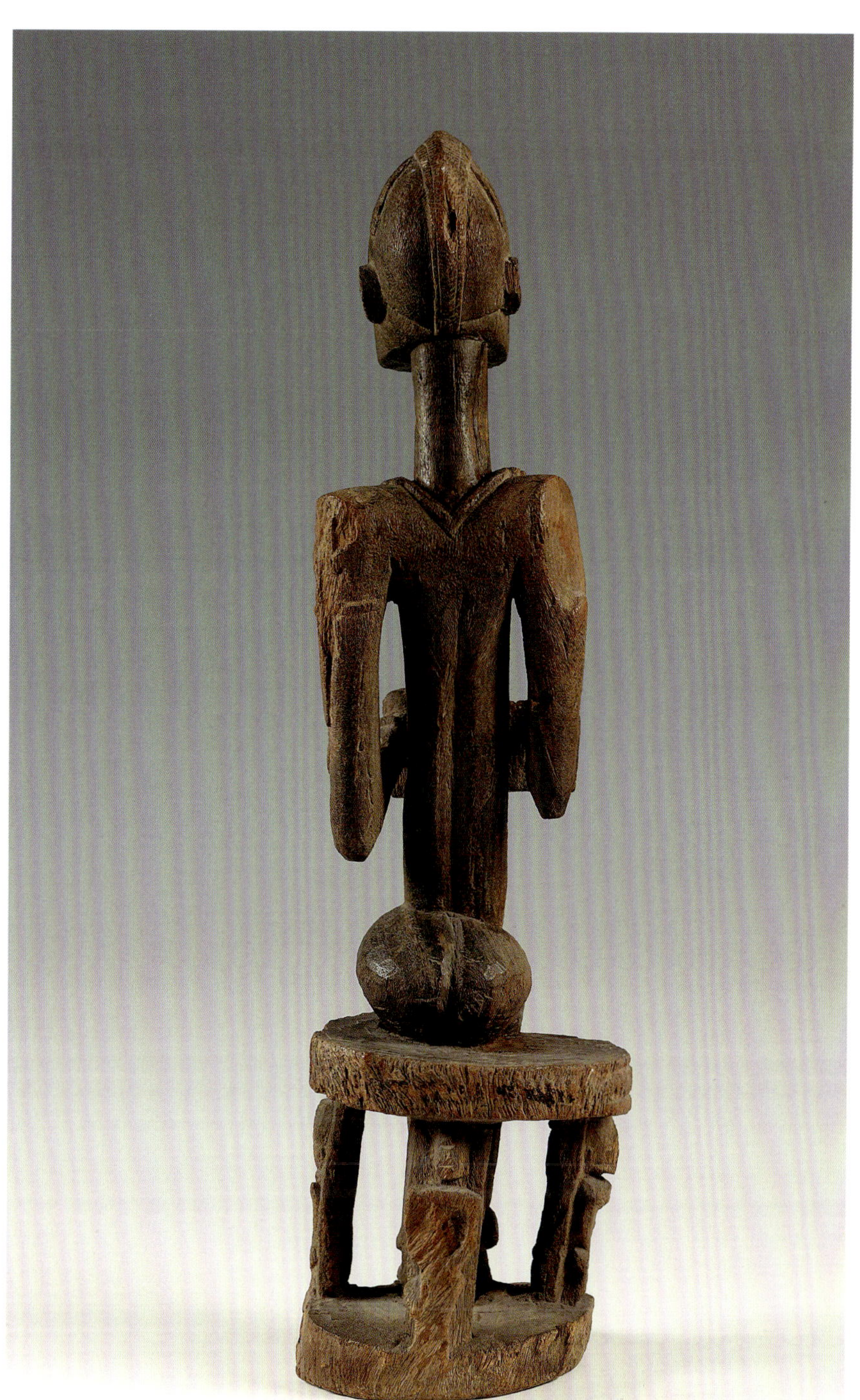

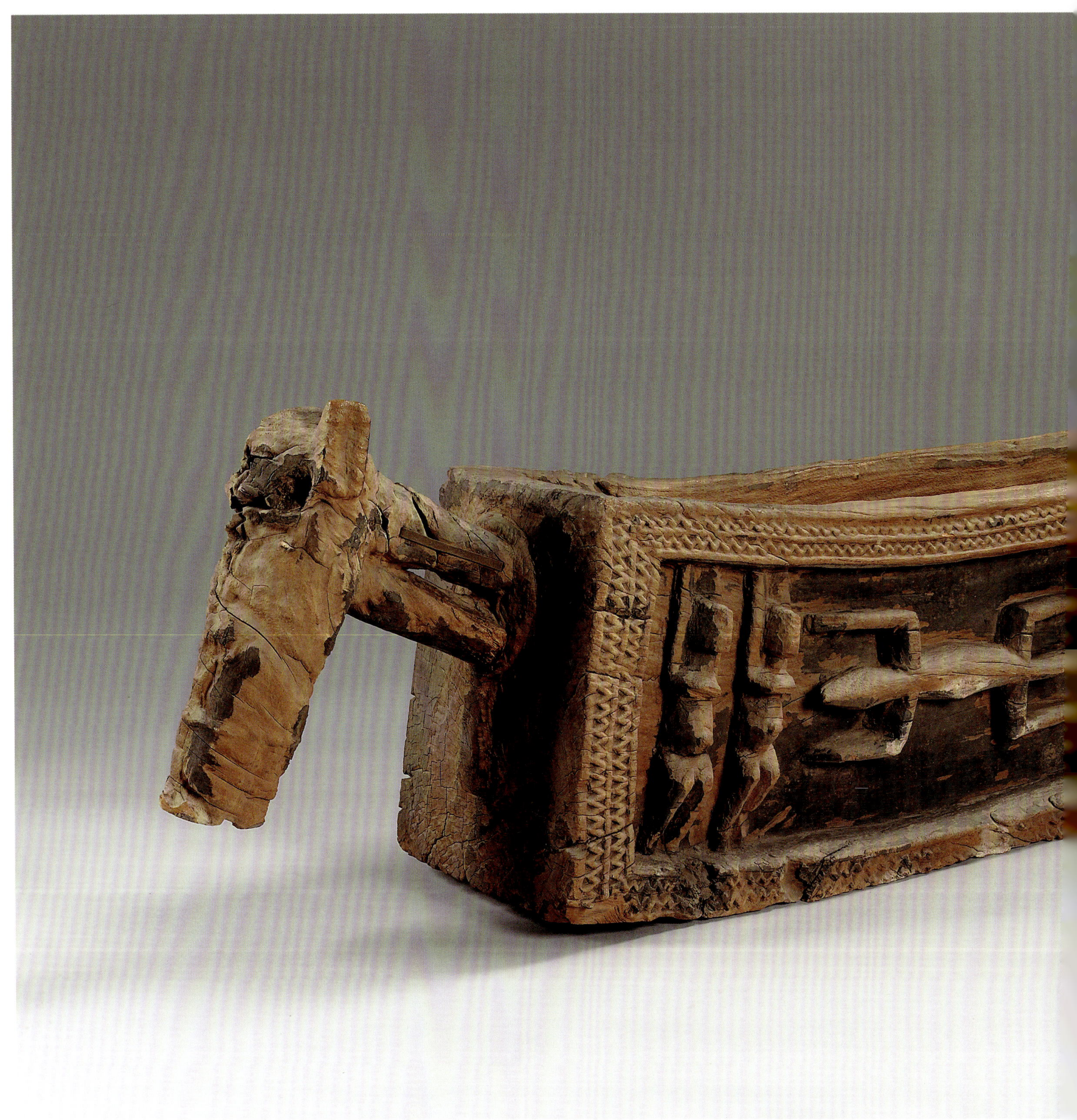

2 Vessel (*aduno koro*), possibly 16th – early 20th century
Unrecorded Dogon artist, Mali
Wood and natural pigment, 46 × 126 × 28 cm

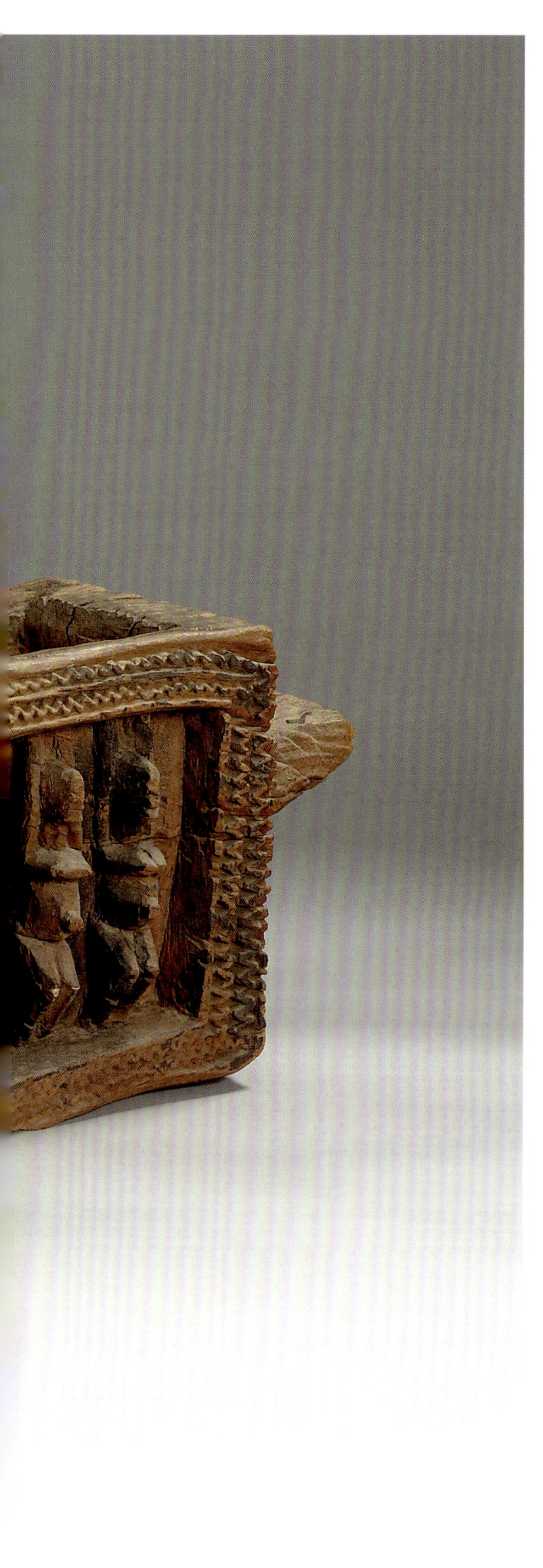

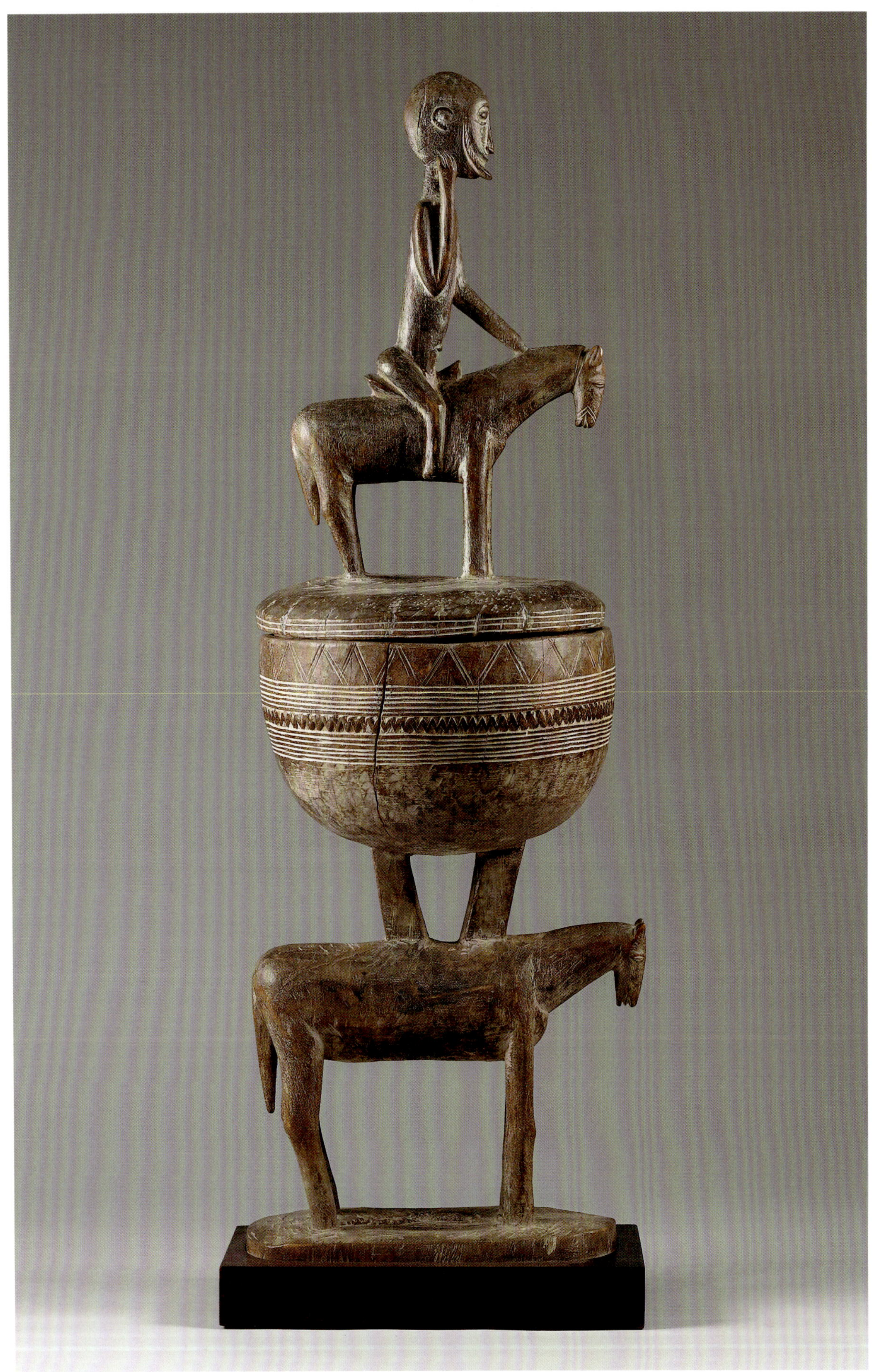

3 Lidded container, probably first half of 20th century
Unrecorded Dogon artist, Mali
Wood, 110 × 42 × 35 cm

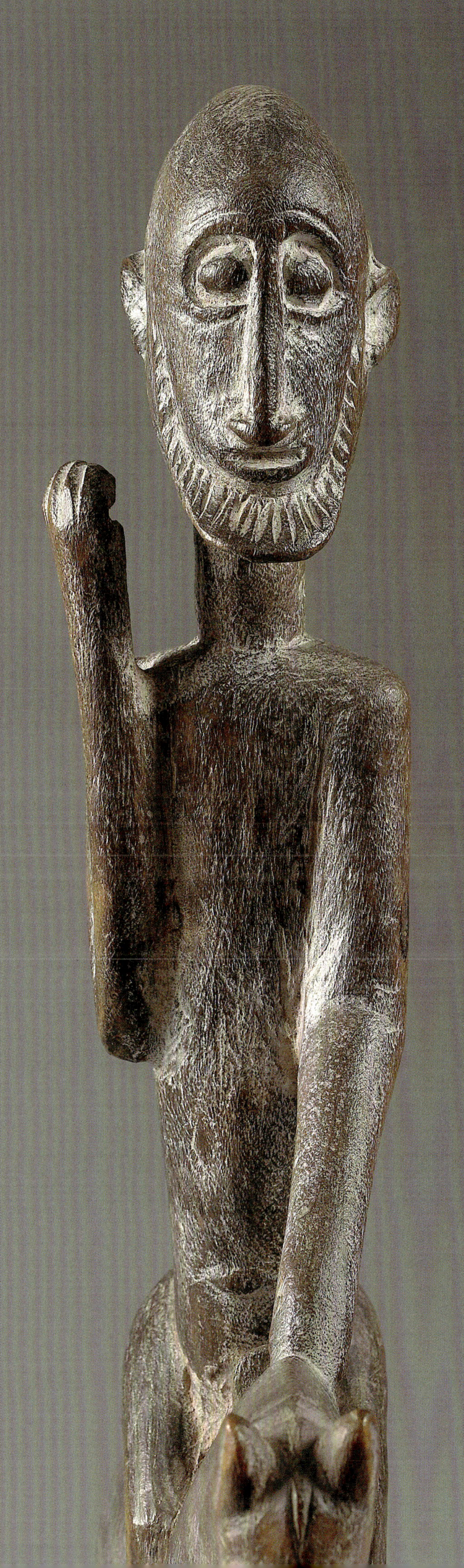

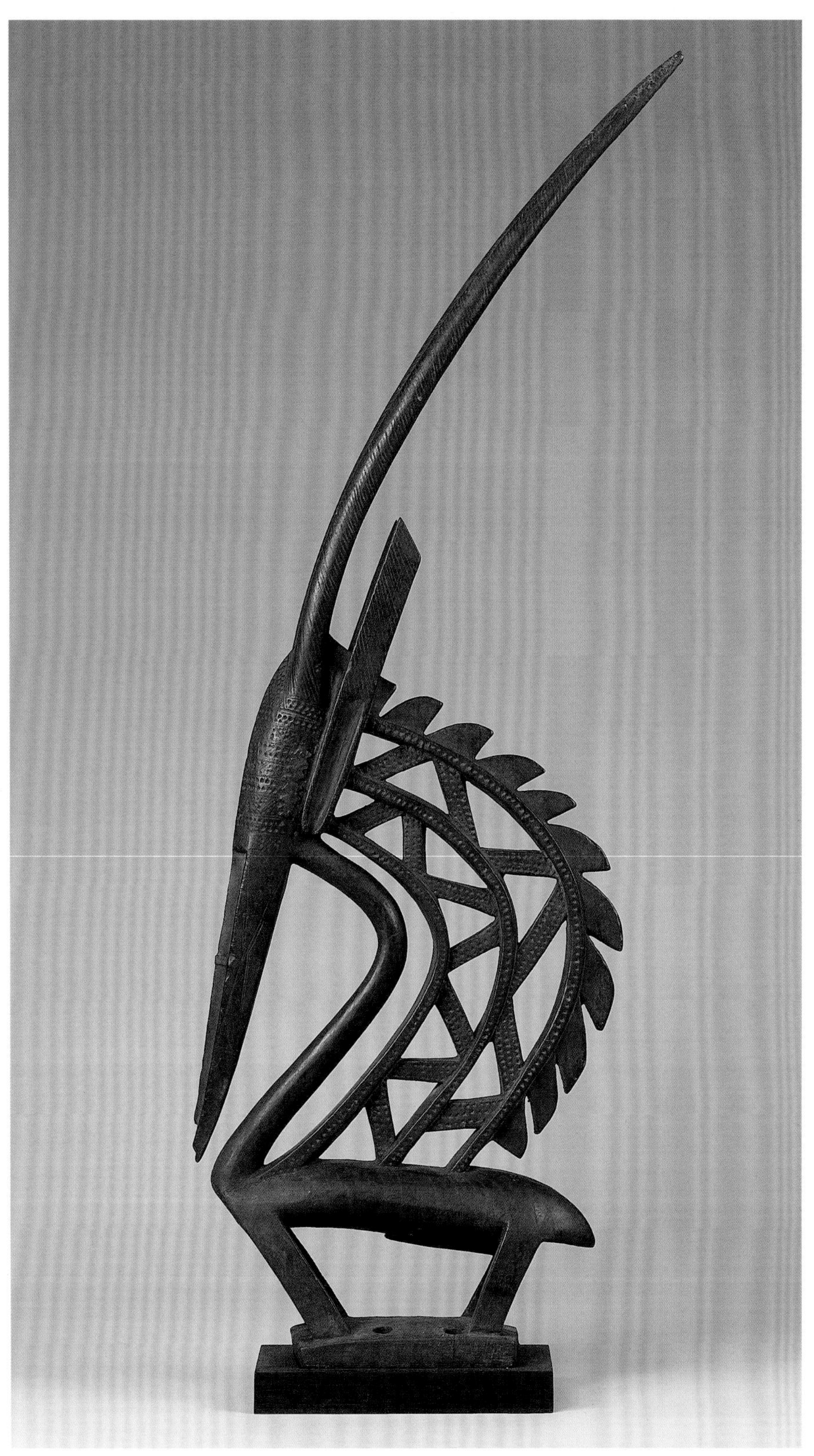

4   Male *Ci Wara* headdress, probably first half of 20th century
Unrecorded Bamana artist, Ségou region, Mali
Wood, 106 × 38 × 10 cm

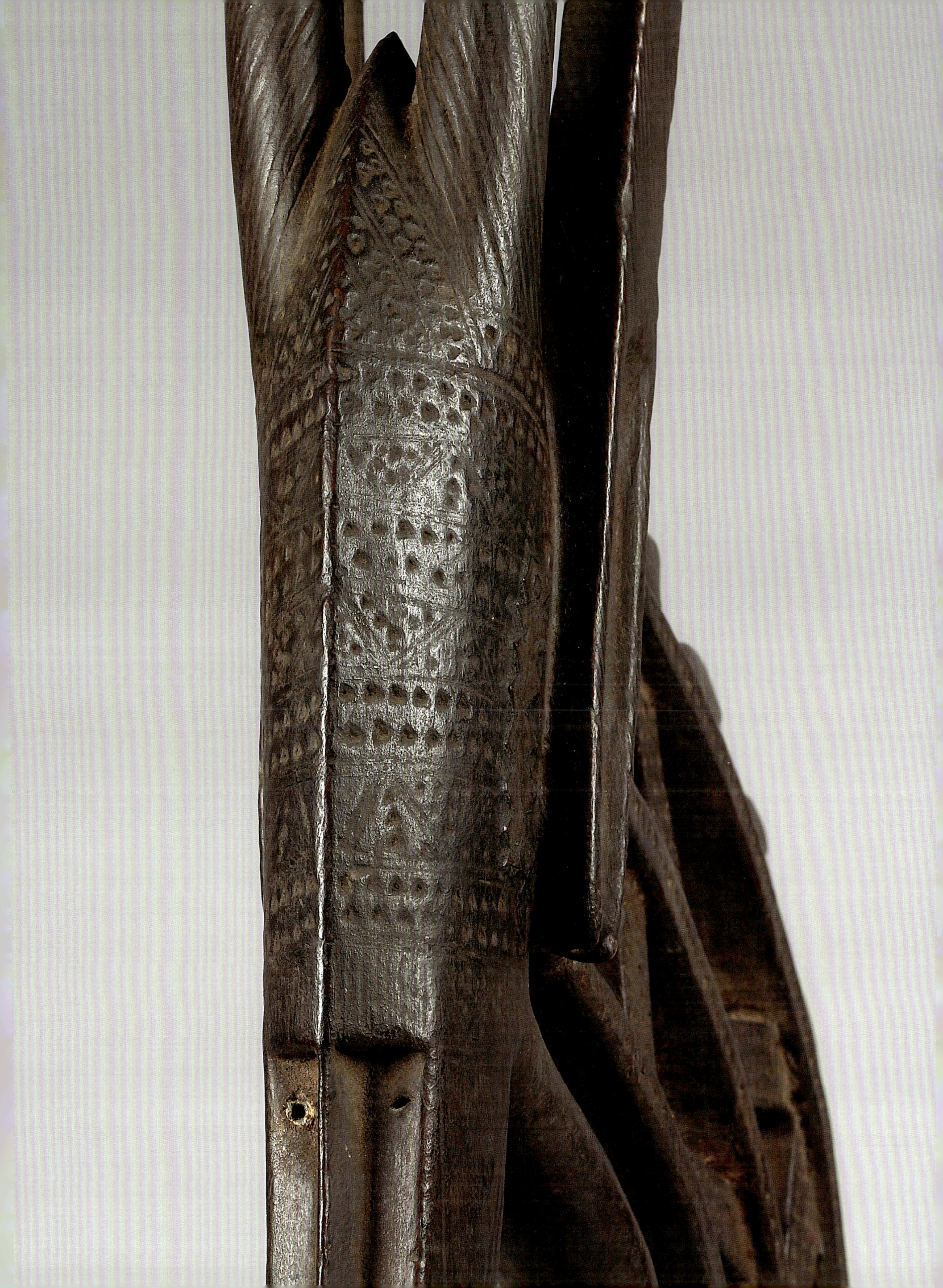

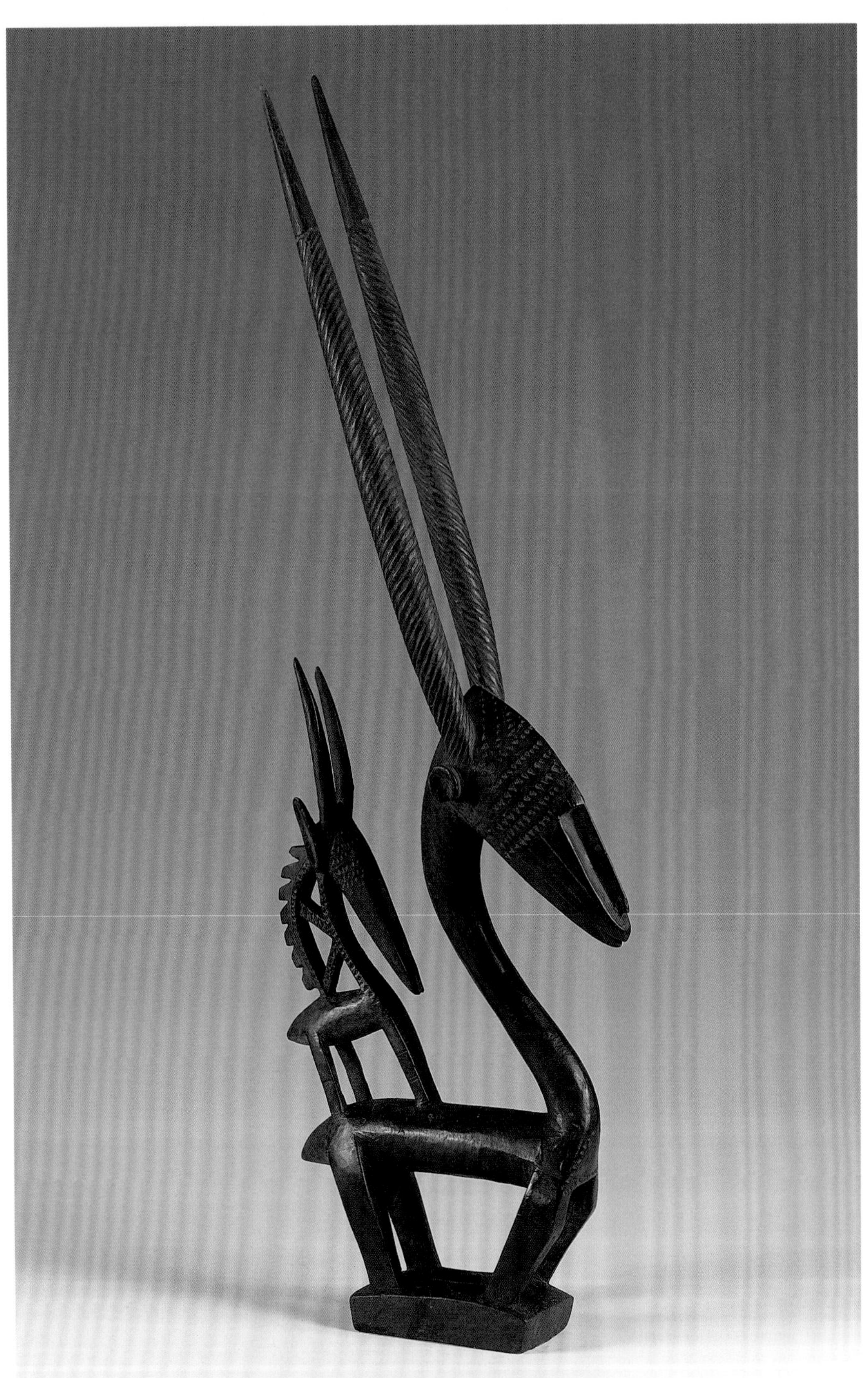

5   Female *Ci Wara* headdress, probably first half of 20th century
Unrecorded Bamana artist, Ségou region, Mali
Wood, 86 × 30 × 10 cm

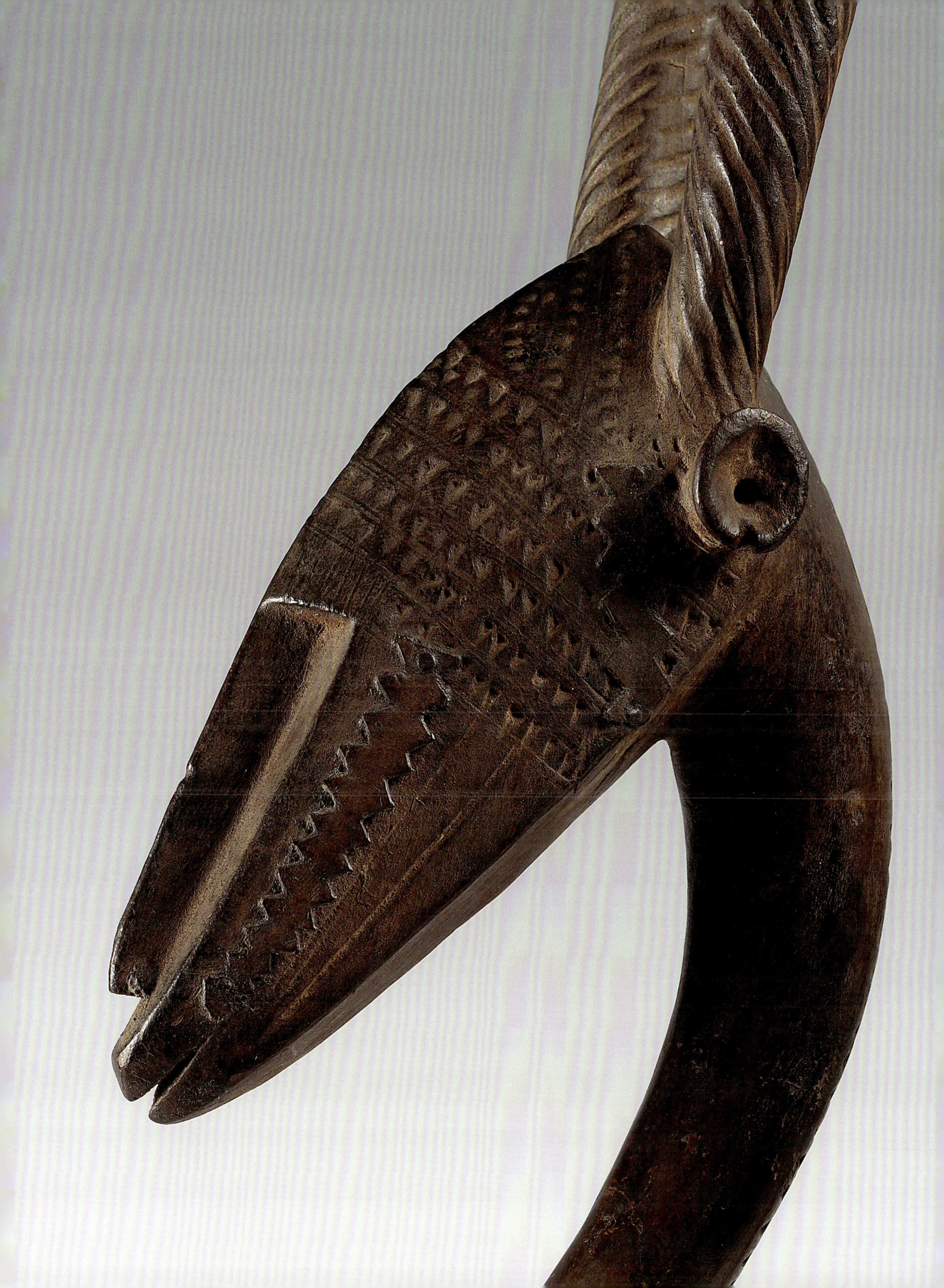

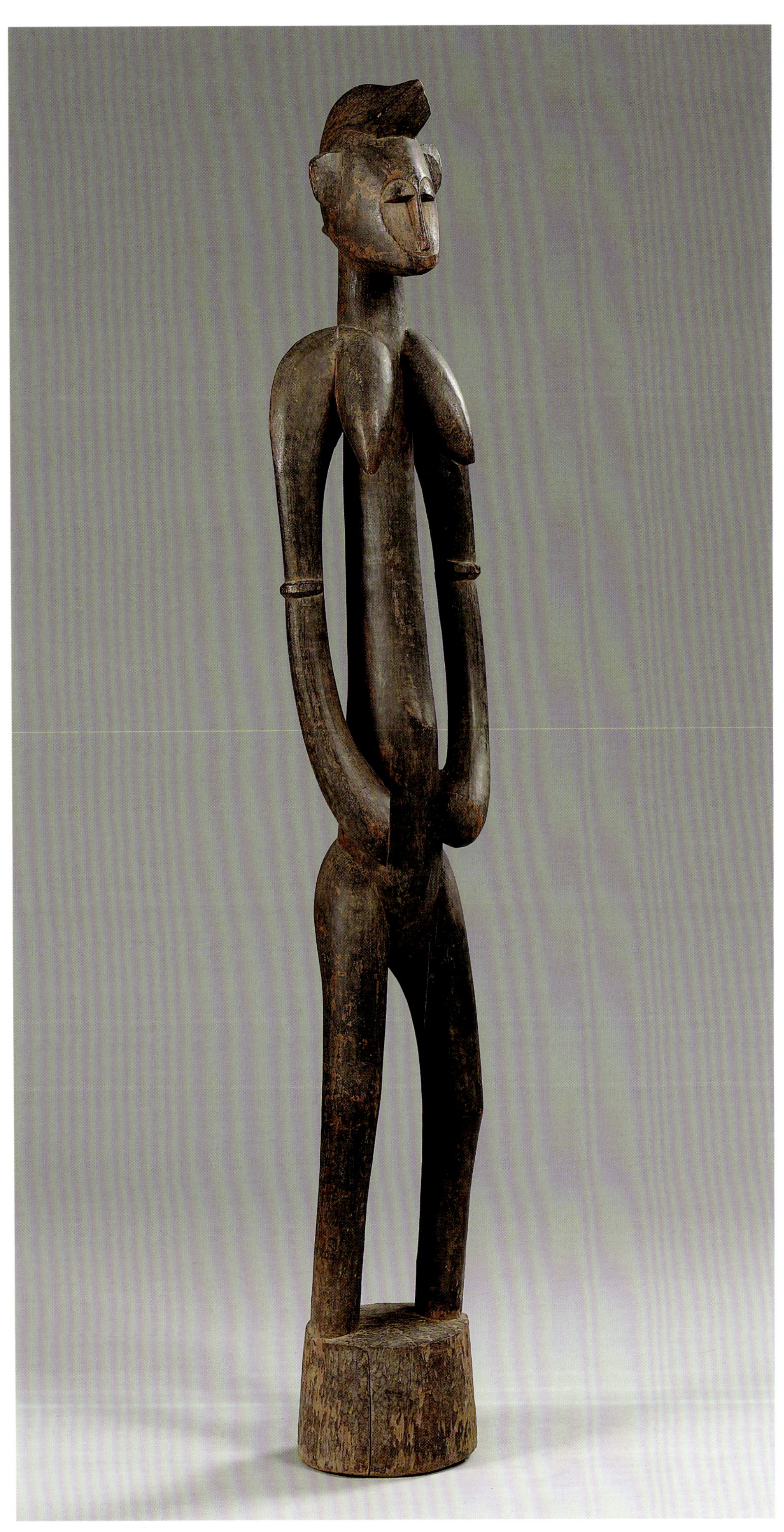

6　Female figure (*pombia*), probably first half of 20th century
Unrecorded Senufo artist, Côte d'Ivoire
Wood, 130 × 18 × 18 cm

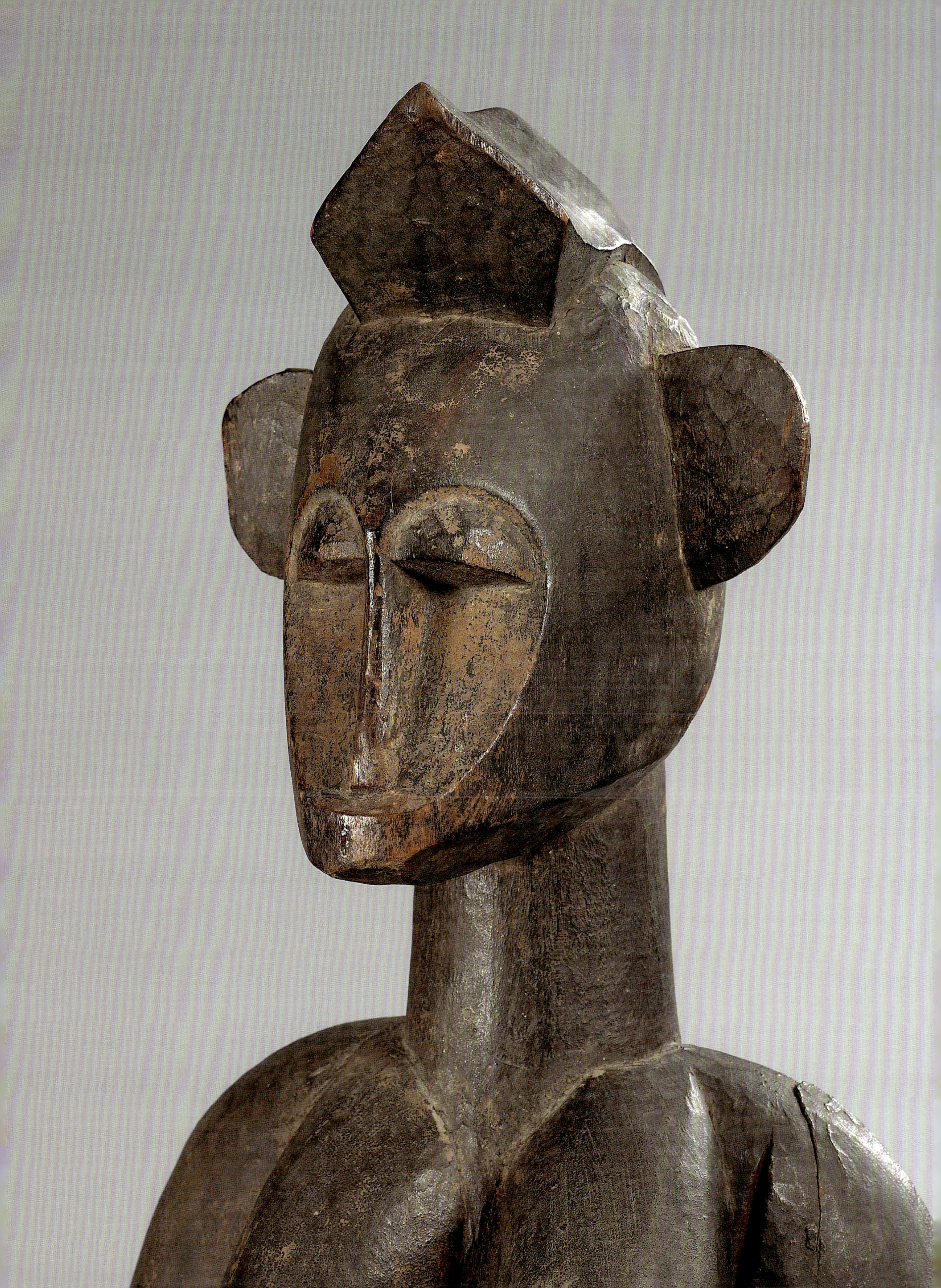

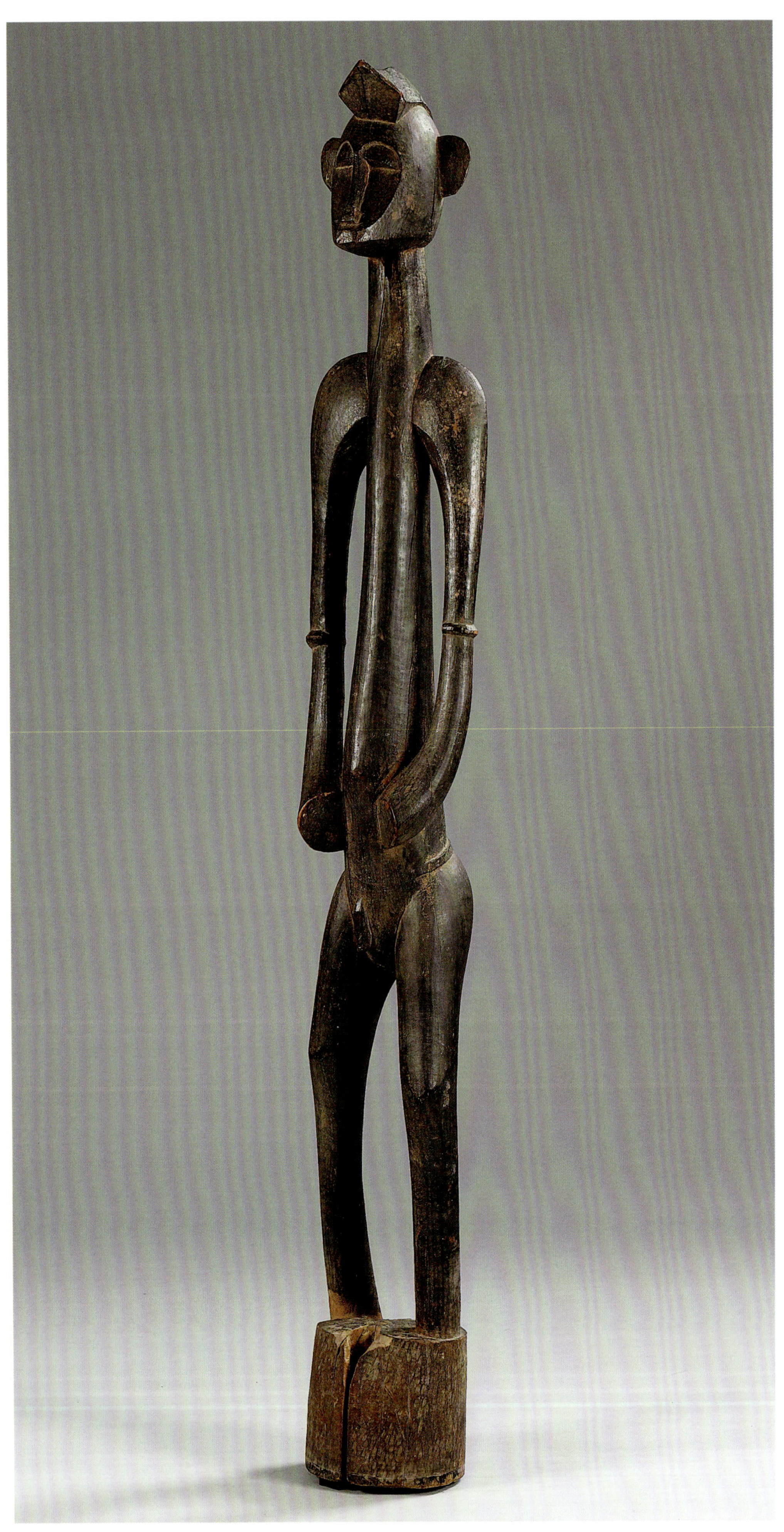

7   Male figure (*pombia*), probably first half of 20th century
Unrecorded Senufo artist, Côte d'Ivoire
Wood, 132 × 18 × 18 cm

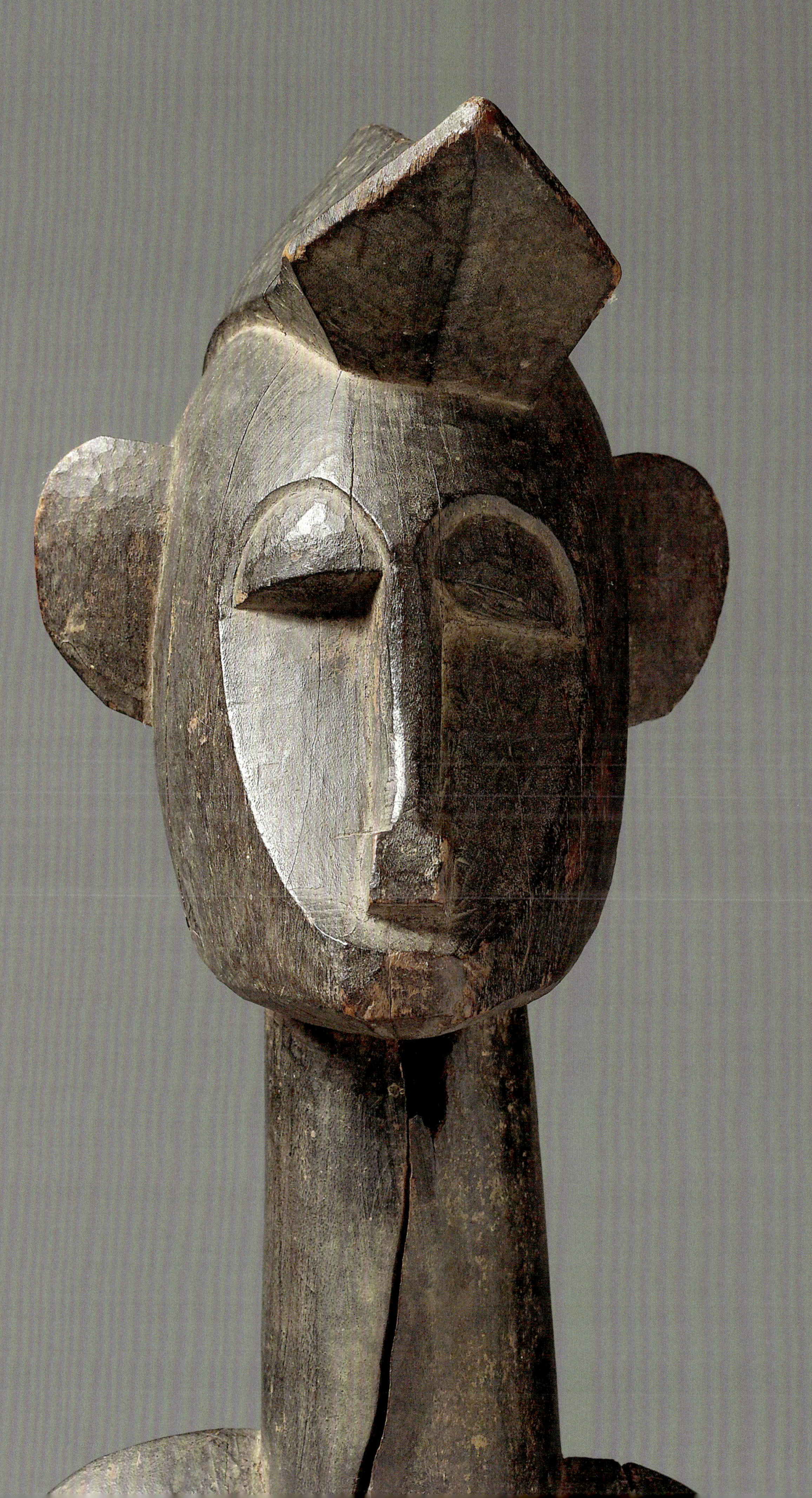

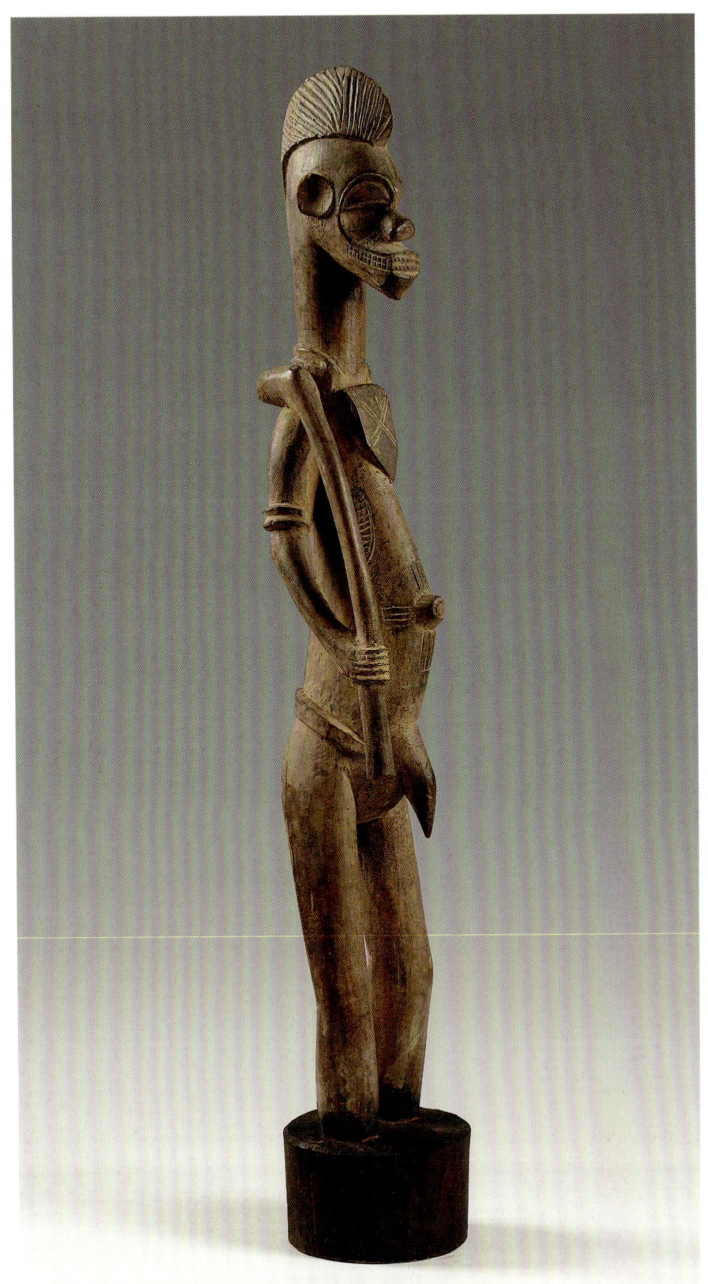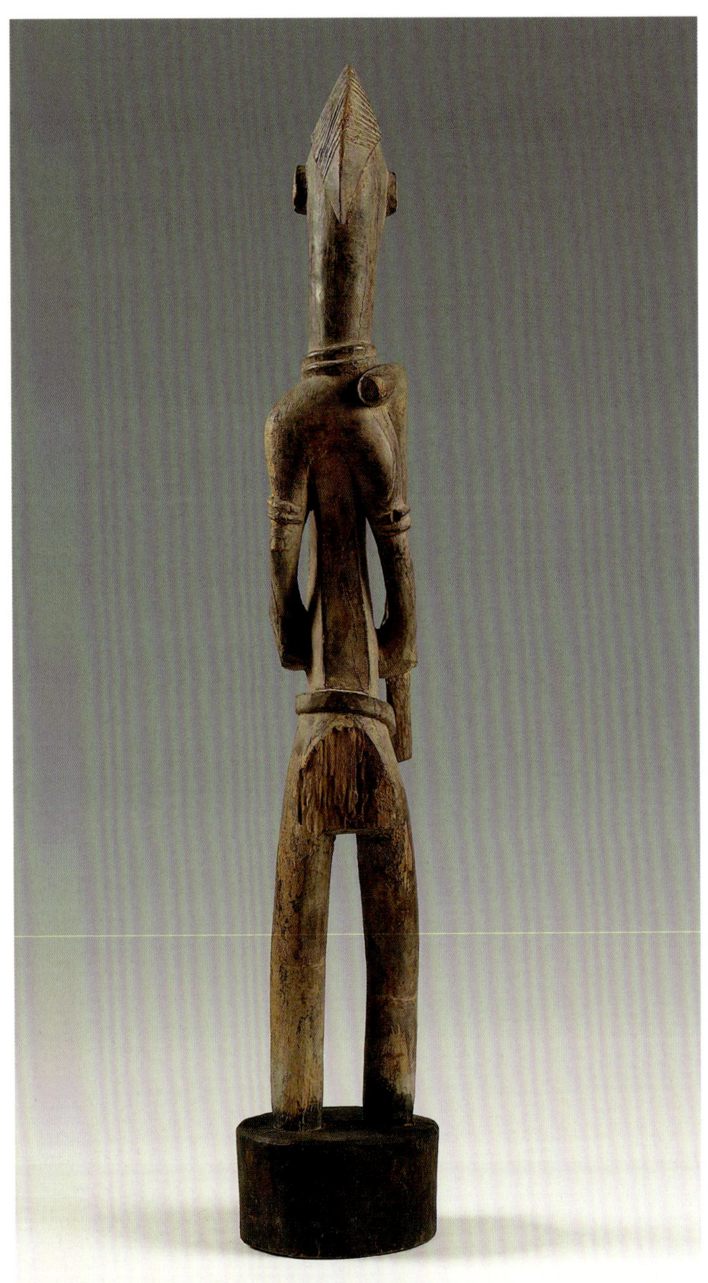

8   Male figure (*pombia*), probably mid-20th century
Unrecorded Senufo artist, Côte d'Ivoire
Wood, 78 × 17 × 17 cm

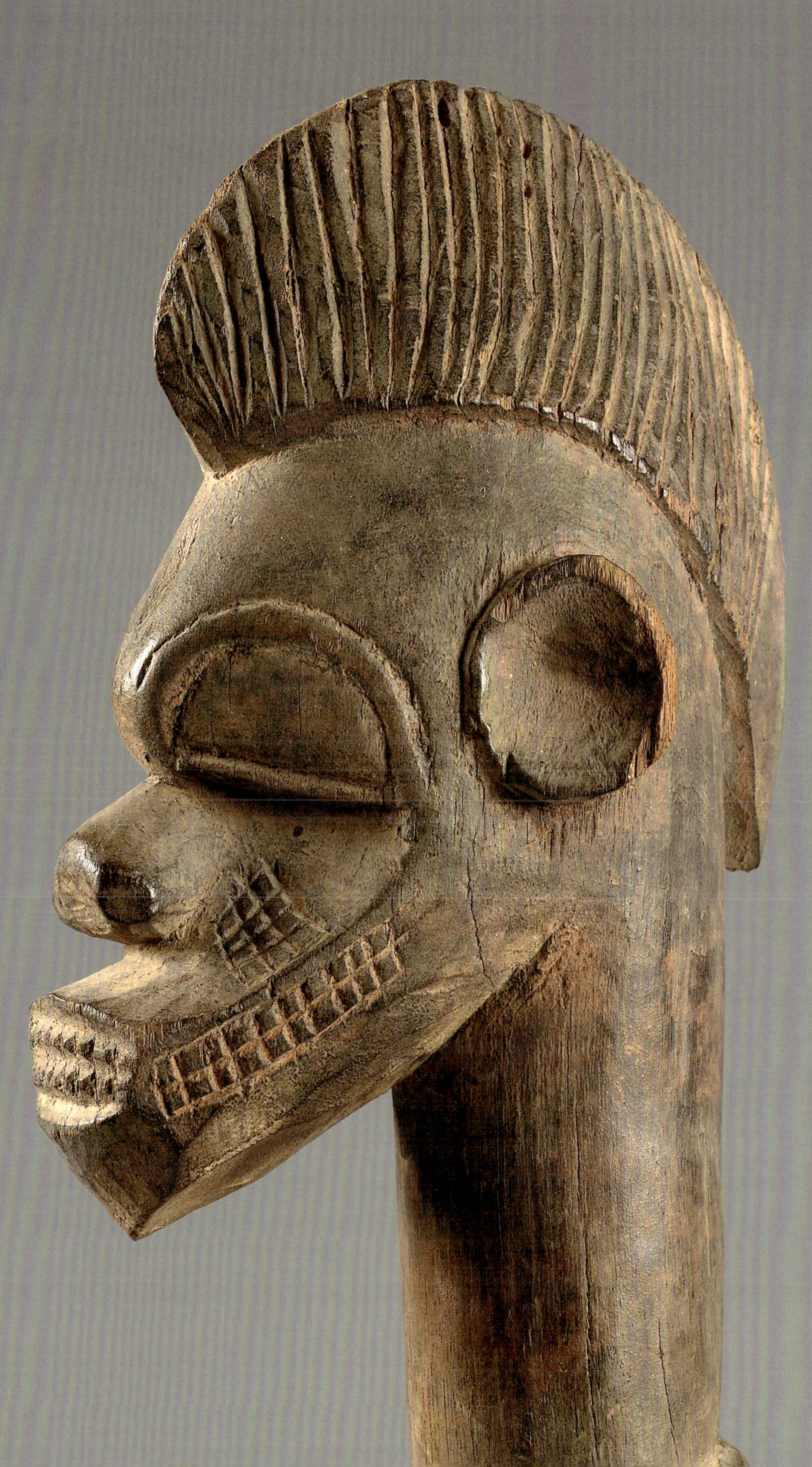

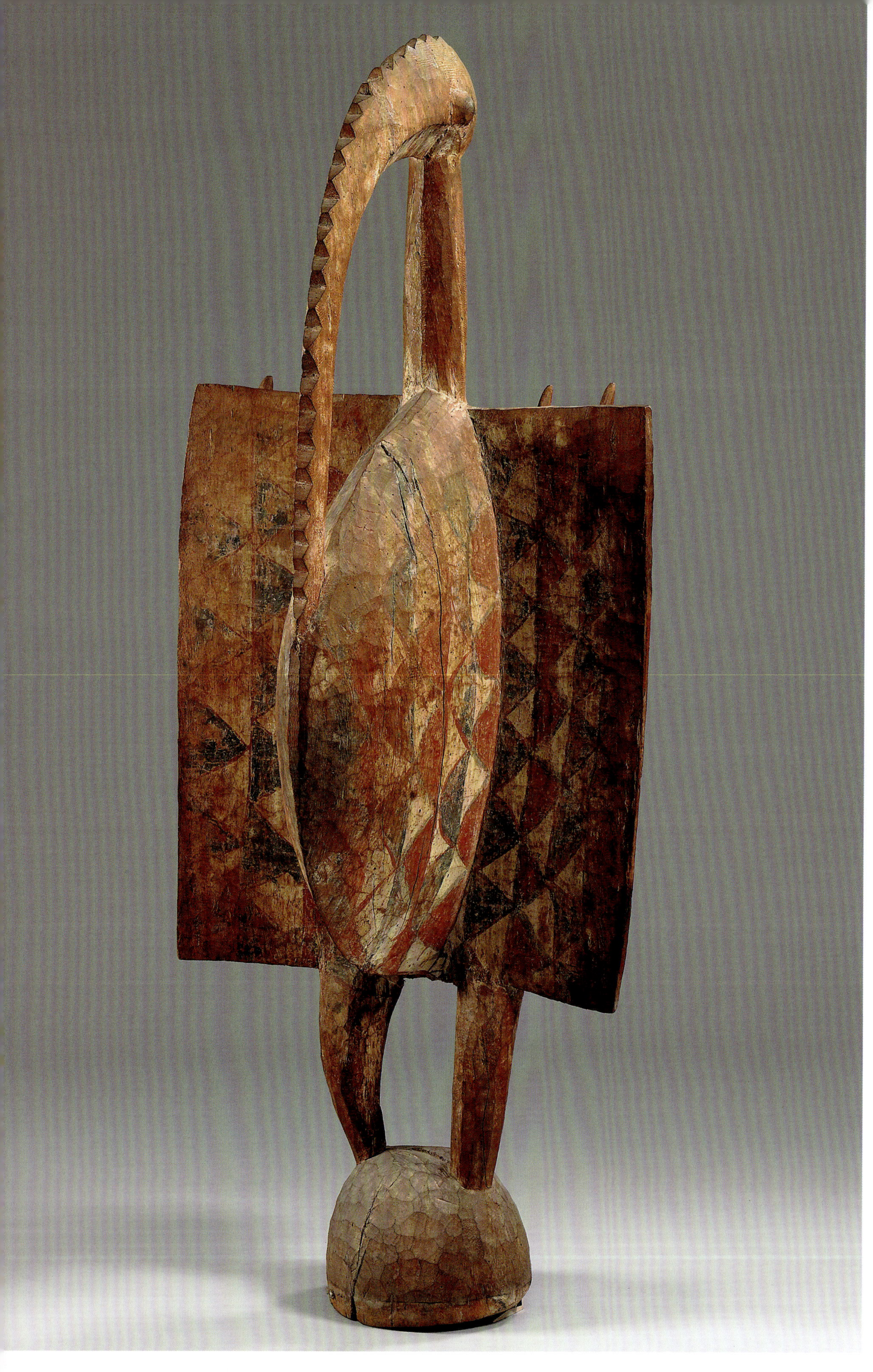

9   Figure of a hornbill, probably first half of 20th century
Unrecorded Senufo artist, Côte d'Ivoire
Wood and natural pigment, 144 × 59 × 47 cm

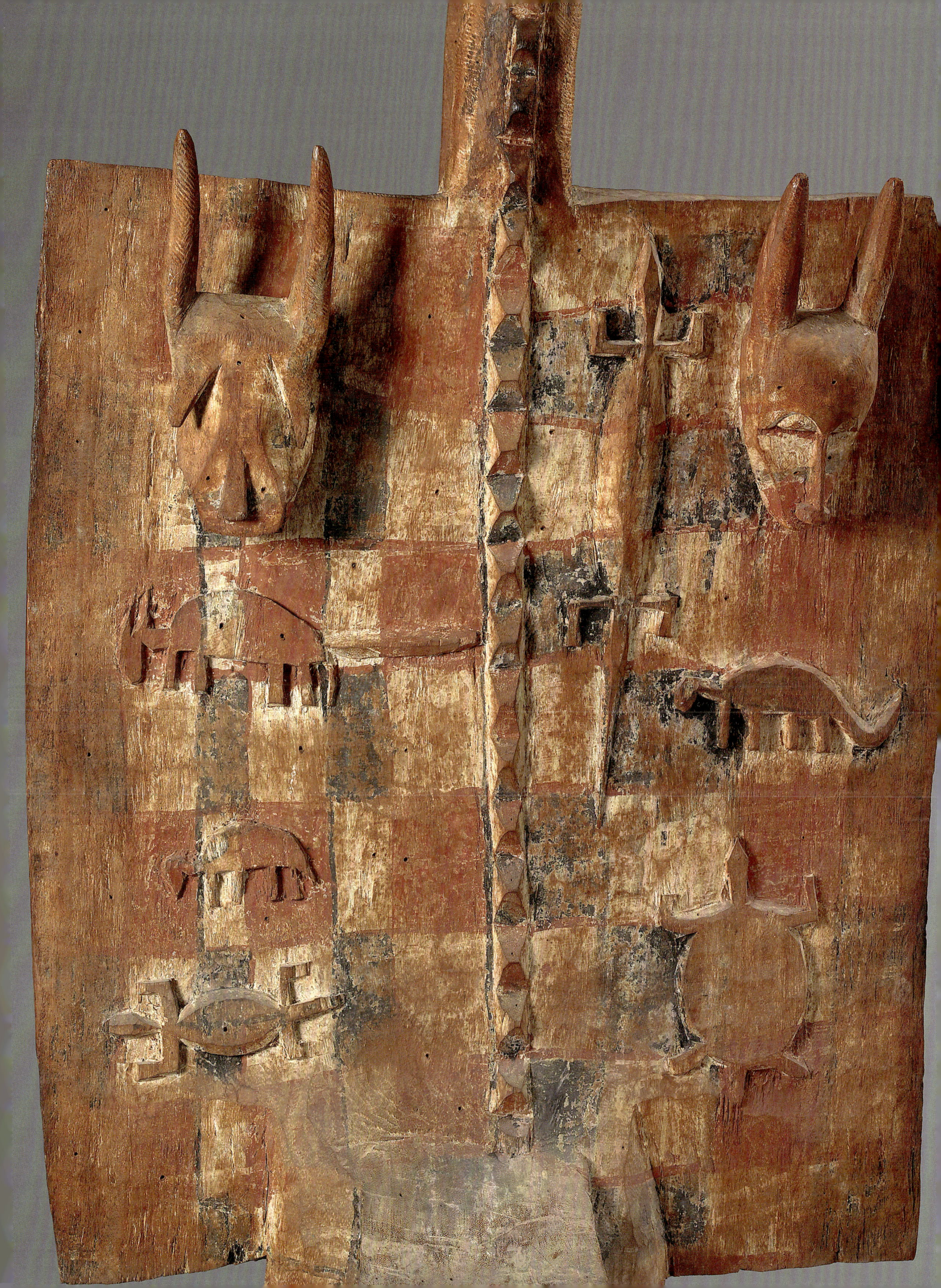

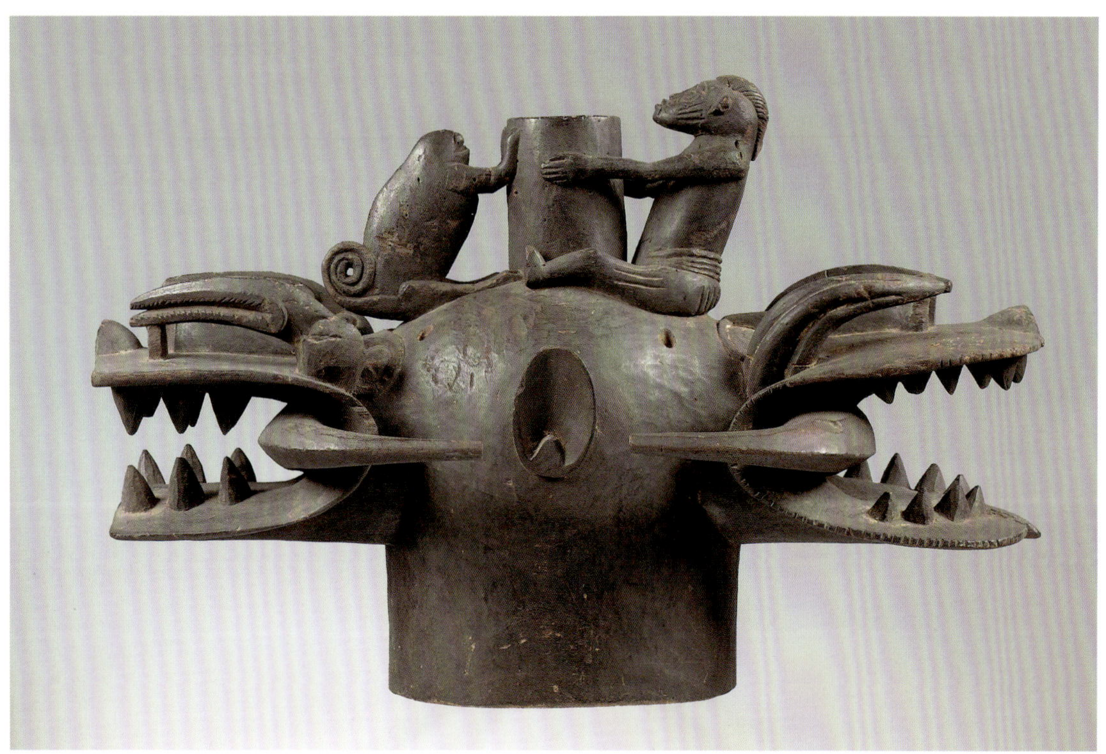

10 Two-faced helmet mask (*wanyugo*), probably mid-20th century
Unrecorded Senufo artist, Côte d'Ivoire
Wood, 44 × 71 × 33 cm

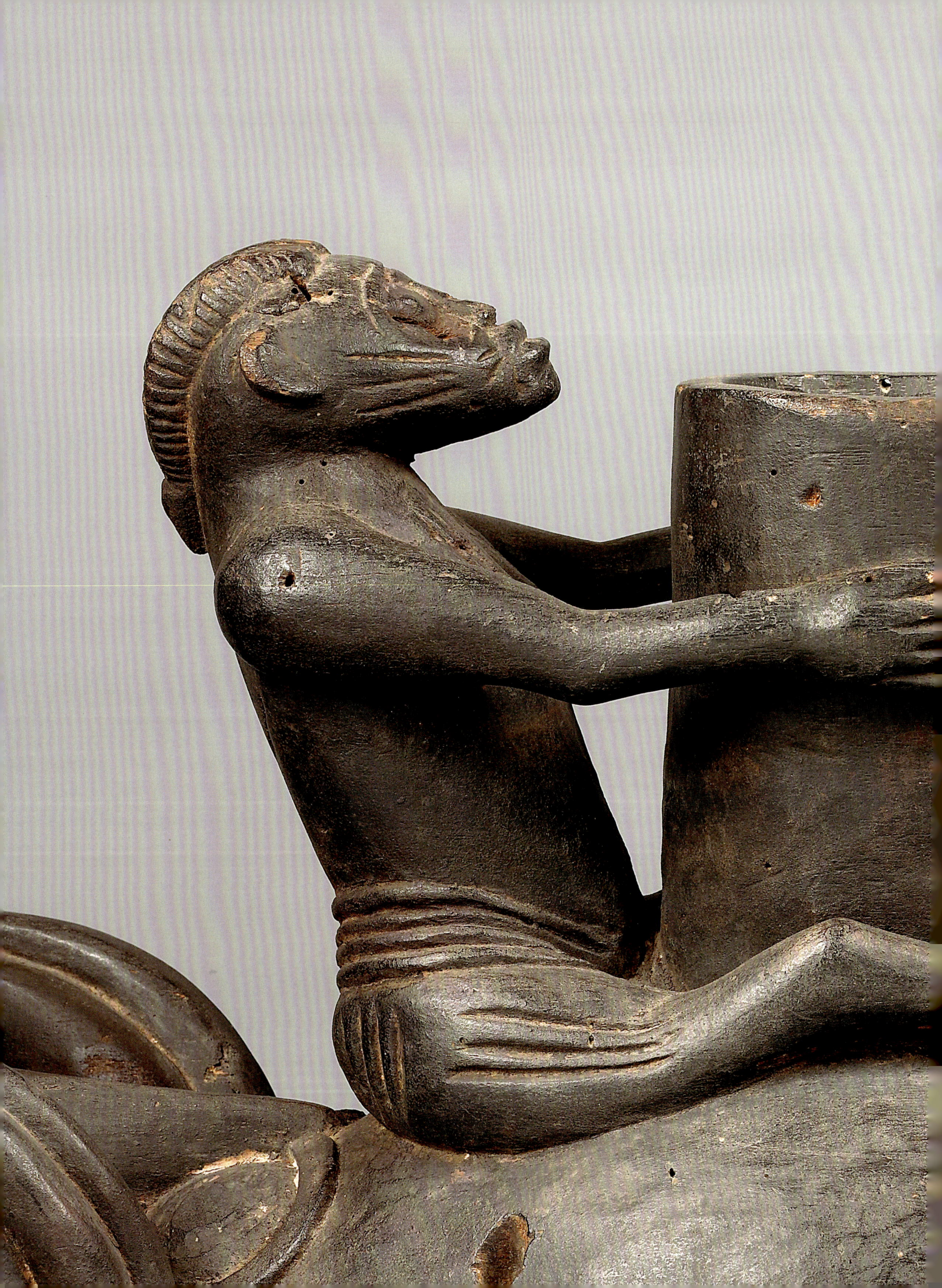

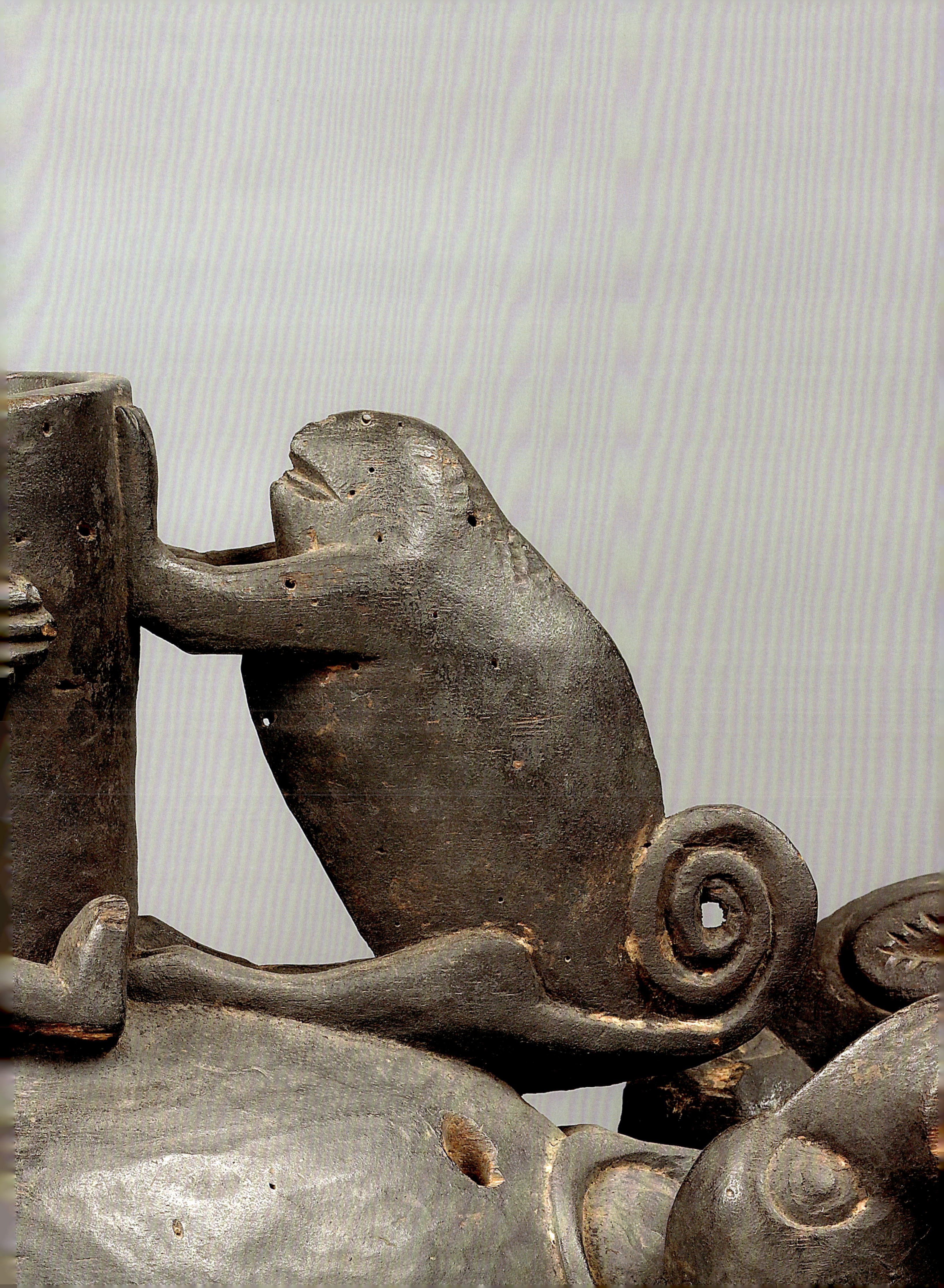

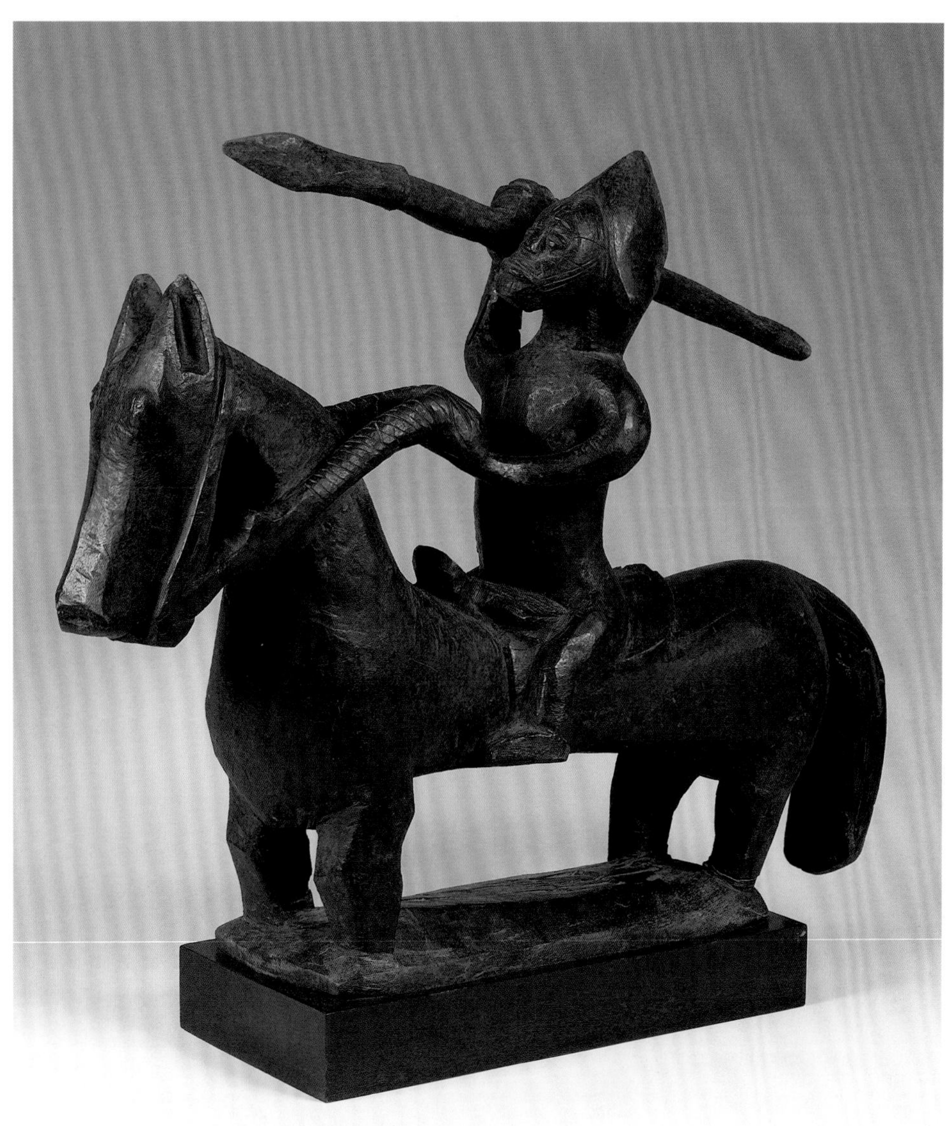

11   Equestrian figure, probably first half of 20th century
Unrecorded Senufo artist, Côte d'Ivoire
Wood, 49 × 20 × 64 cm

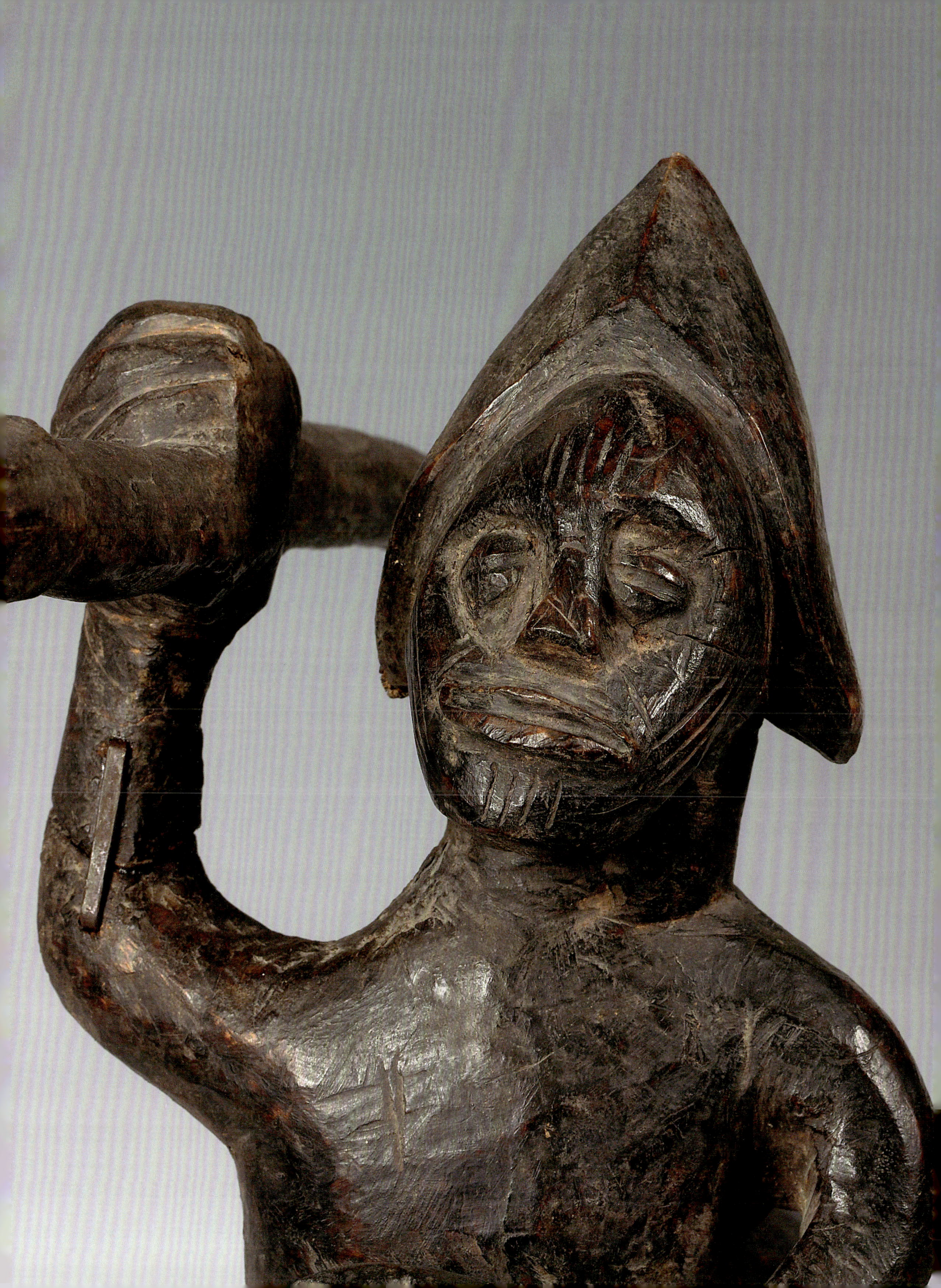

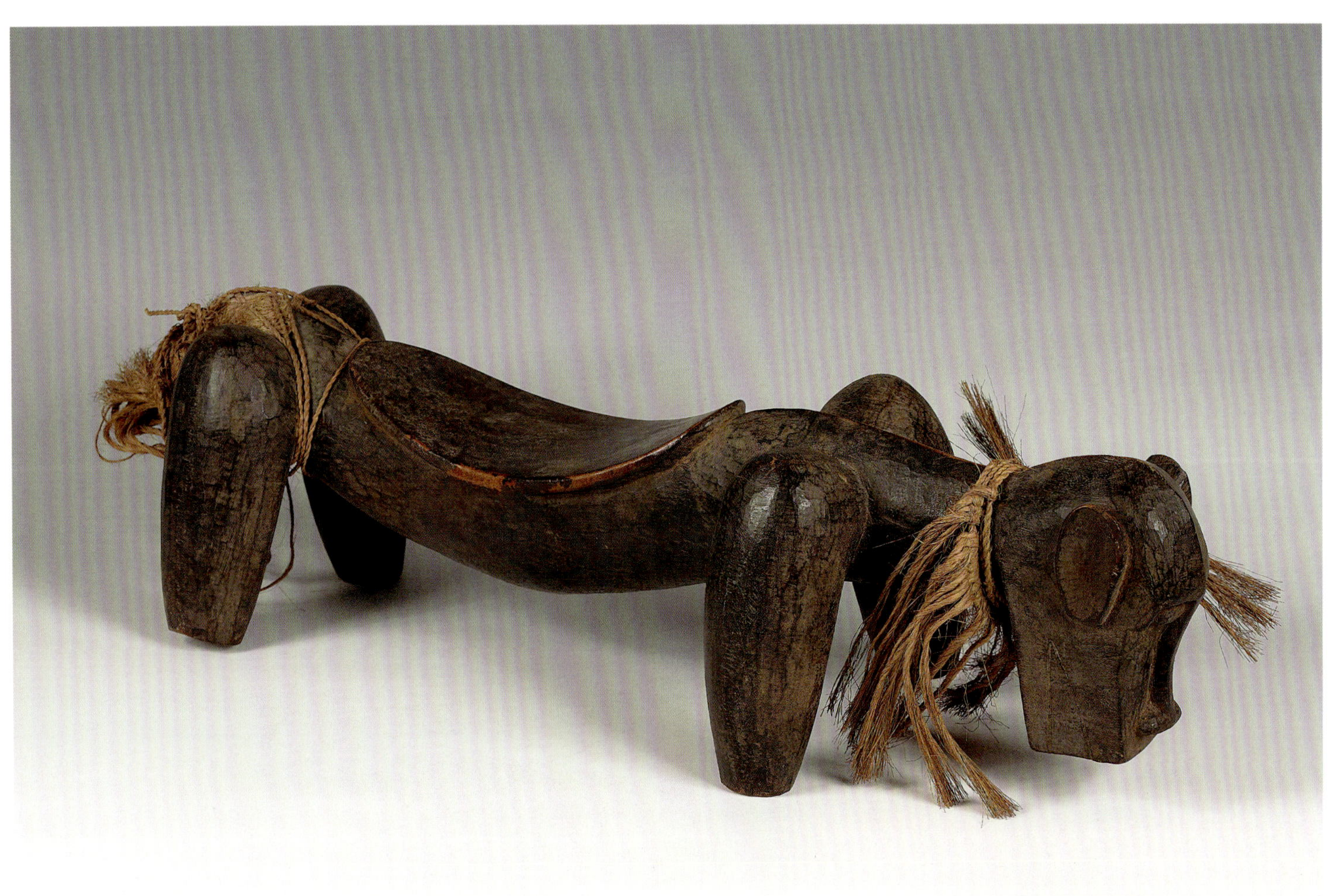

12   Figure of a horse (*syon*), probably mid-20th century
Unrecorded Senufo artist, Côte d'Ivoire
Wood and plant fiber, 18 × 72 × 19 cm

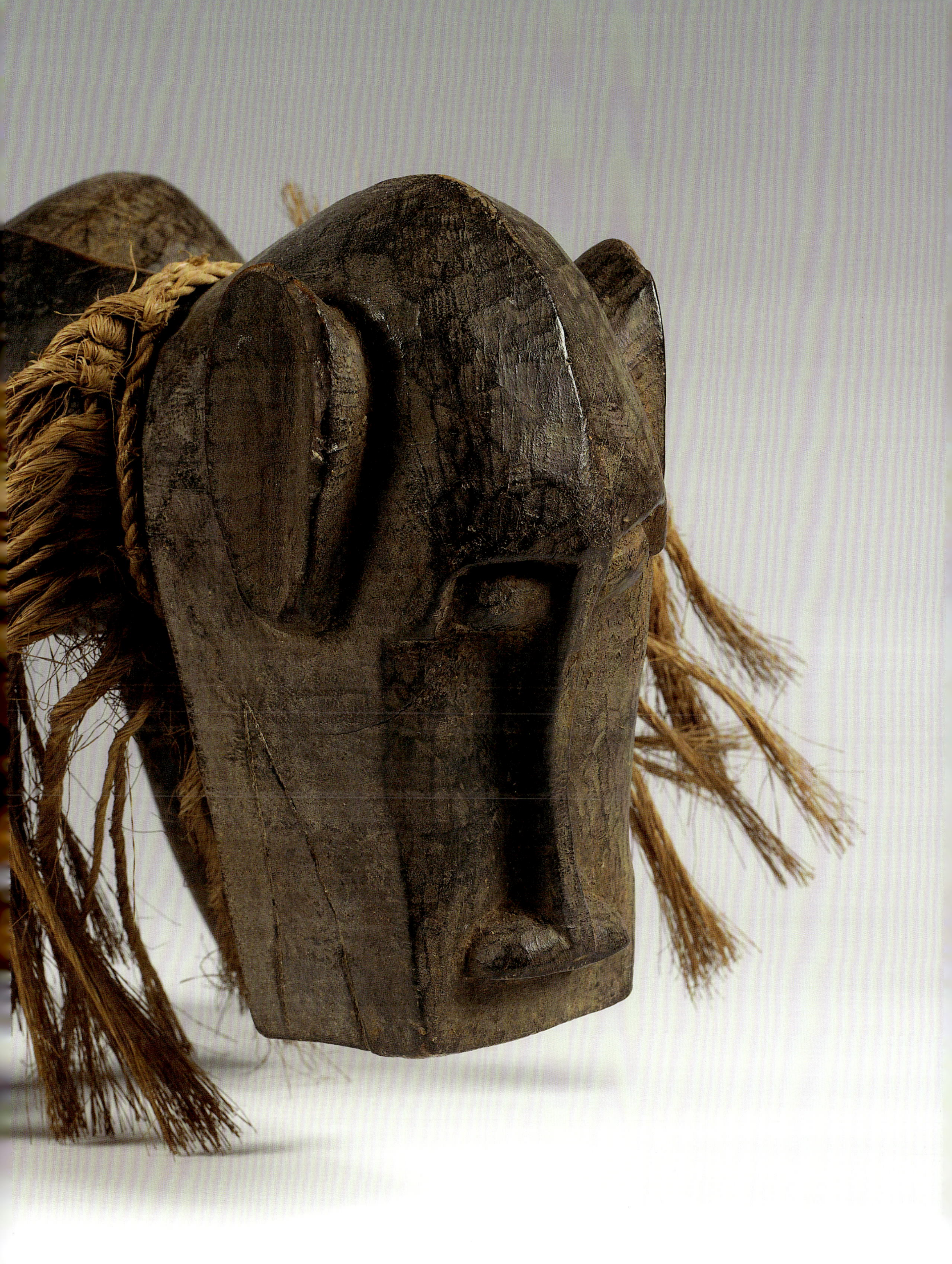

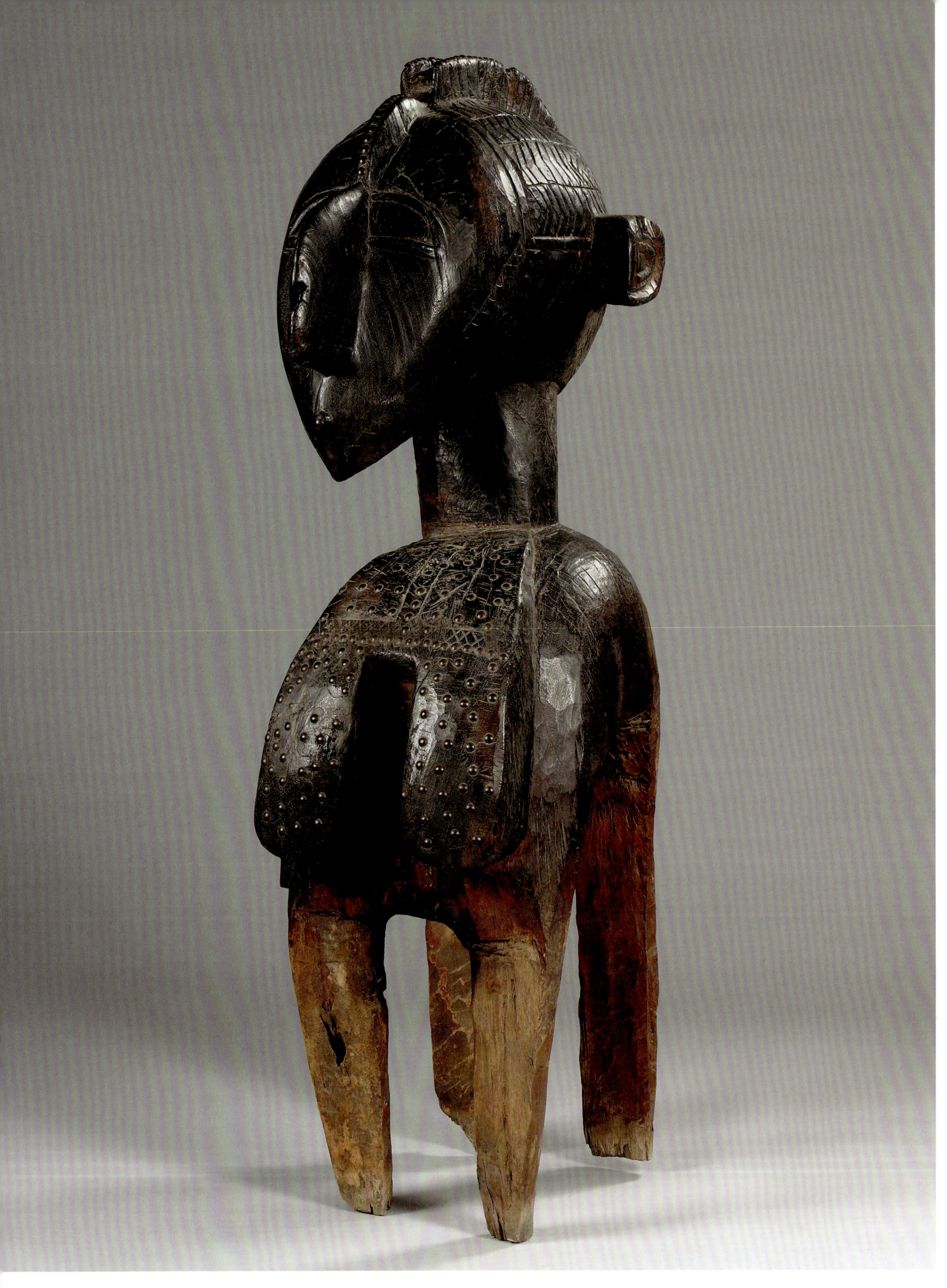

13 *D'mba* headdress, probably first half of 20th century
Unrecorded Baga artist, Guinea
Wood and brass tacks, 142 × 40 × 75 cm

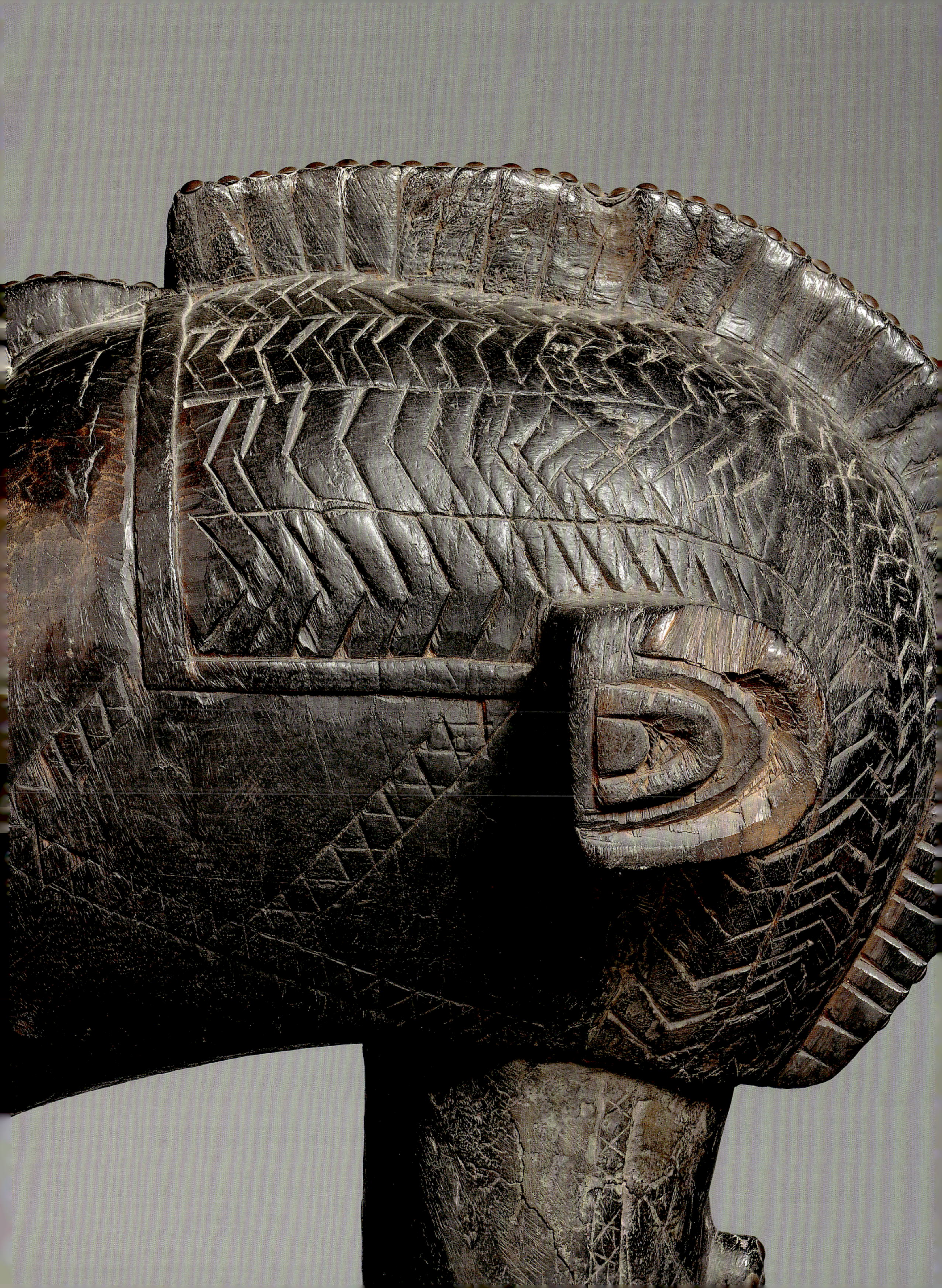

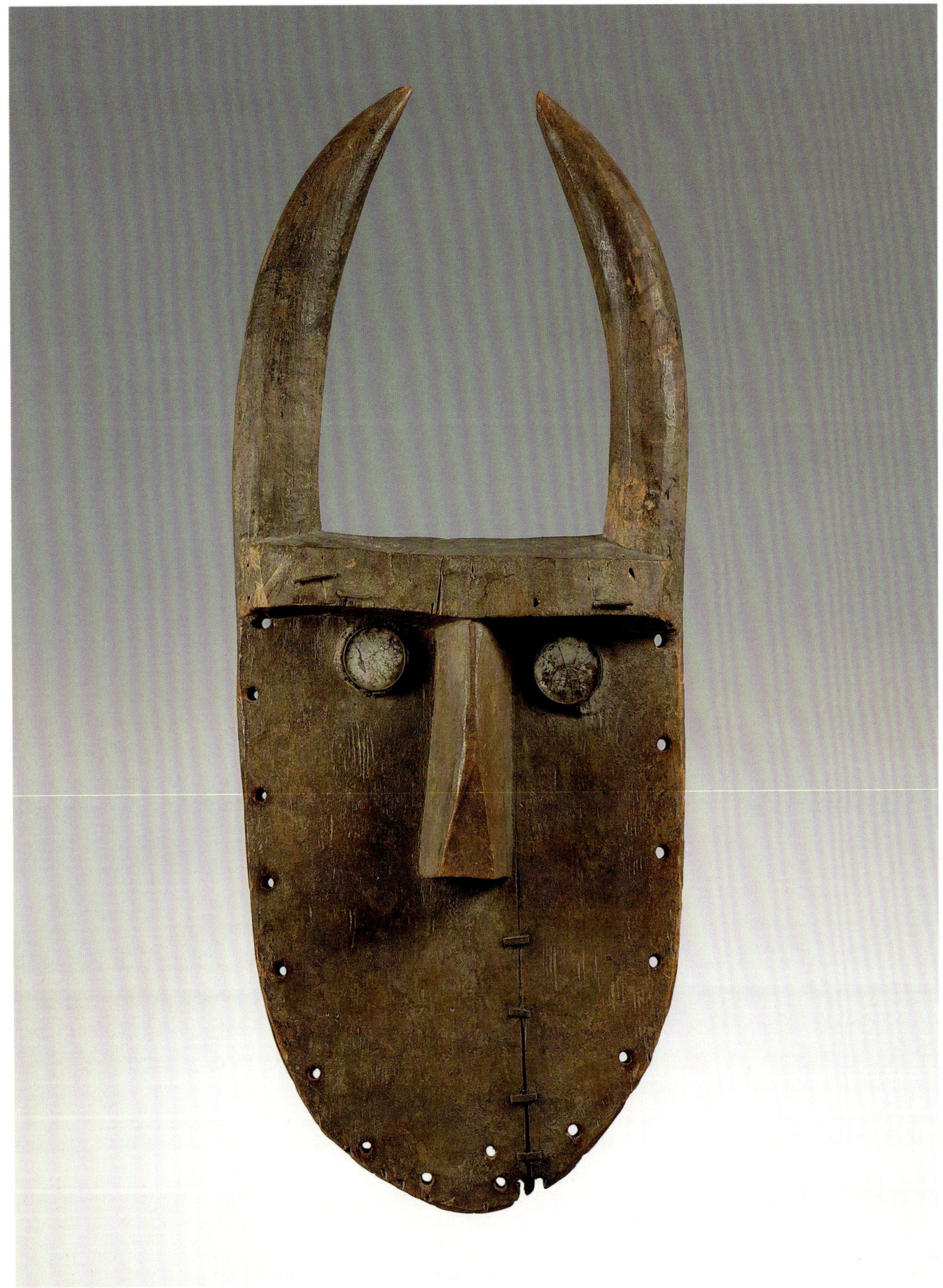

14   Mask (*angbai* or *nyanbai*), probably first half of 20th century
Unrecorded Toma or Loma artist, Guinea
Wood, iron nails, glass, metal, and resin, 88 × 39 × 15 cm

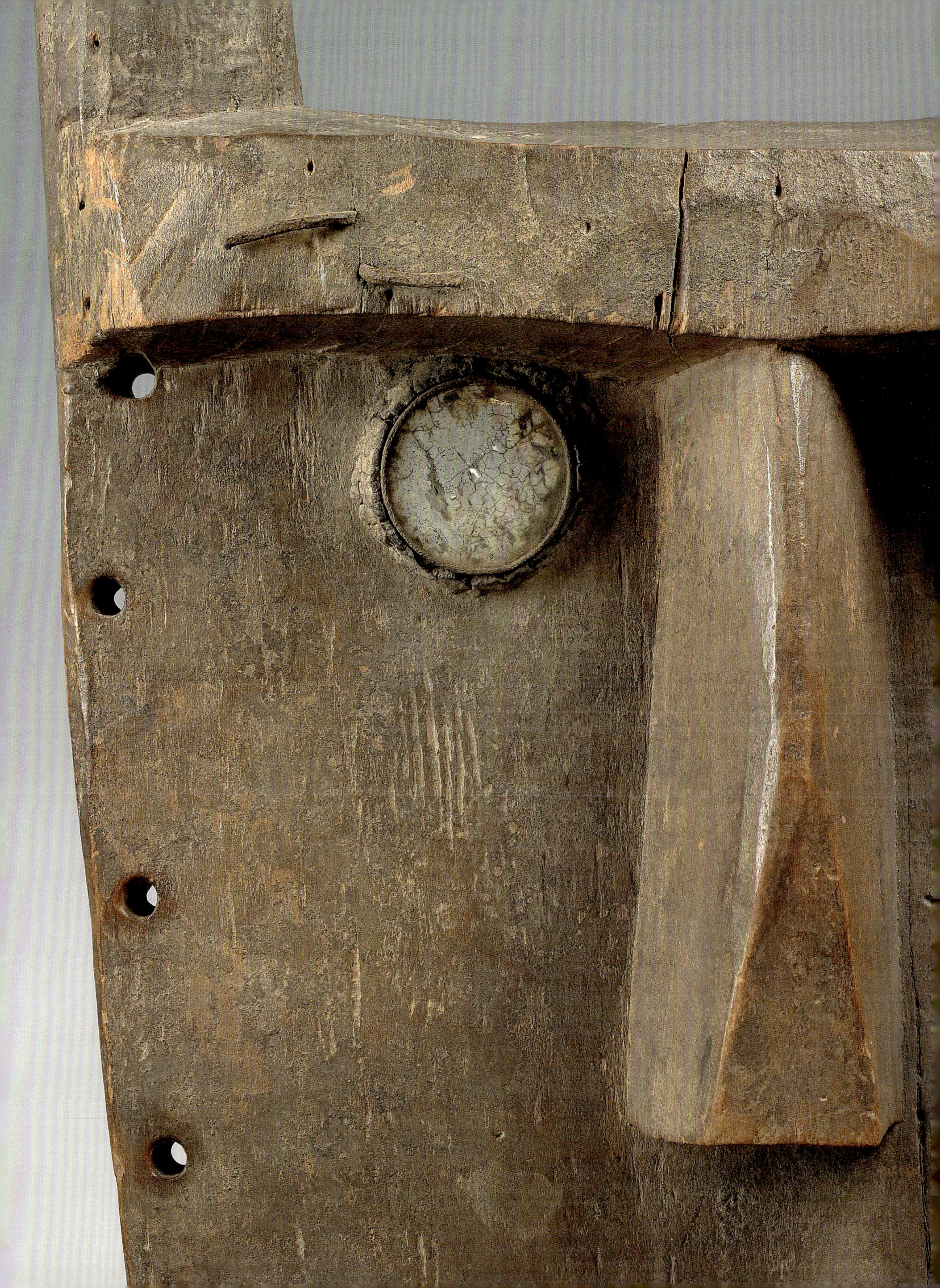

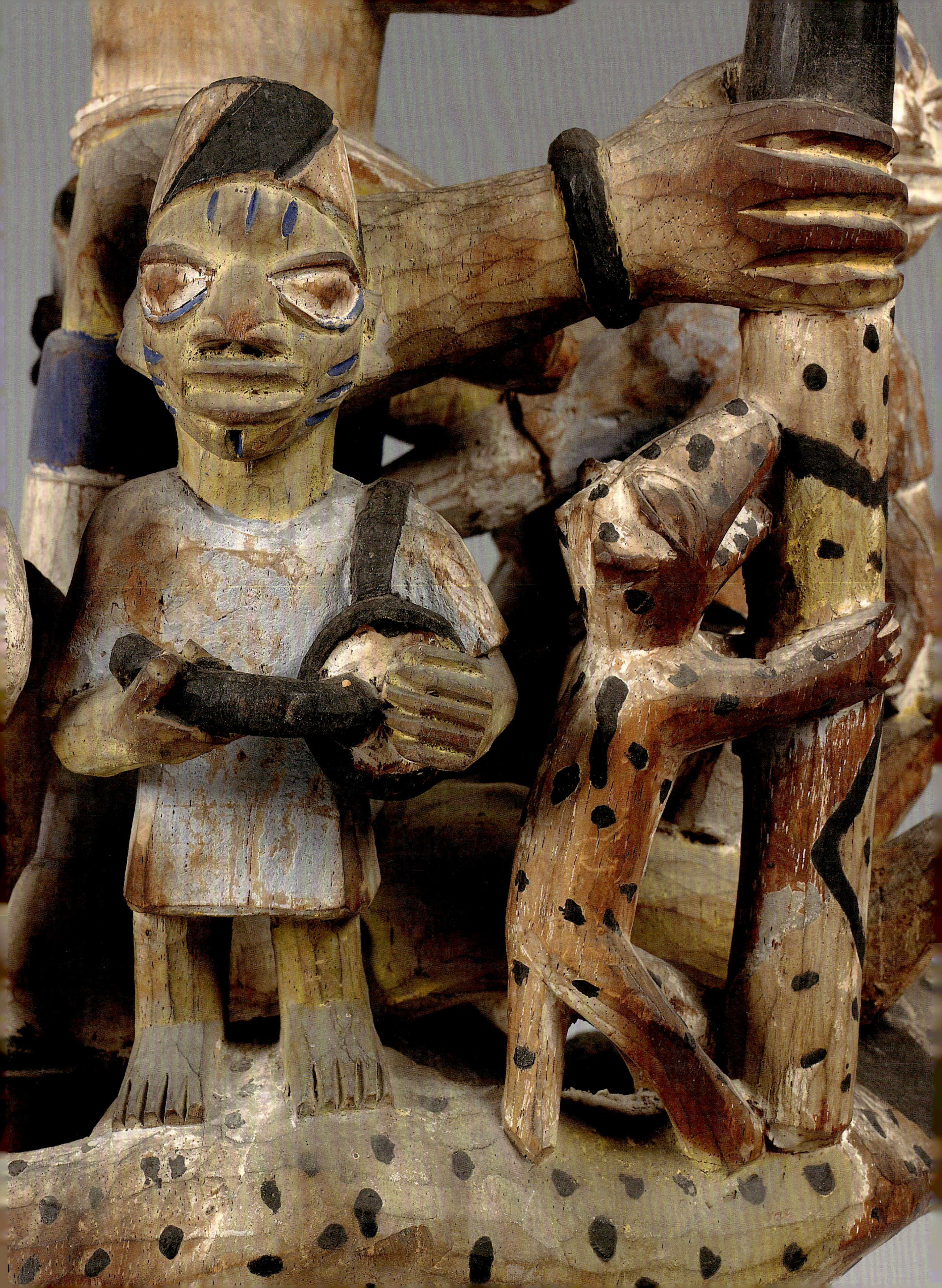

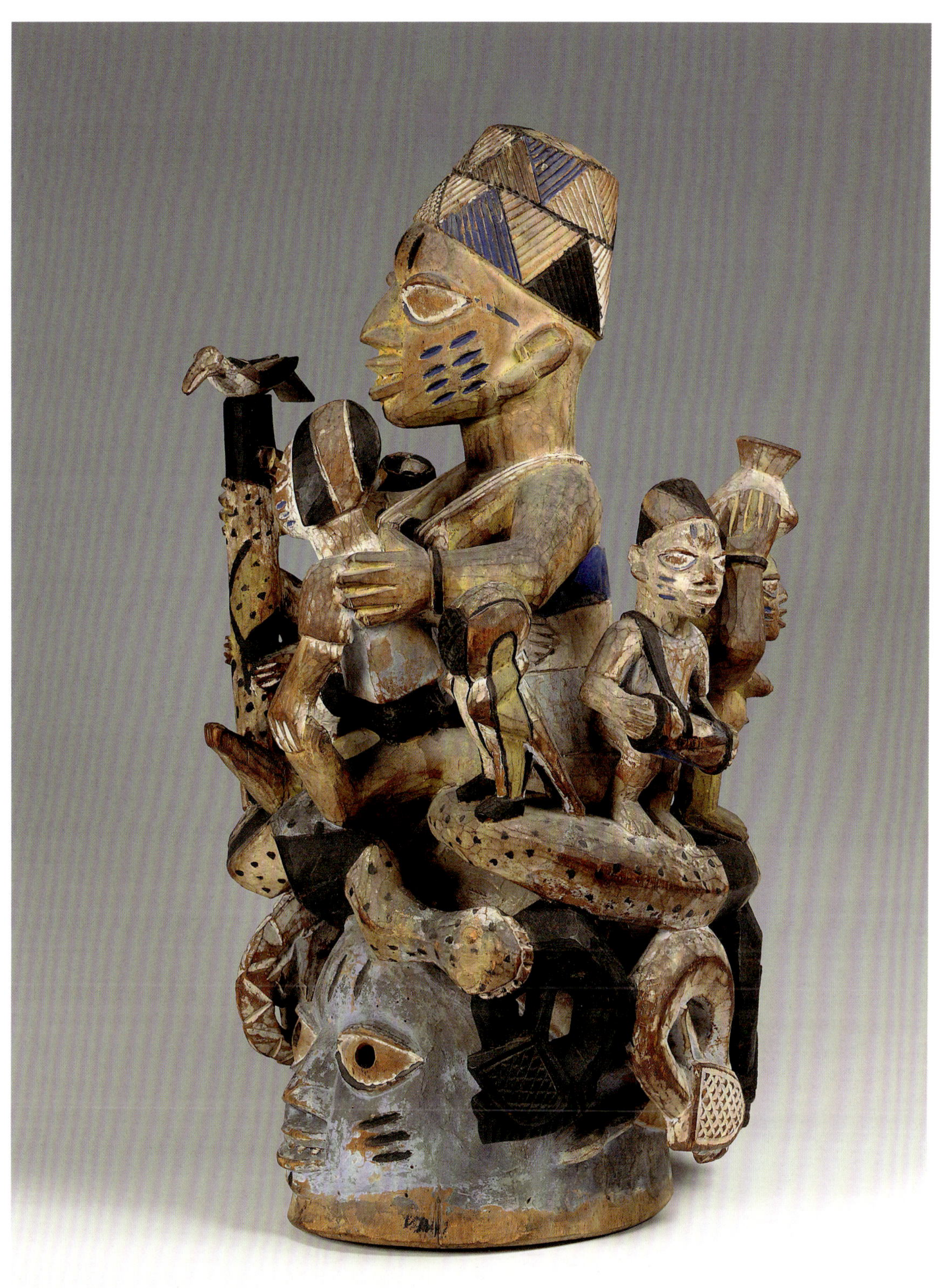

15   Headdress (*Ago Egungun*), probably first half of 20th century
Workshop of Oniyide Adugbologe (ca. 1875–1949; Yoruba artist), Abeokuta, Nigeria
Wood and natural pigment and coloring, 70 × 33 × 35 cm

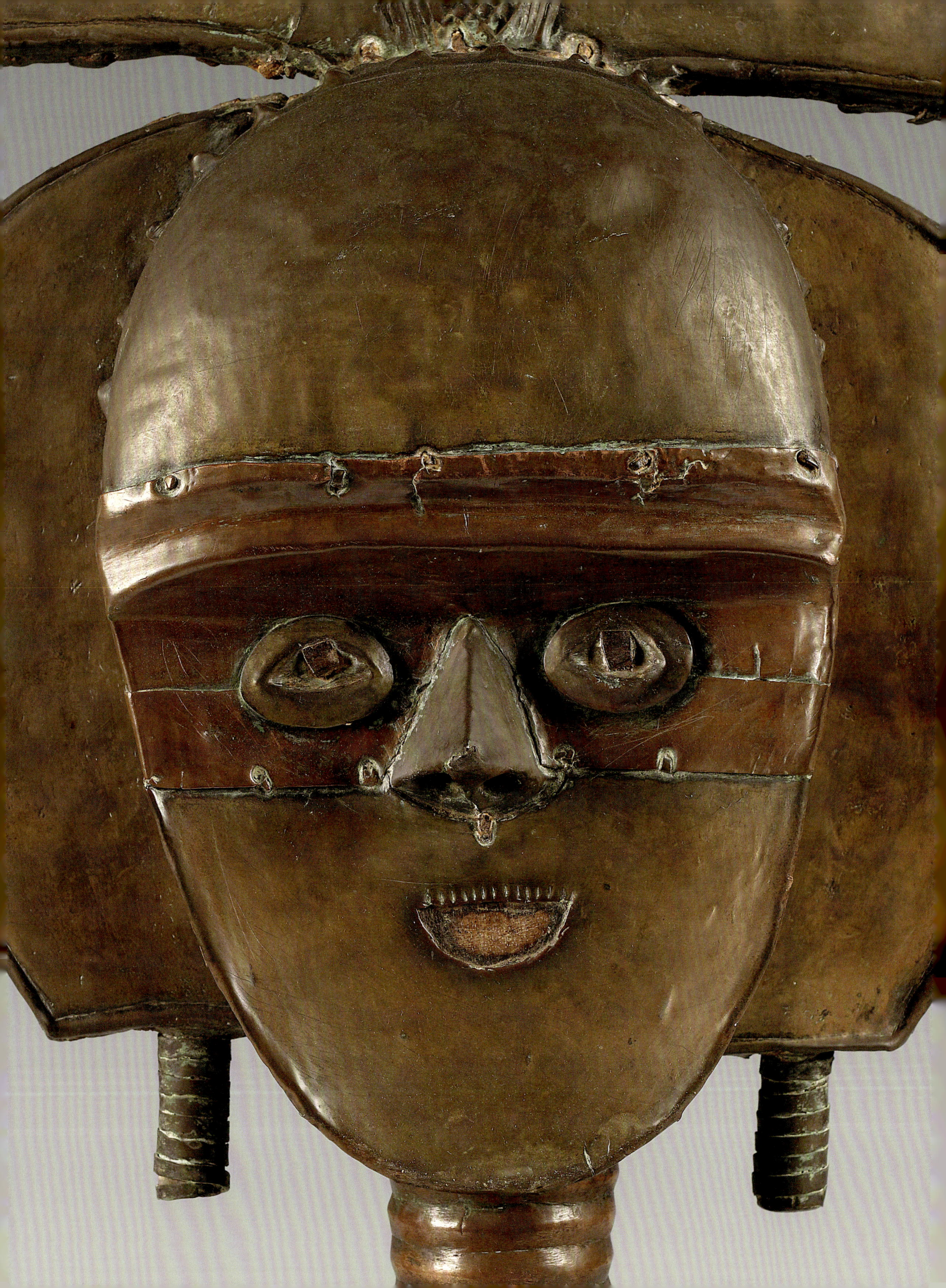

16   Figure from a reliquary ensemble (*mbulu ngulu*),
probably late 19th – early 20th century
Unrecorded Kota artist, Gabon
Wood, copper, and iron, 61 × 35 × 11 cm

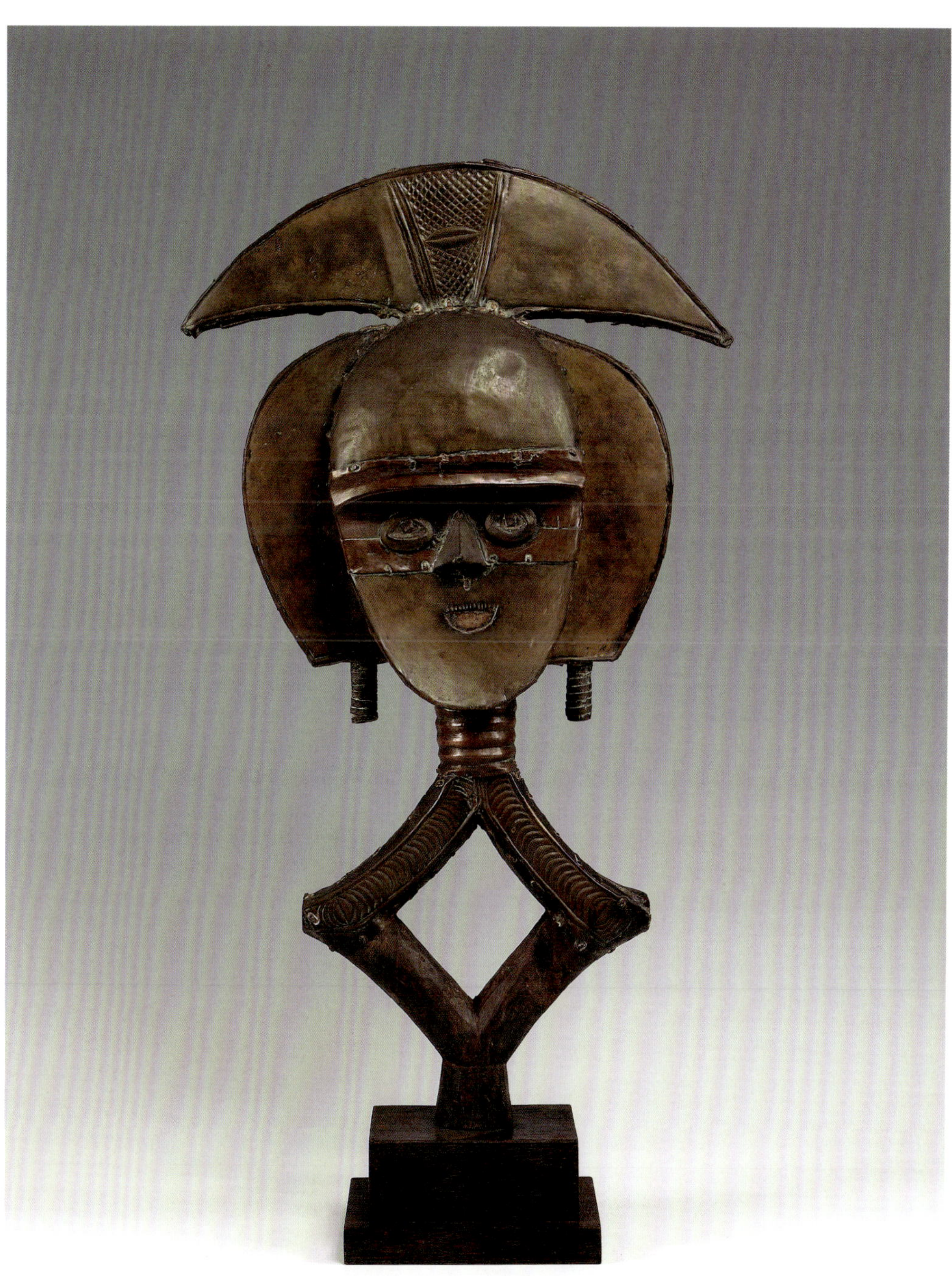

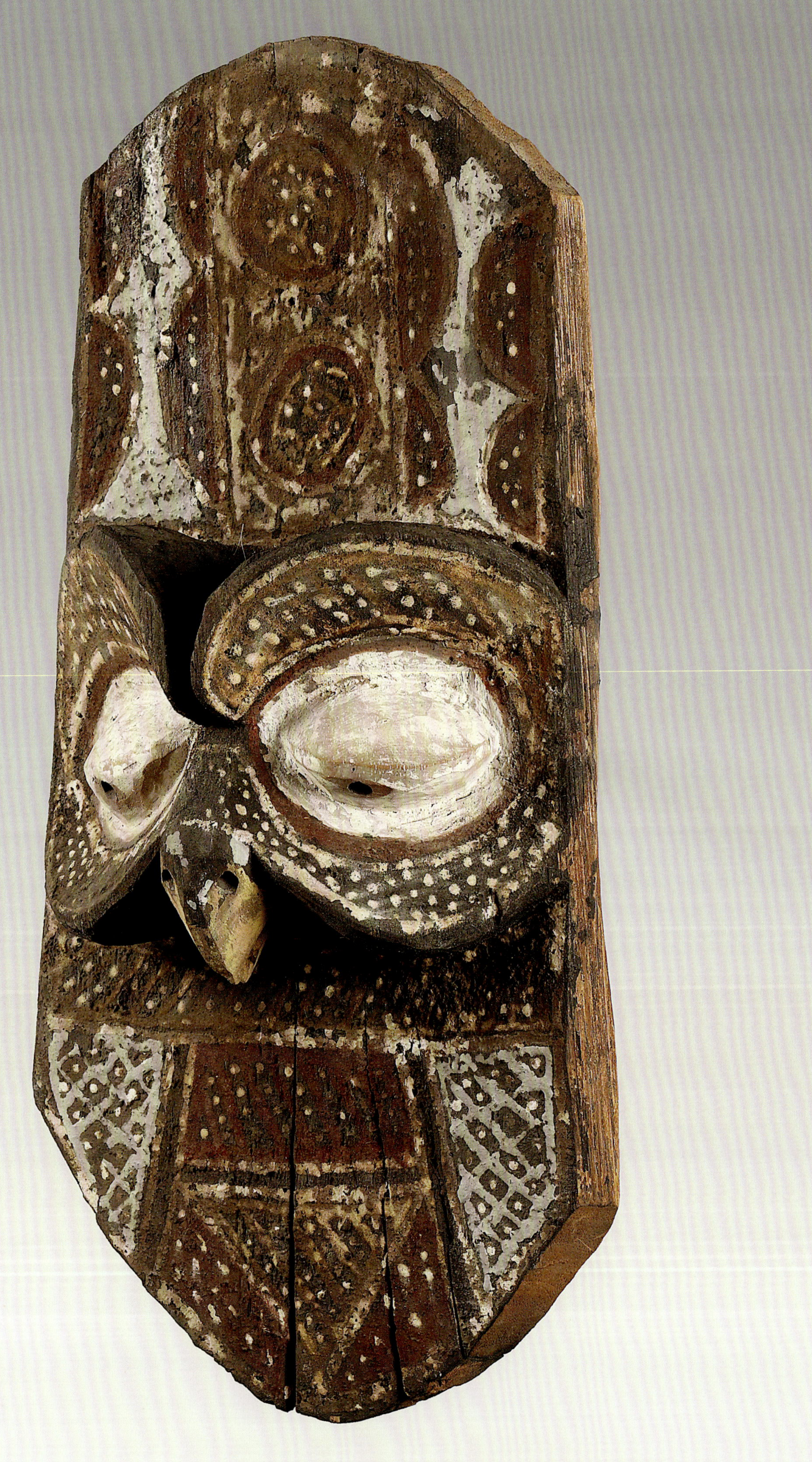

17   Panel, probably first half of 20th century
Unrecorded Nkanu artist, Democratic Republic of the Congo
Wood, kaolin, and natural pigment, 48 × 23 × 12 cm

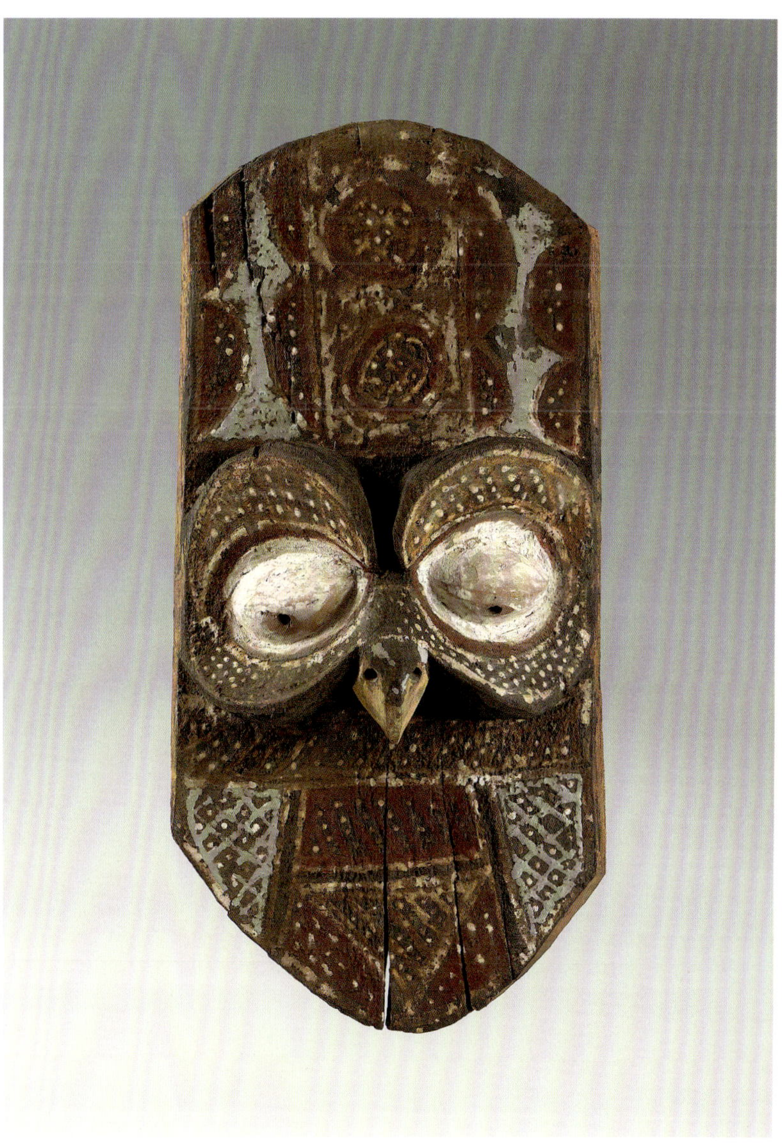

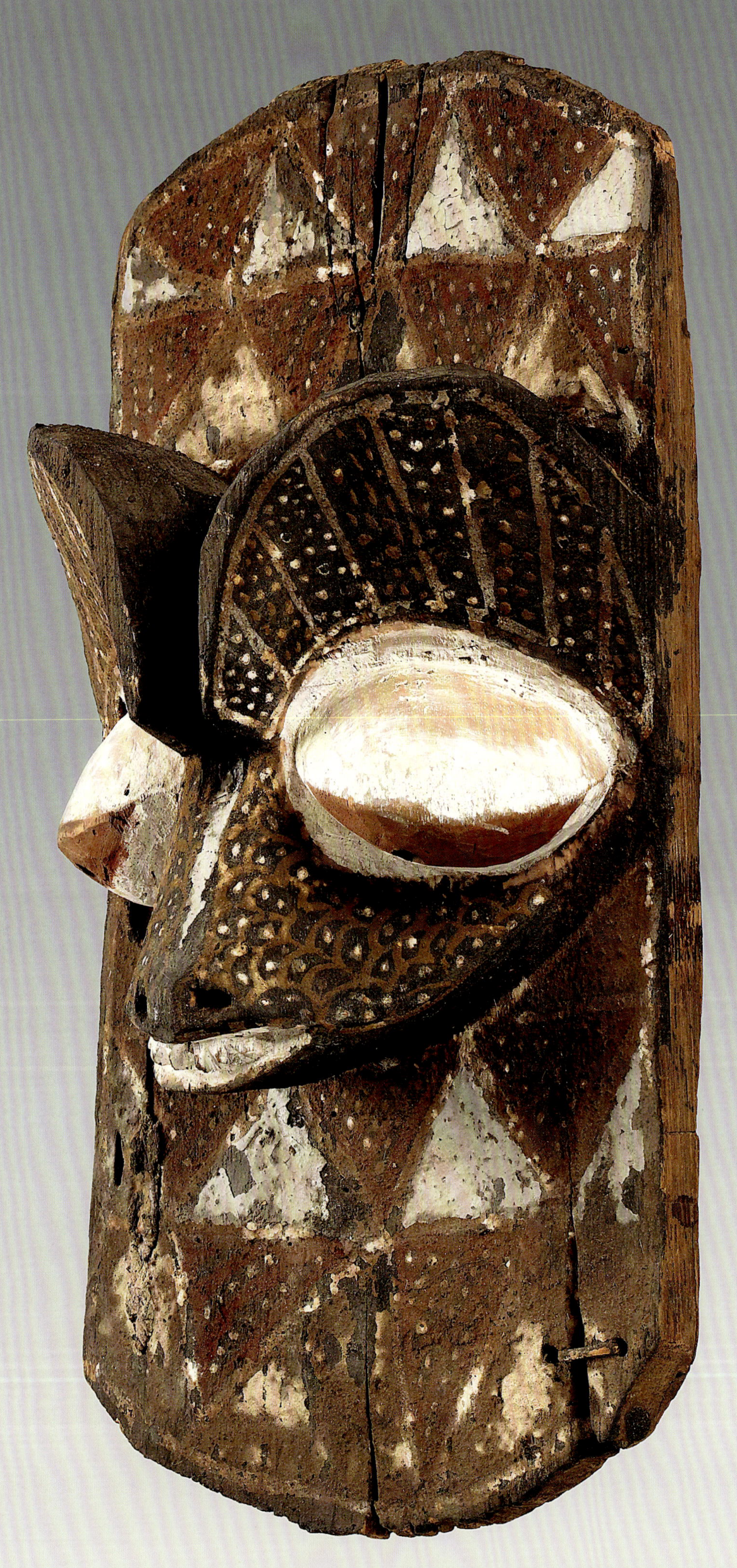

18   Panel, probably first half of 20th century
Unrecorded Nkanu artist, Democratic Republic of the Congo
Wood, kaolin, and natural pigment, 49 × 26 × 15 cm

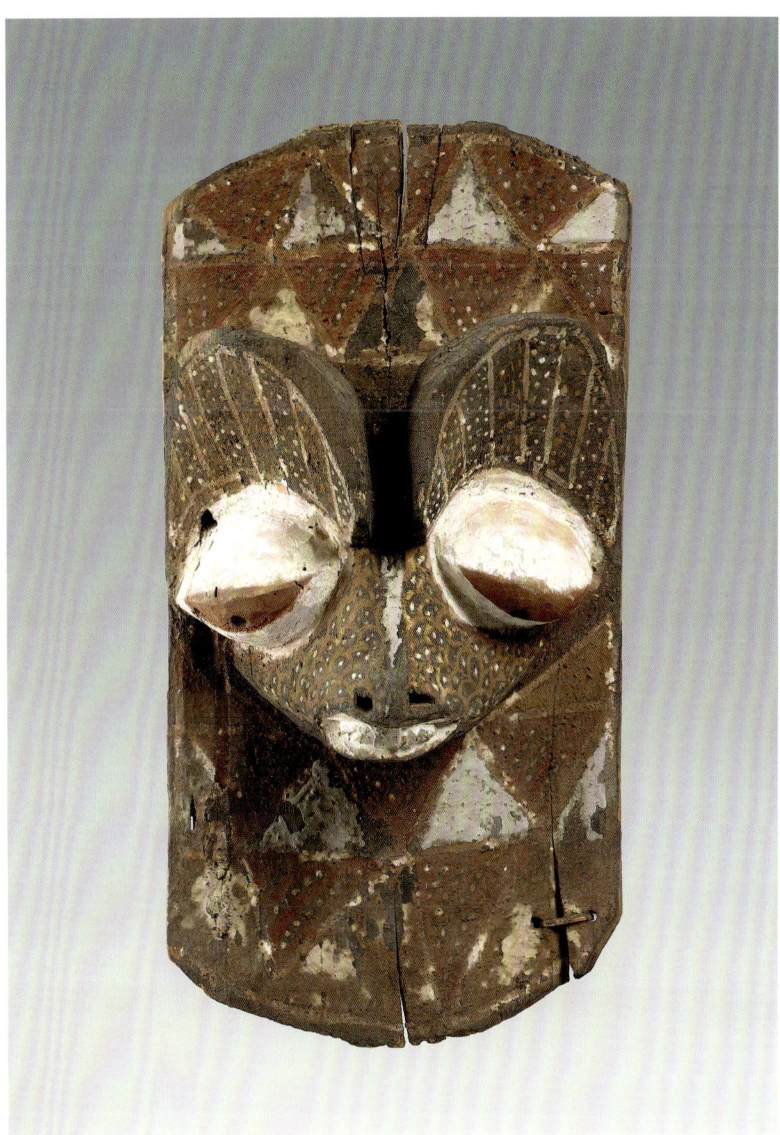

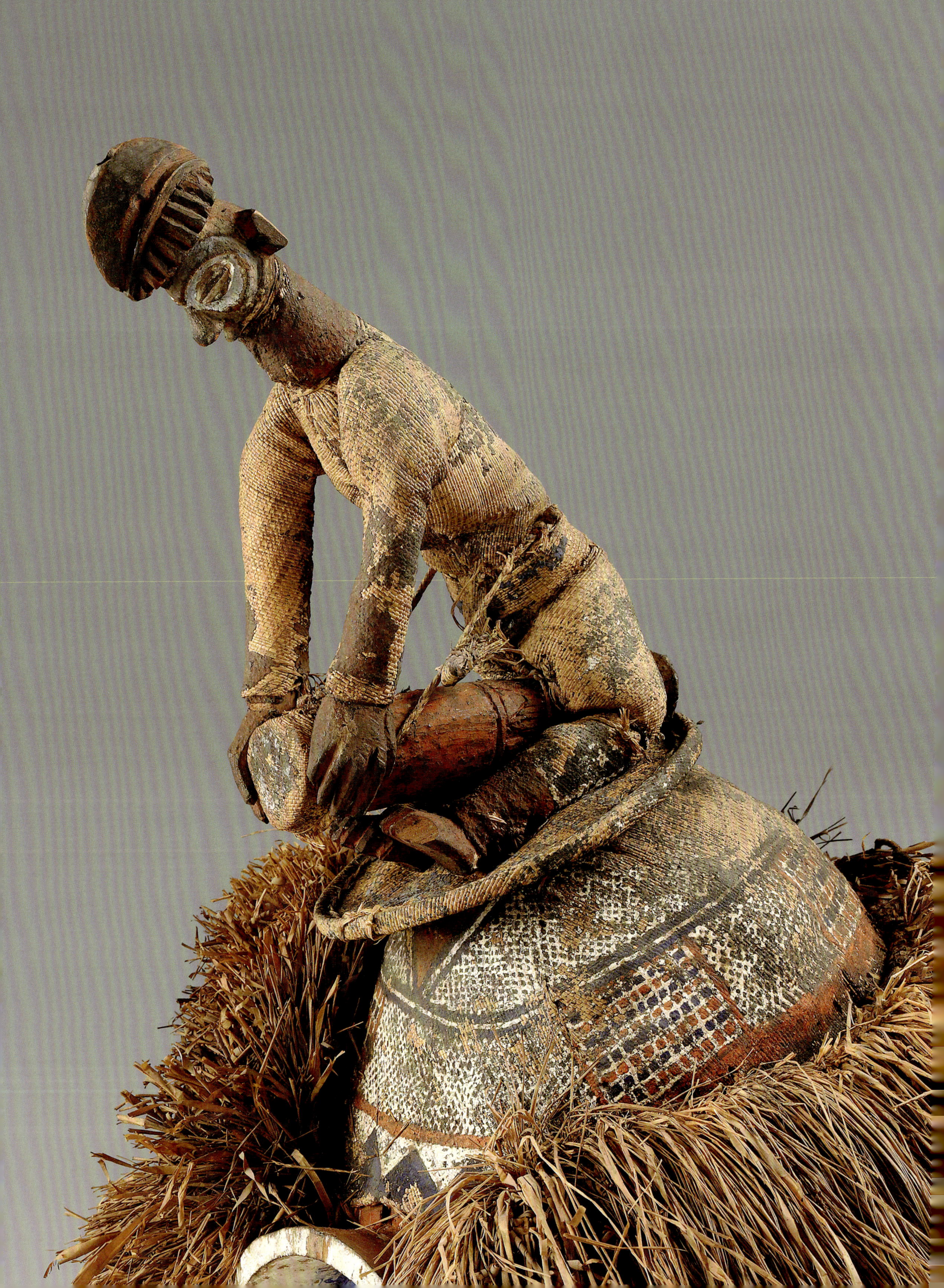

19   Headdress (*kholuka* or *mbala*), probably first half of 20th century
Unrecorded Yaka artist, Democratic Republic of the Congo
Wood, plant fiber, resin, and natural pigment and coloring, 57 × 40 × 38 cm

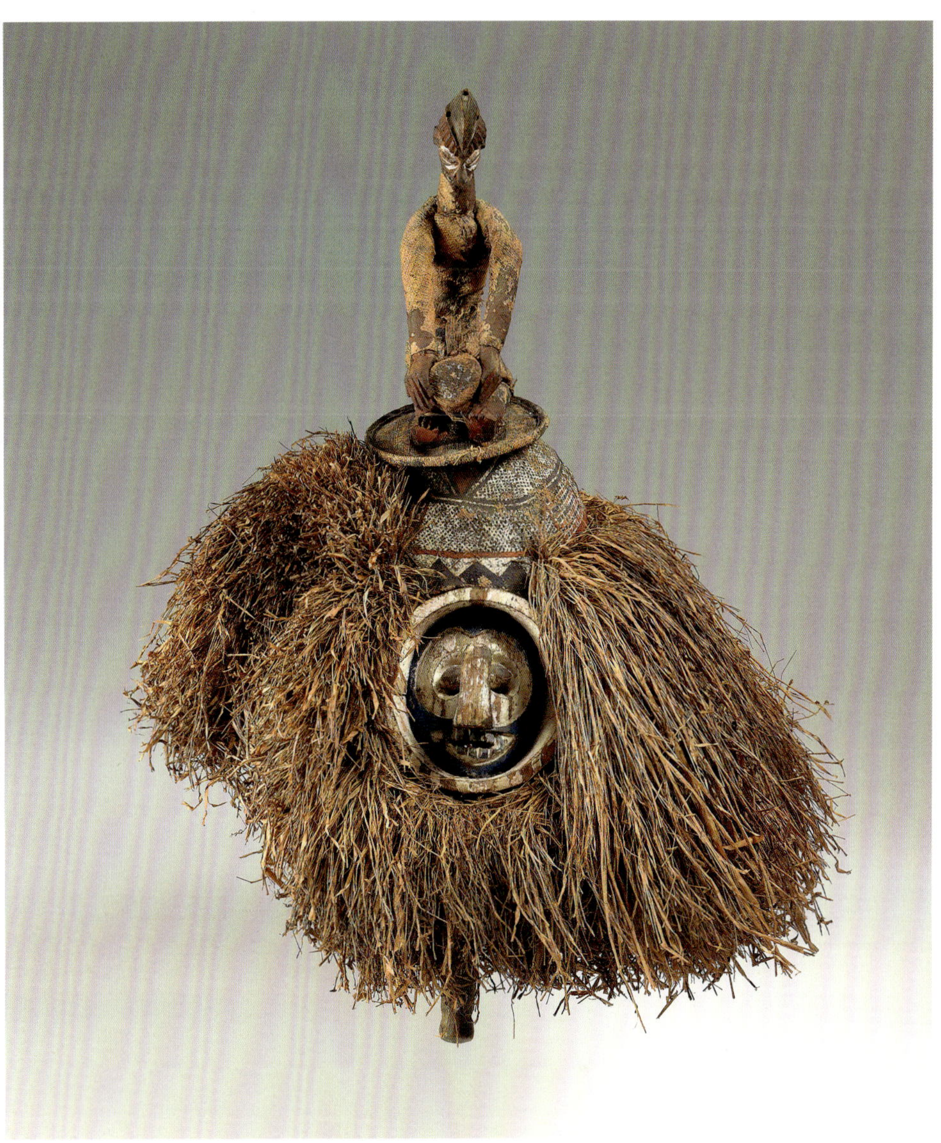

20   Mask (*mukinka*), probably first half of 20th century
Unrecorded Salampasu artist, Democratic Republic of the Congo
Wood, copper, plant fiber, kaolin, and natural pigment, 62 × 26 × 28 cm

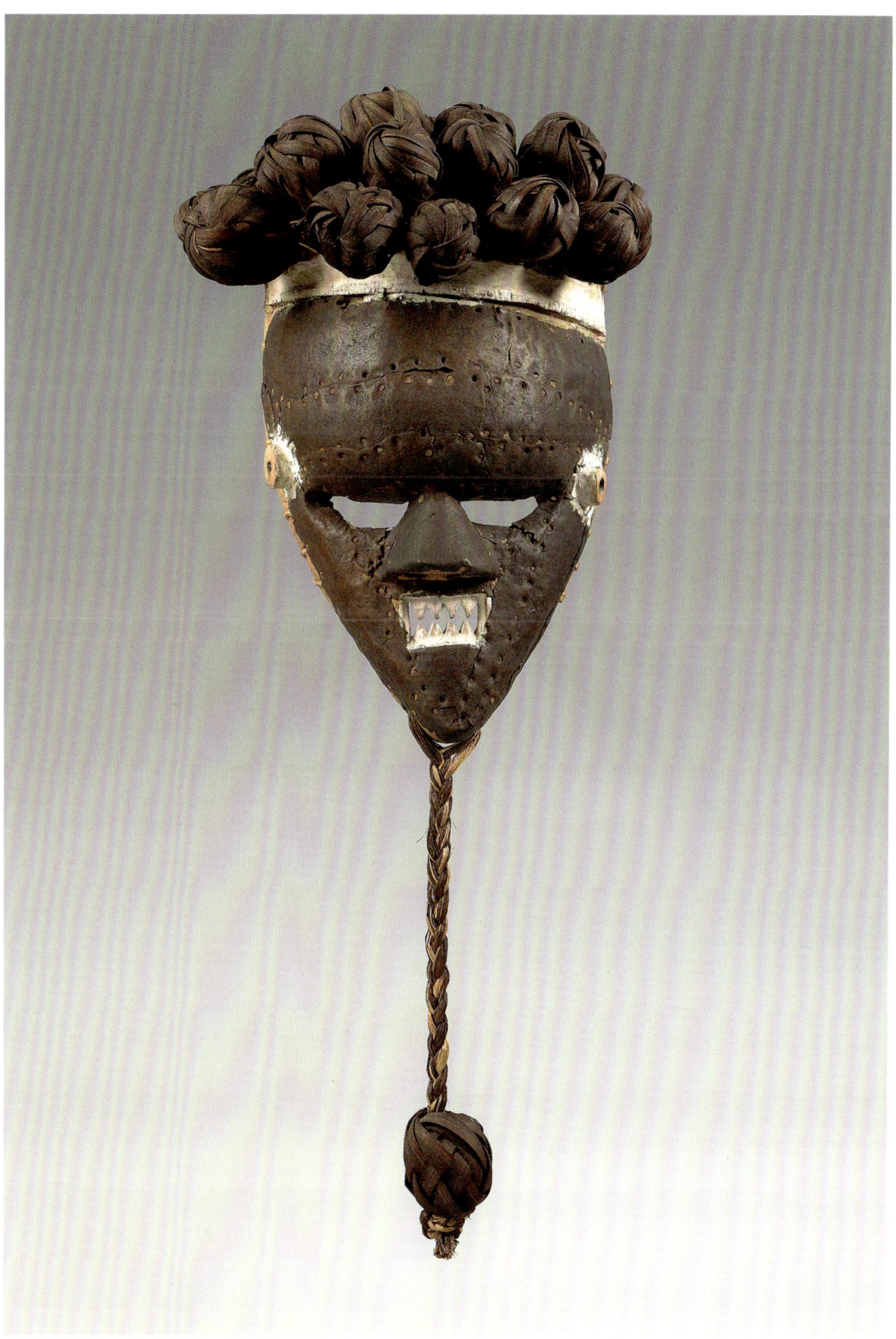

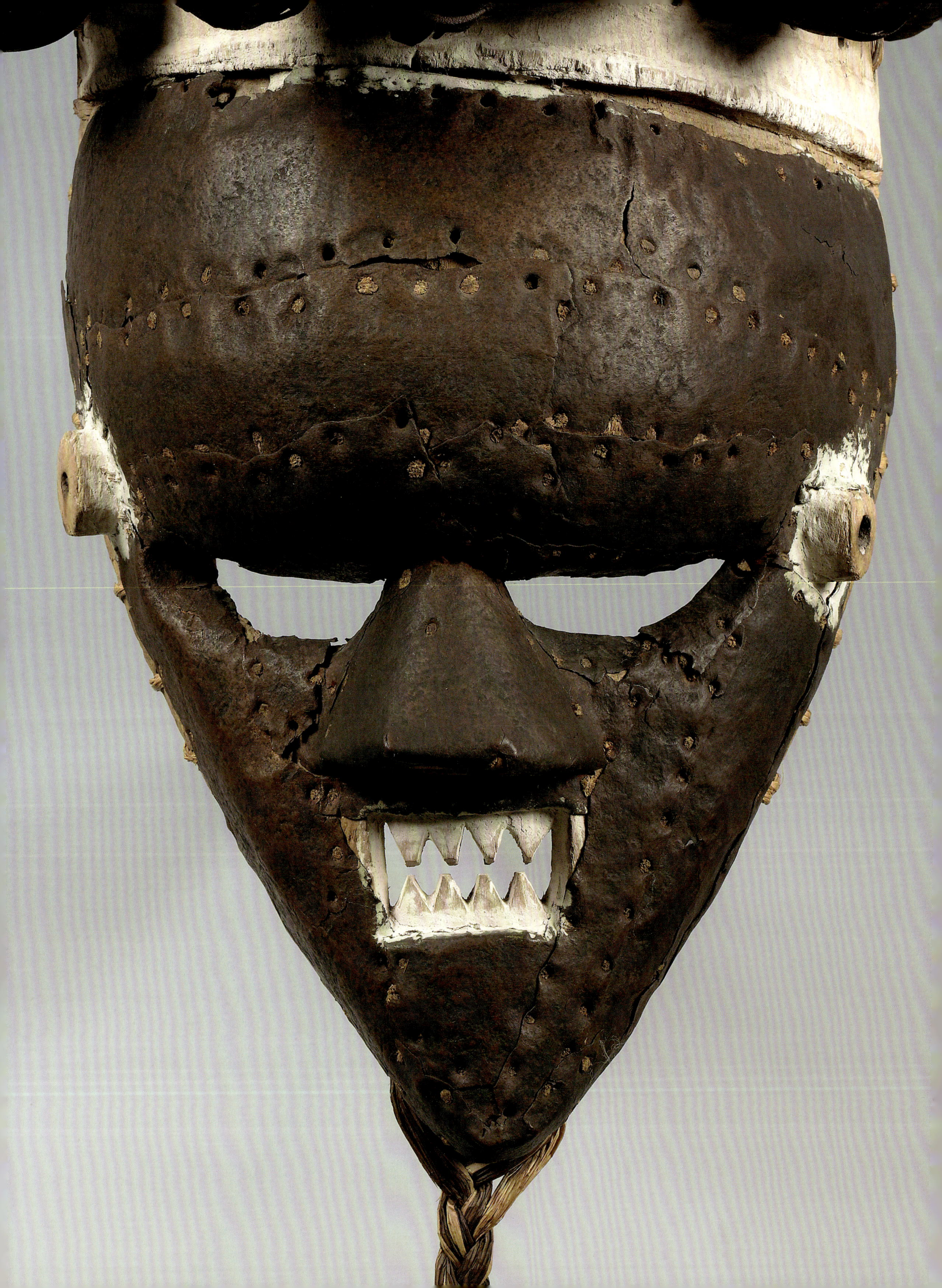

Oceania

22
21, 23–29

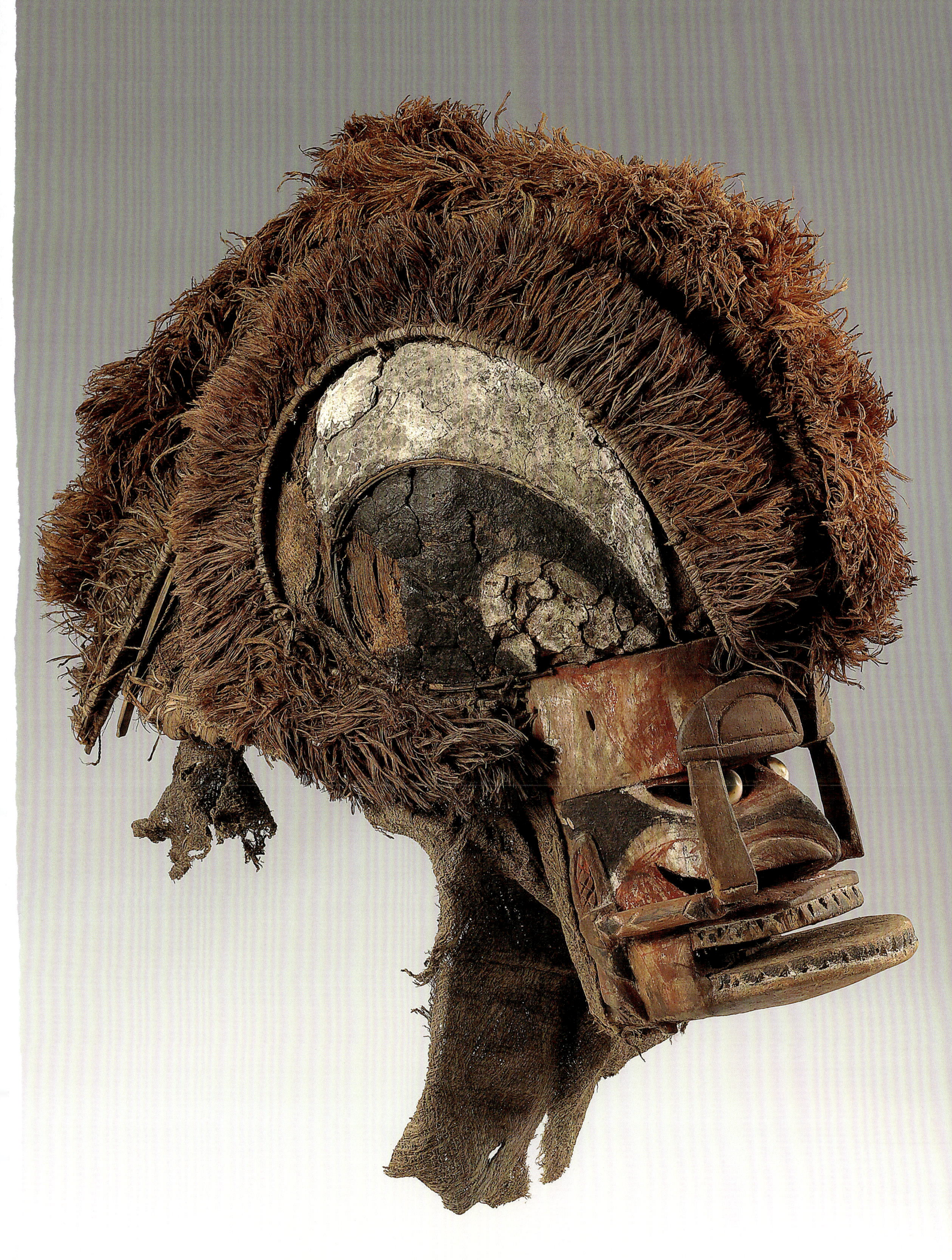

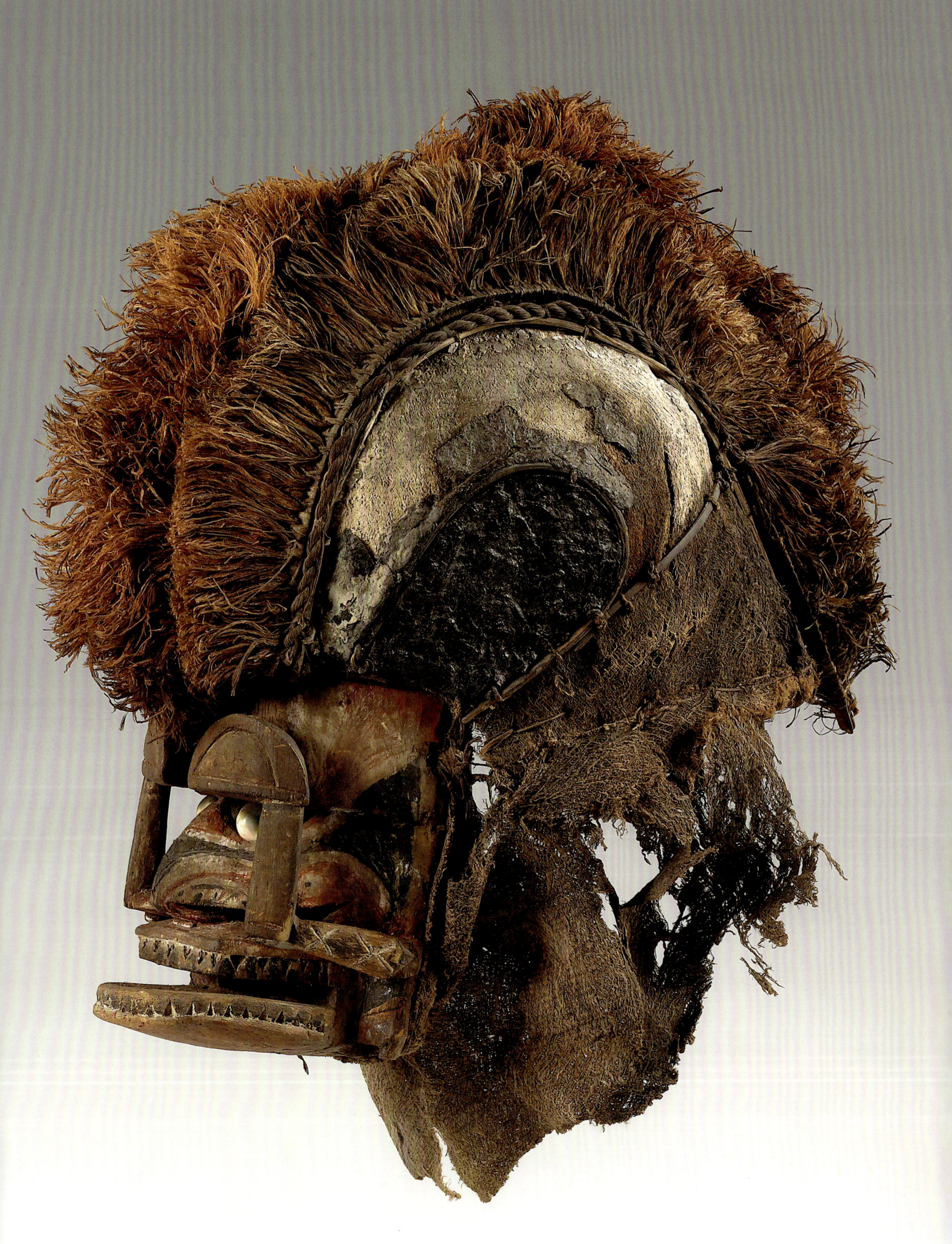

21   *Tatanua* mask (*malangan*), early 20th century
Unrecorded Madak artist, Northern New Ireland,
Papua New Guinea
Wood, natural pigment, plant fiber, and sea-snail
opercula, 46 × 20 × 39 cm

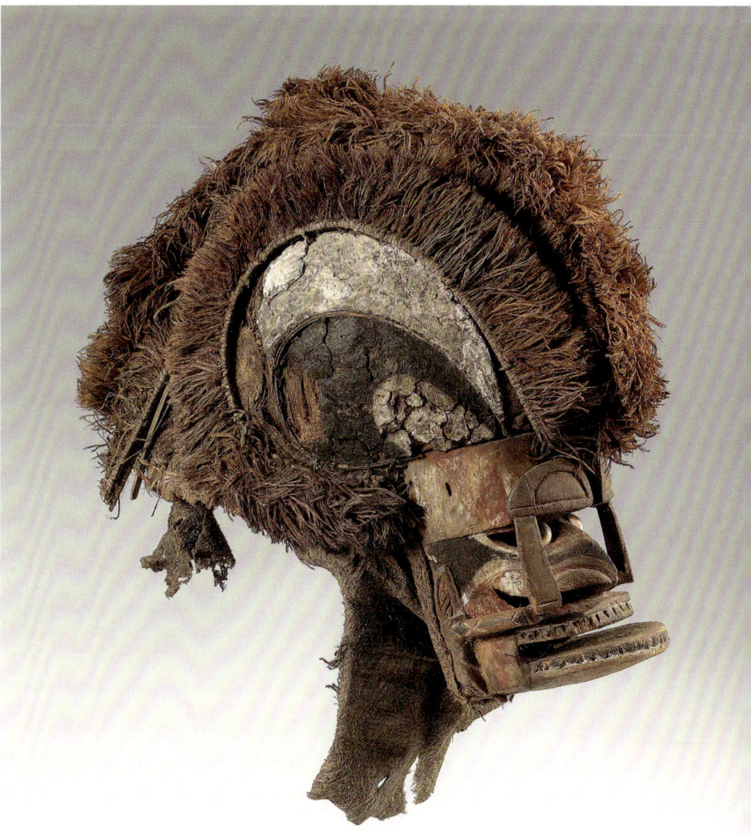

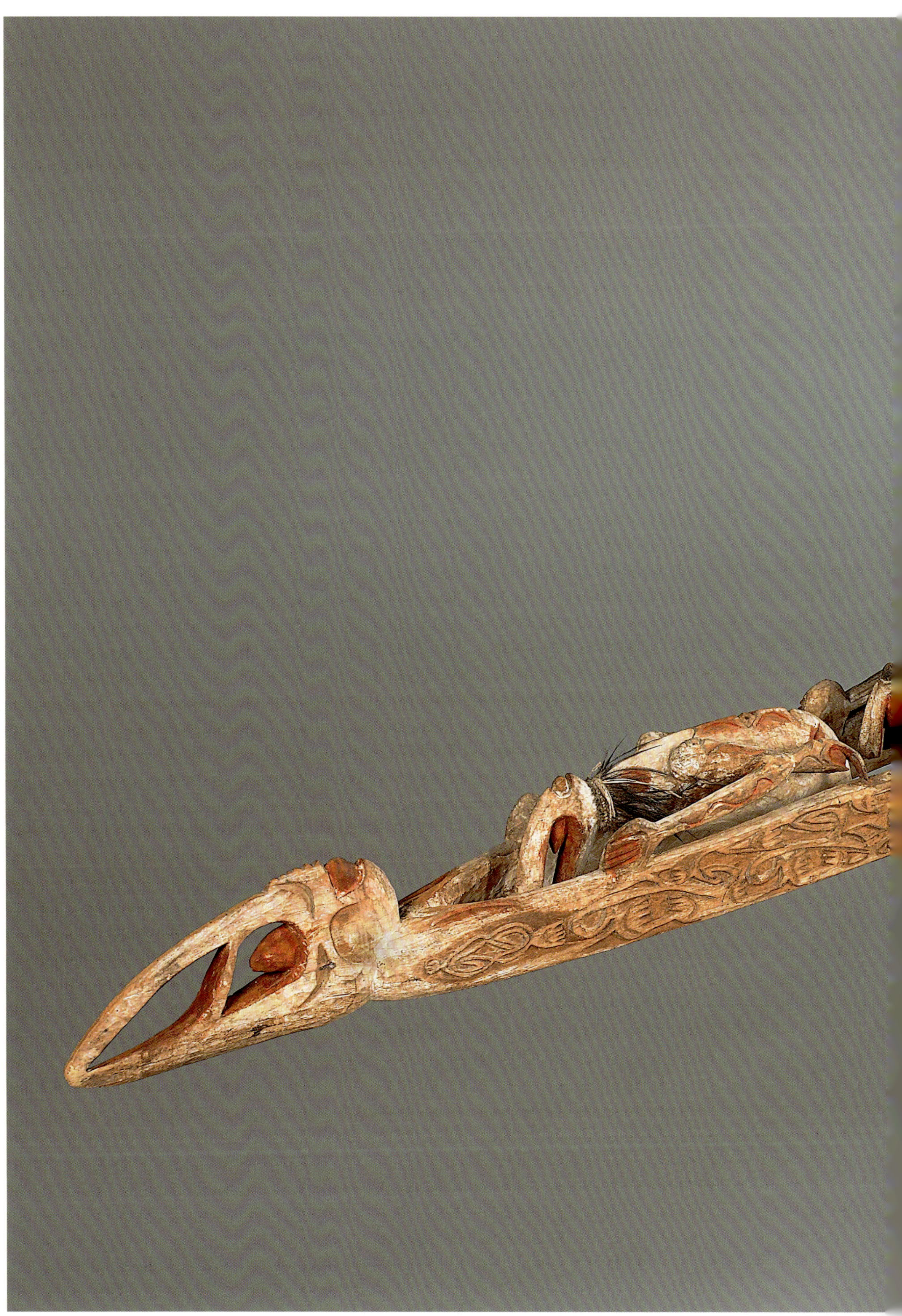

22   Soul canoe (*wuramon*), mid-20th century
Unrecorded Asmat artists, Papua (Western New Guinea), Indonesia
Wood, cassowary feathers, natural pigment, and plant fiber, 18 × 123 × 18 cm

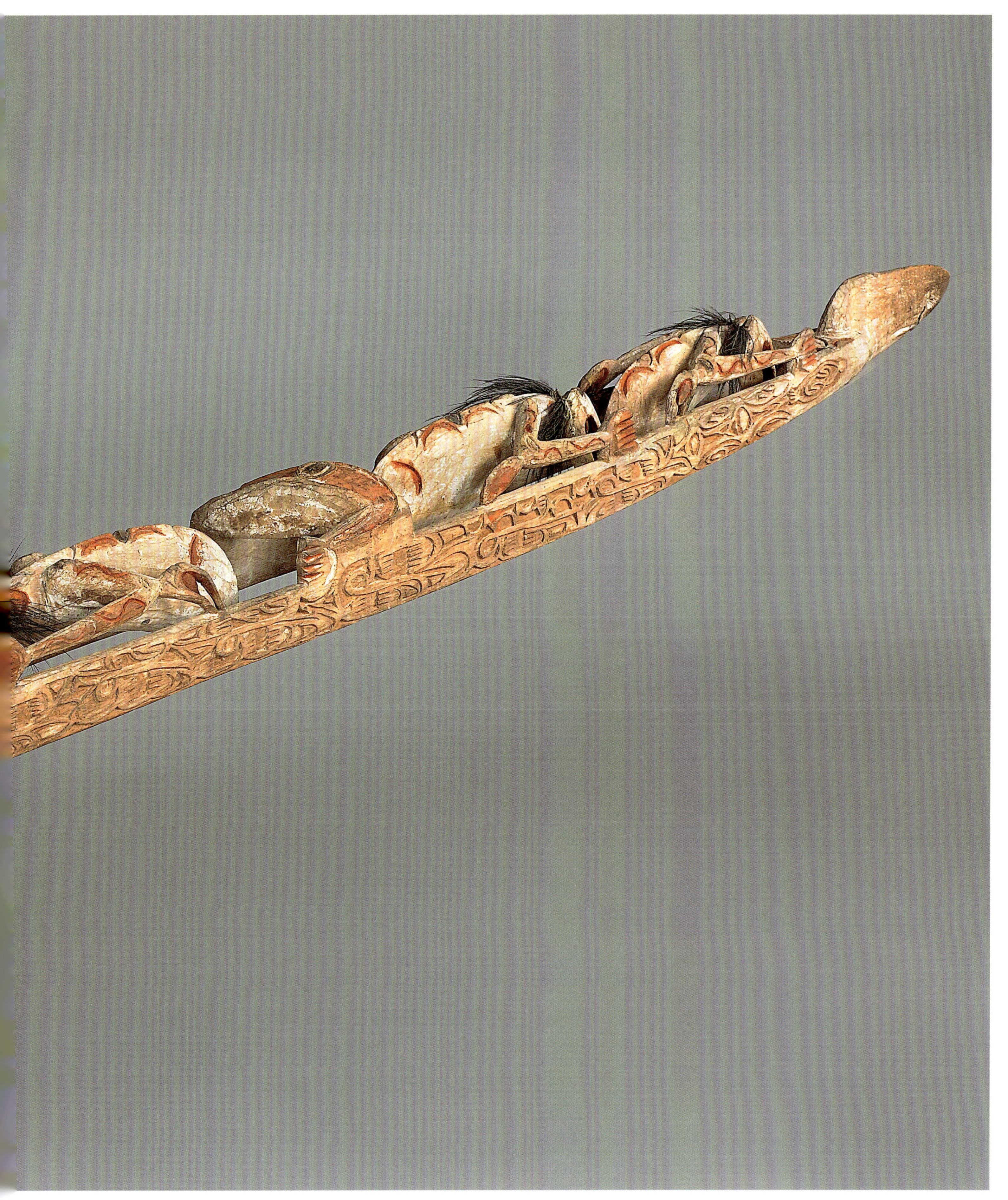

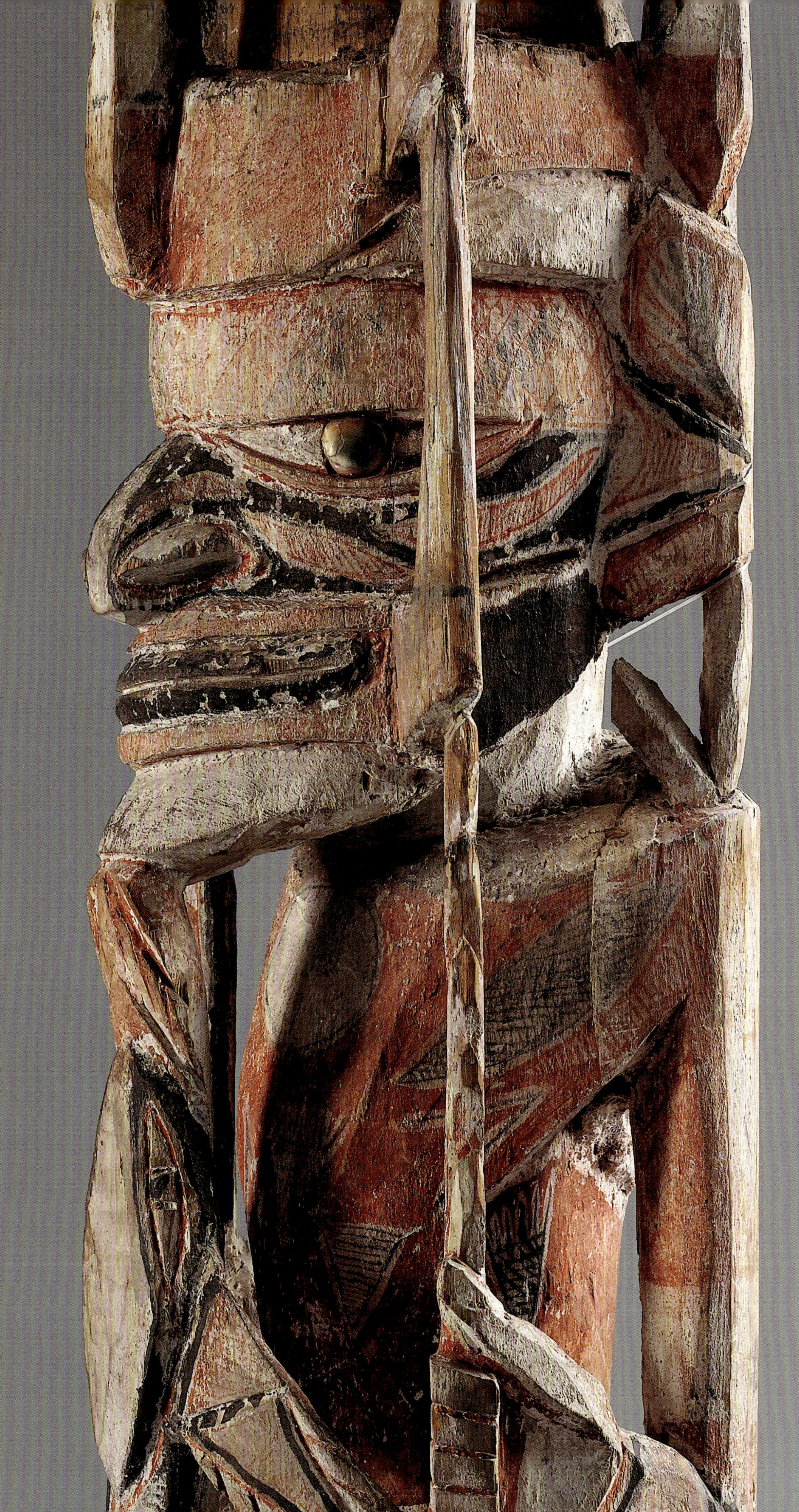

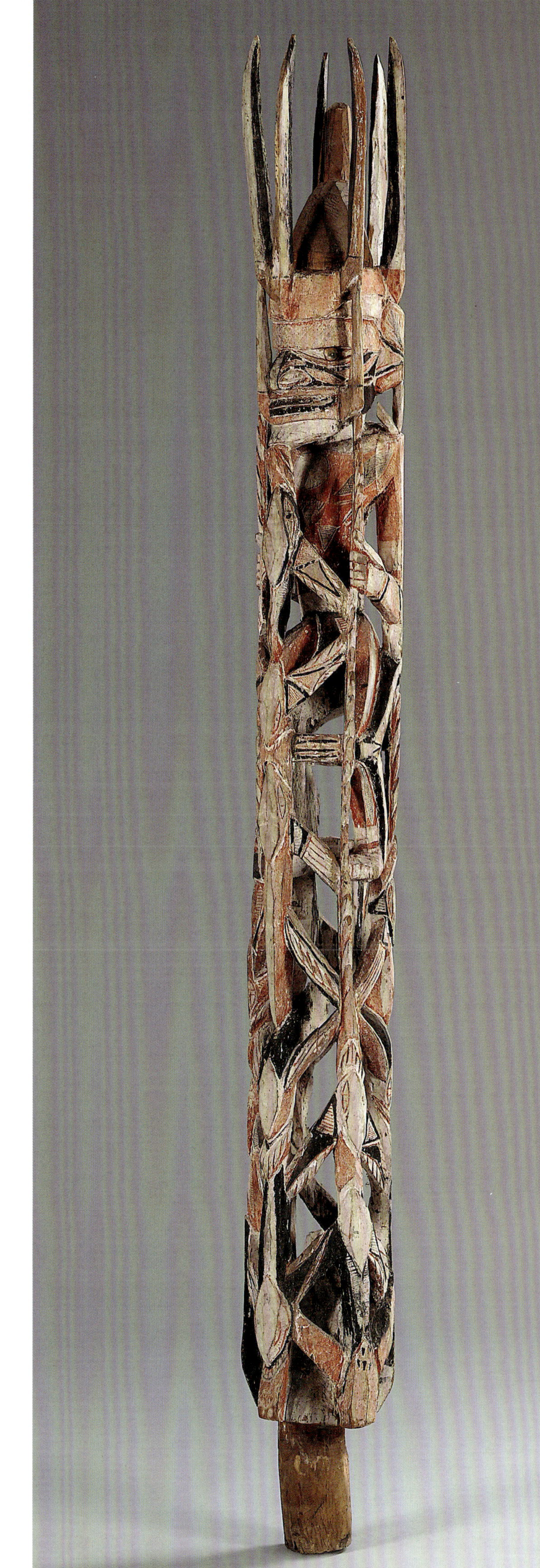

23   Funerary carving (*malangan maramarua*),
early 20th century
Unrecorded Mandara (or Tabar) artist, Tabar Island,
Northern New Ireland, Papua New Guinea
Wood, natural pigment, and sea-snail opercula,
170 × 22 × 22 cm

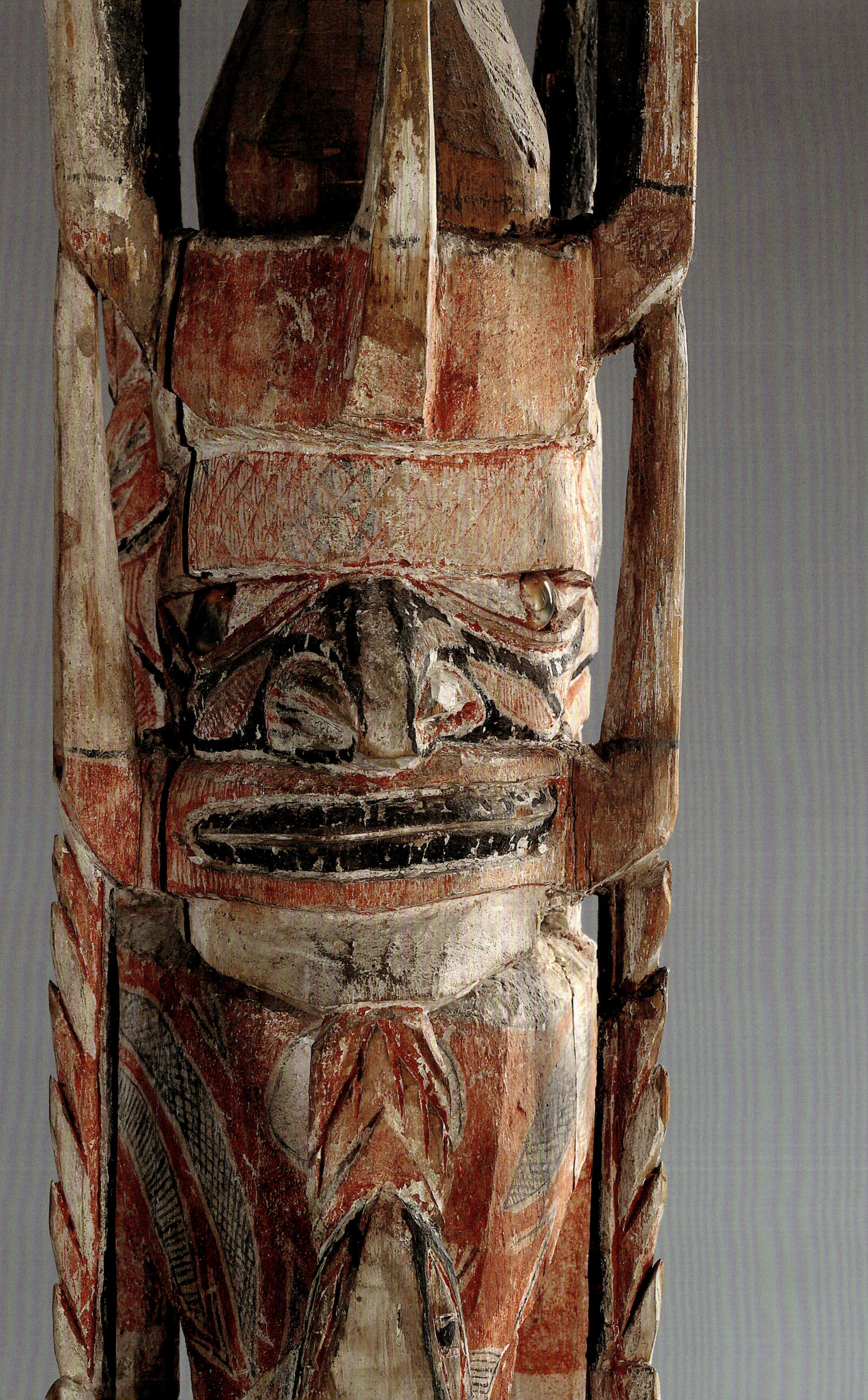

24   Suspension hook, early 20th century
Unrecorded Western Iatmul artist, East Sepik Province,
Papua New Guinea
Wood and natural pigment, 67 × 20 × 10 cm

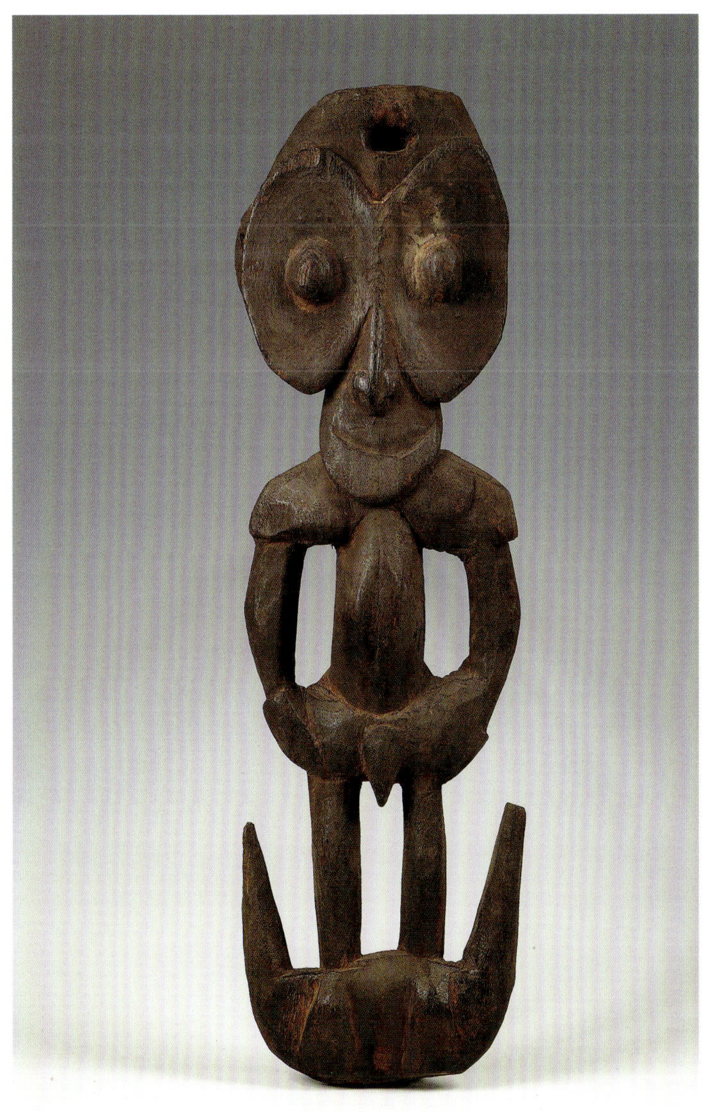

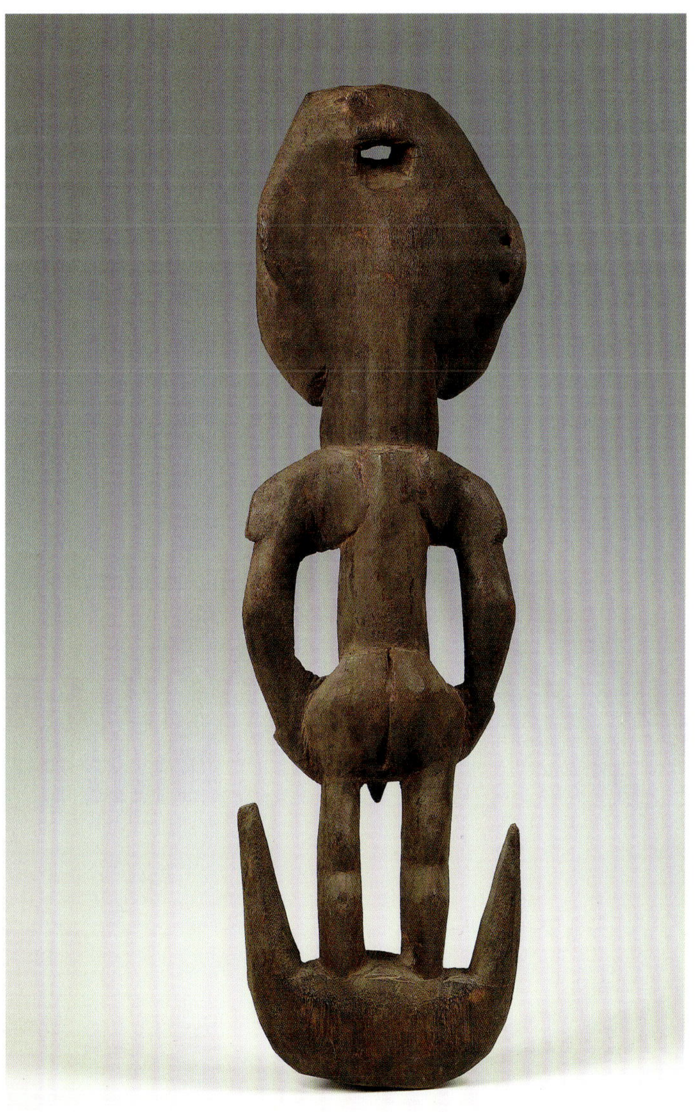

25   Ancestor figure, 1900–1960
Unrecorded Sawos artist, Yamok village,
East Sepik Province, Papua New Guinea
Wood and natural pigment, 140 × 30 × 17 cm

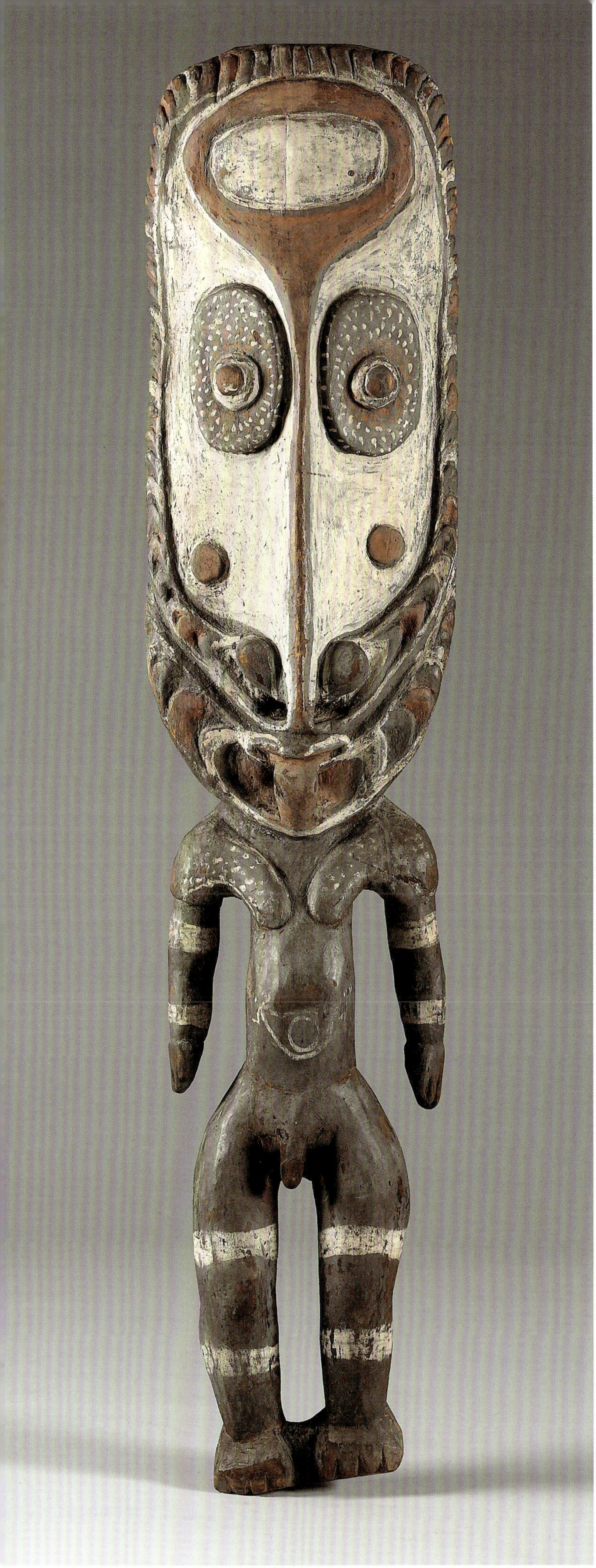

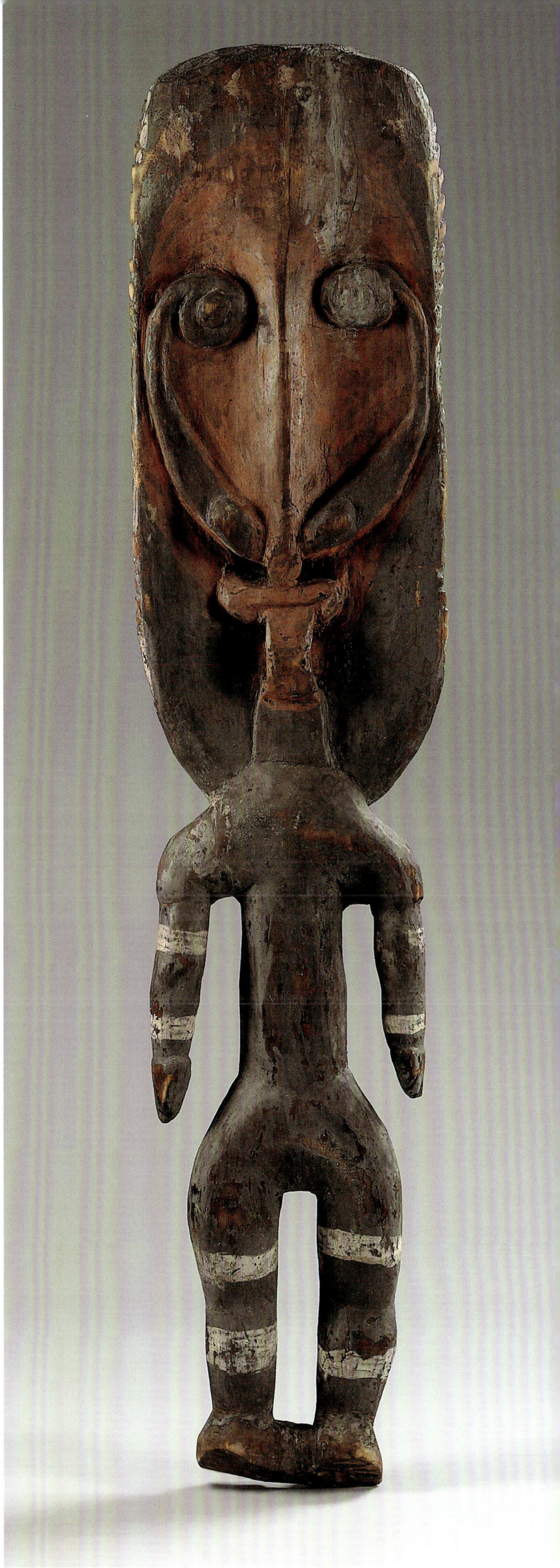

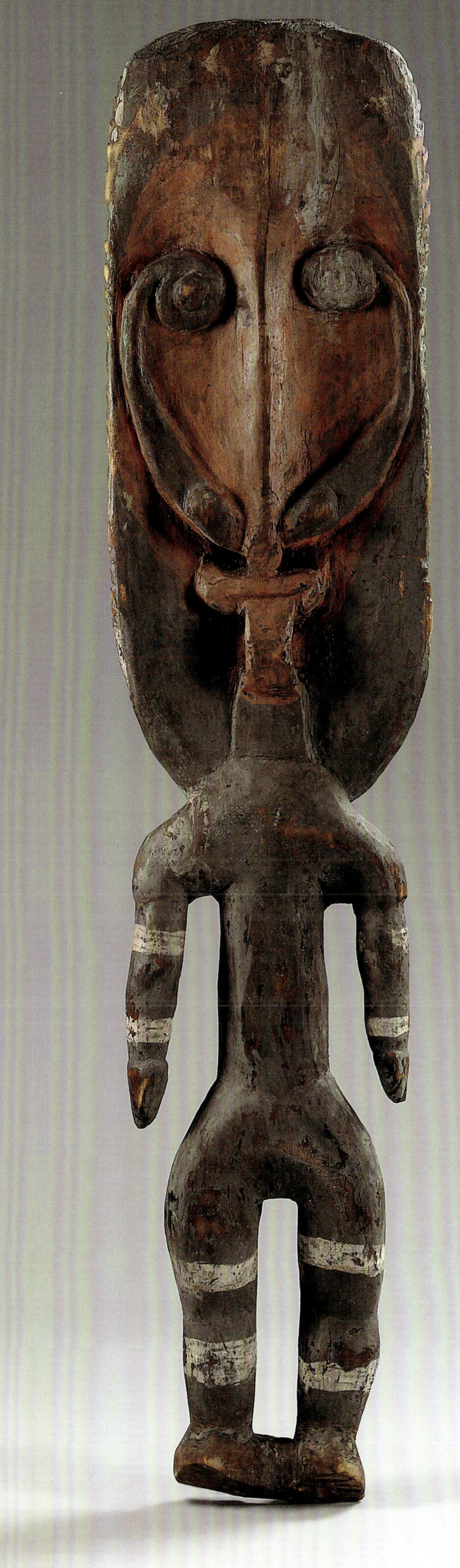

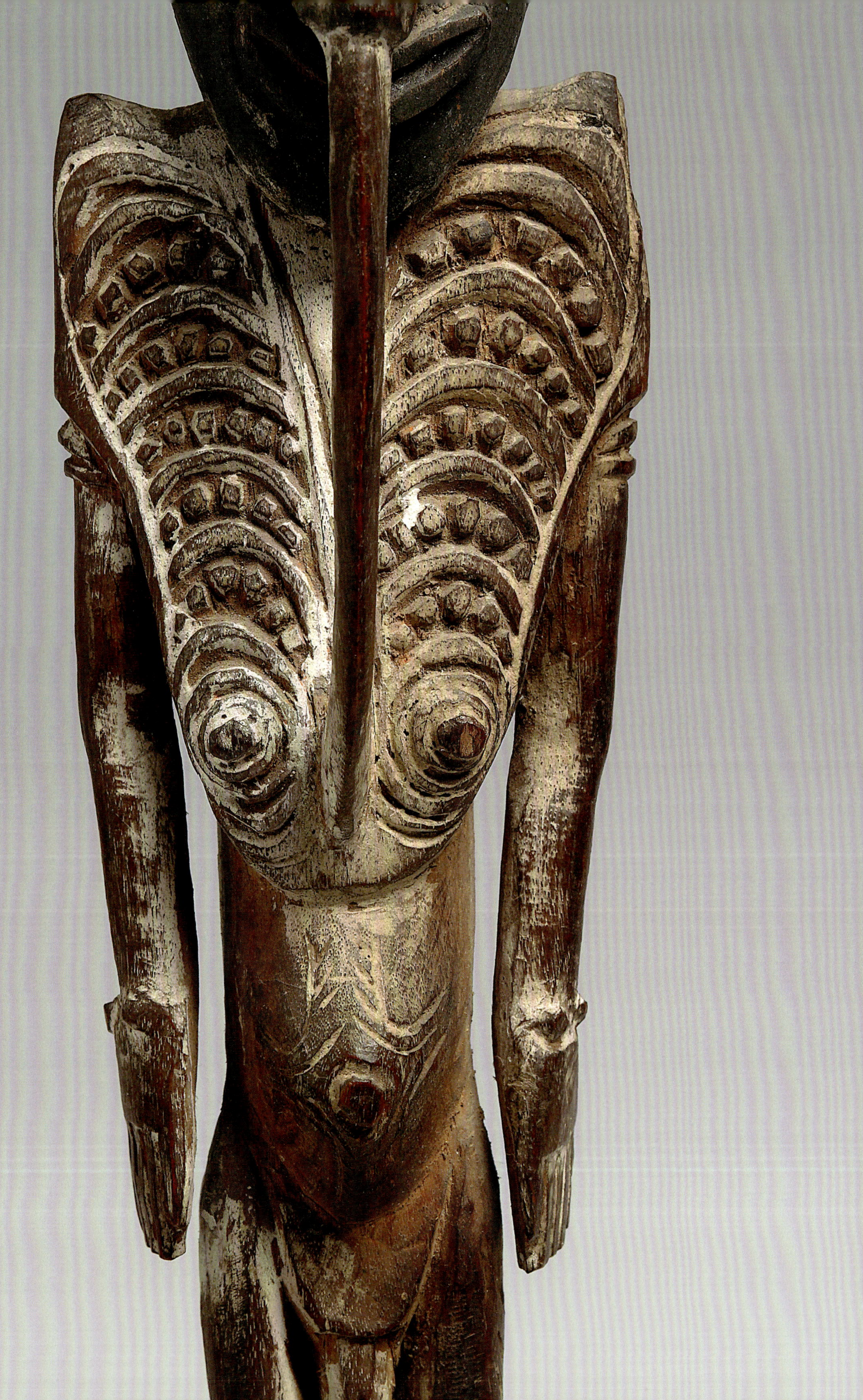

26   Flute figure, late 19th – early 20th century
Unrecorded Chambri artist, East Sepik Province,
Papua New Guinea
Wood, dog teeth, conus shell, plant fiber, and
natural pigment, 49 × 8 × 6 cm

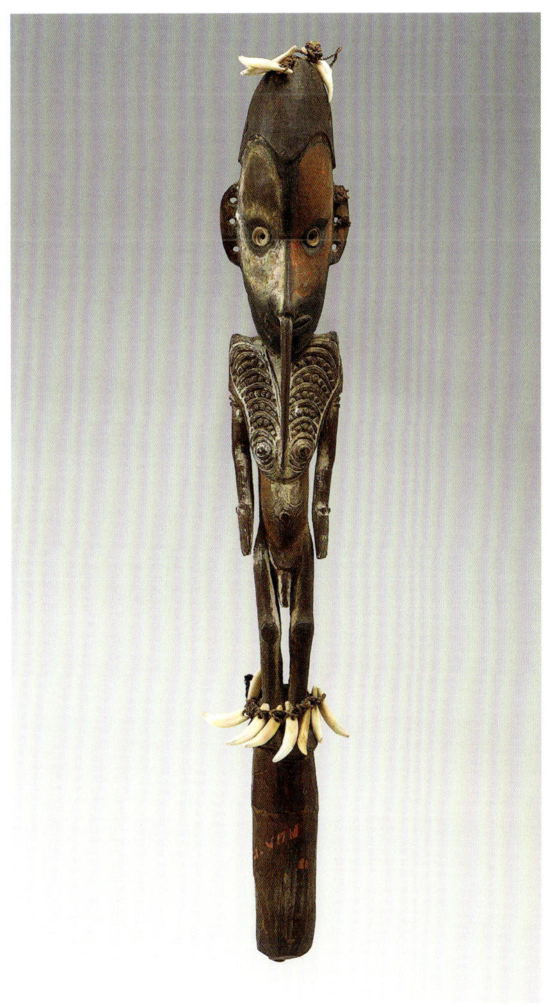

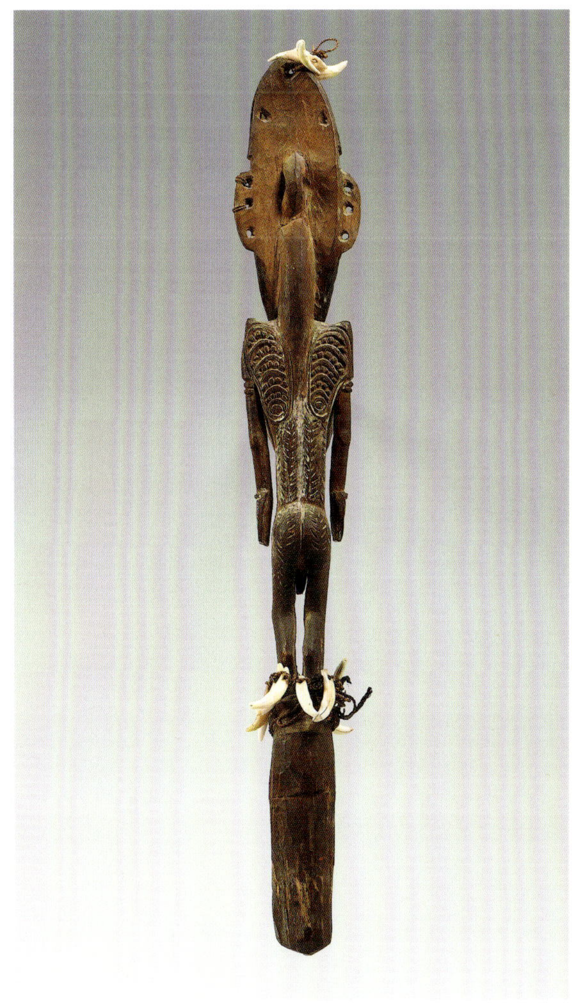

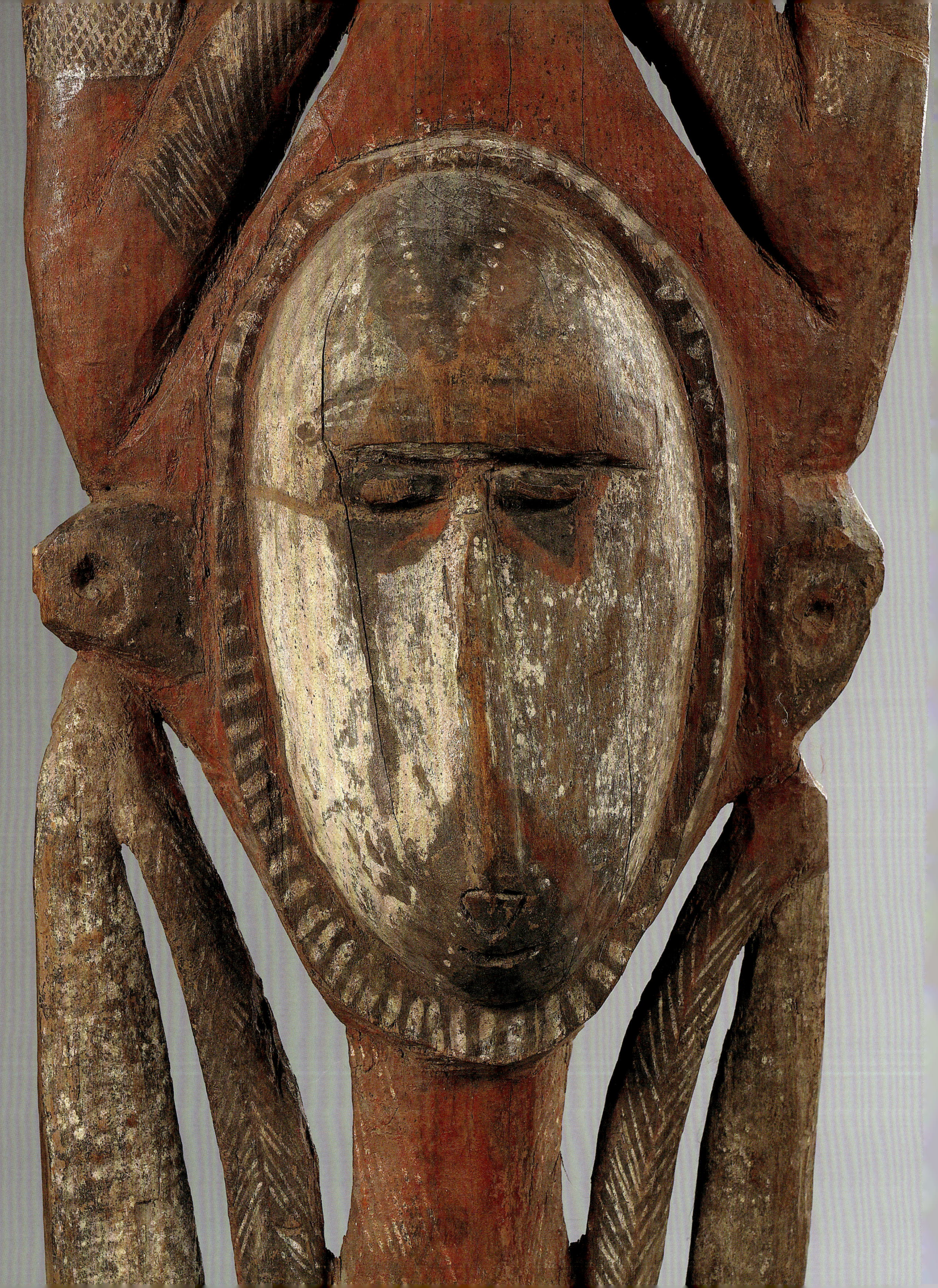

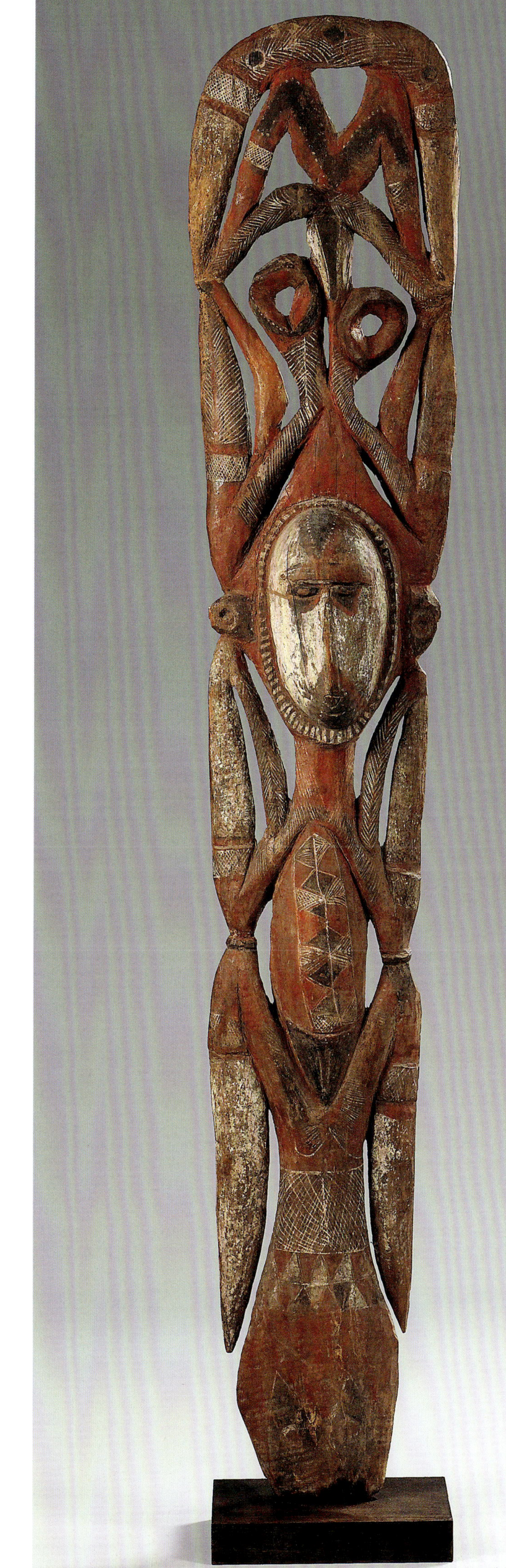

27   Ancestor figure (*miamba maira*), mid-20th century
Unrecorded Wosera artist, Southern Abelam,
Bobmagum (or Bogmuken) village, East Sepik Province,
Papua New Guinea
Wood and natural pigment, 168 × 31 × 14 cm

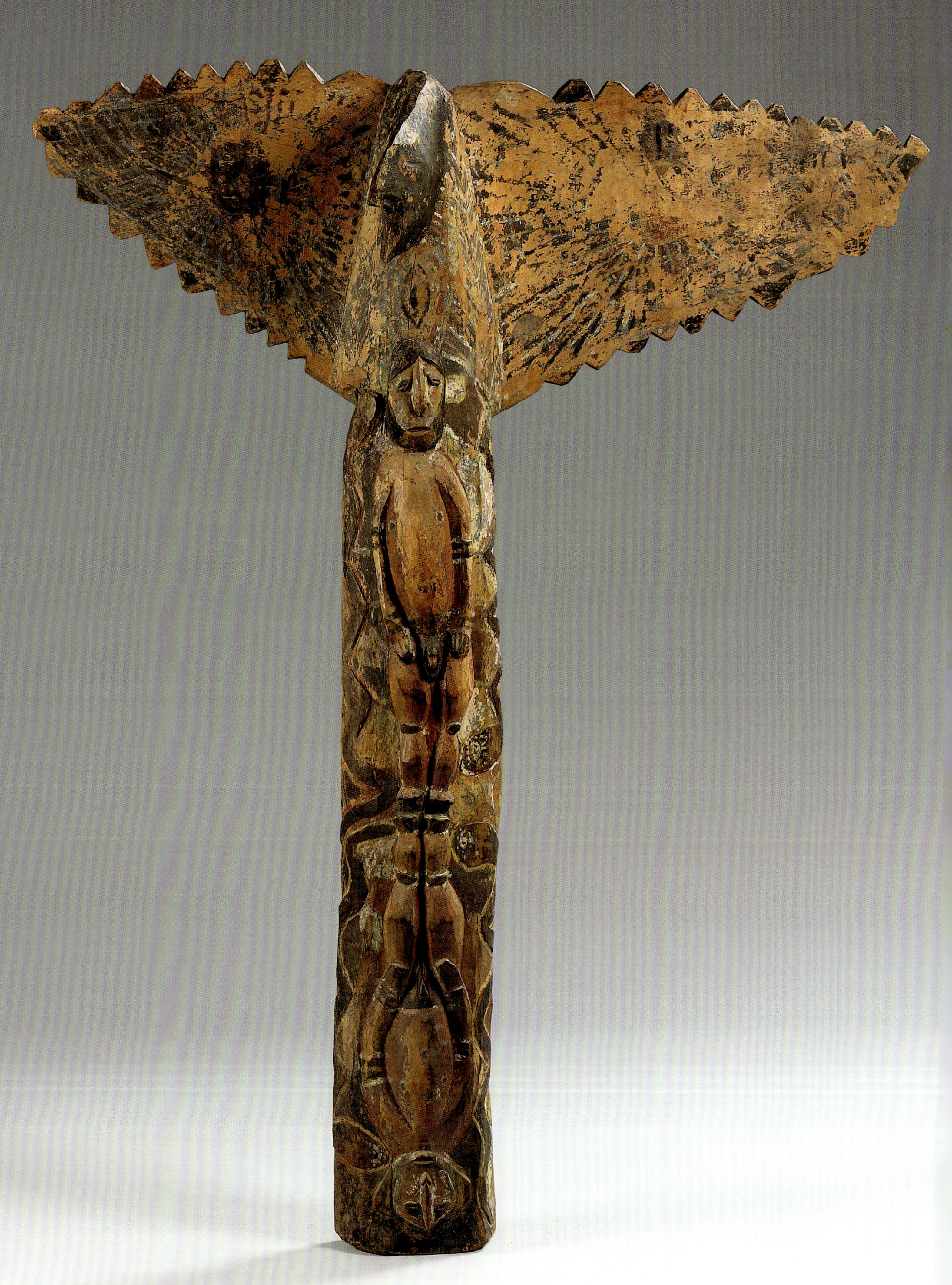

28   Element of ceremonial house, mid-20th century
Unrecorded Abelam or Boiken artist, Maprik, East Sepik
Province, Papua New Guinea
Wood and natural pigment, 142 × 112 × 37 cm

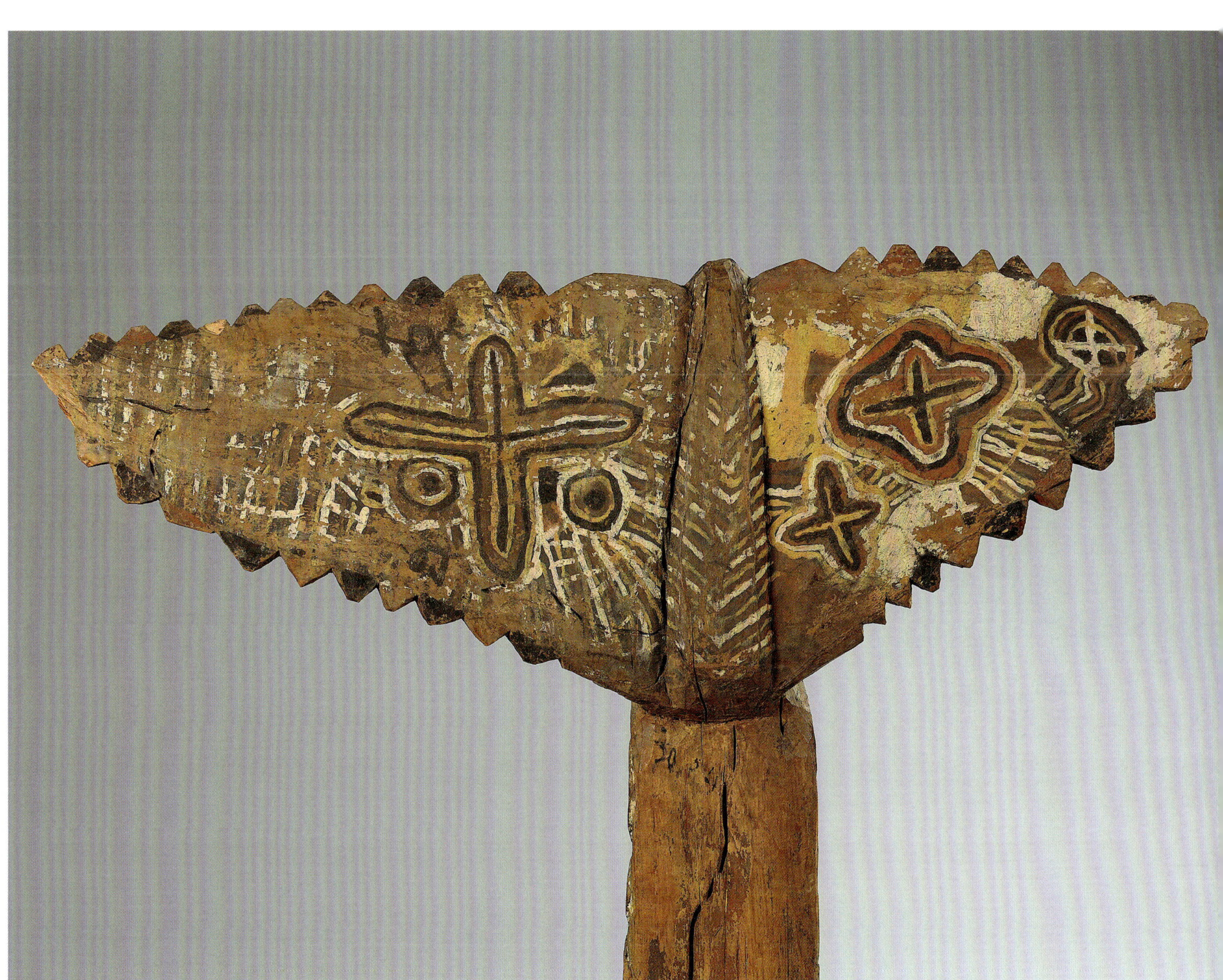

29   Male figure (*kadibon* or *kandimbog*), early 20th century
Unrecorded artist, Murik Lake, East Sepik Province, Papua New Guinea
Wood, pigment, and plant fiber, 80 × 15 × 18 cm

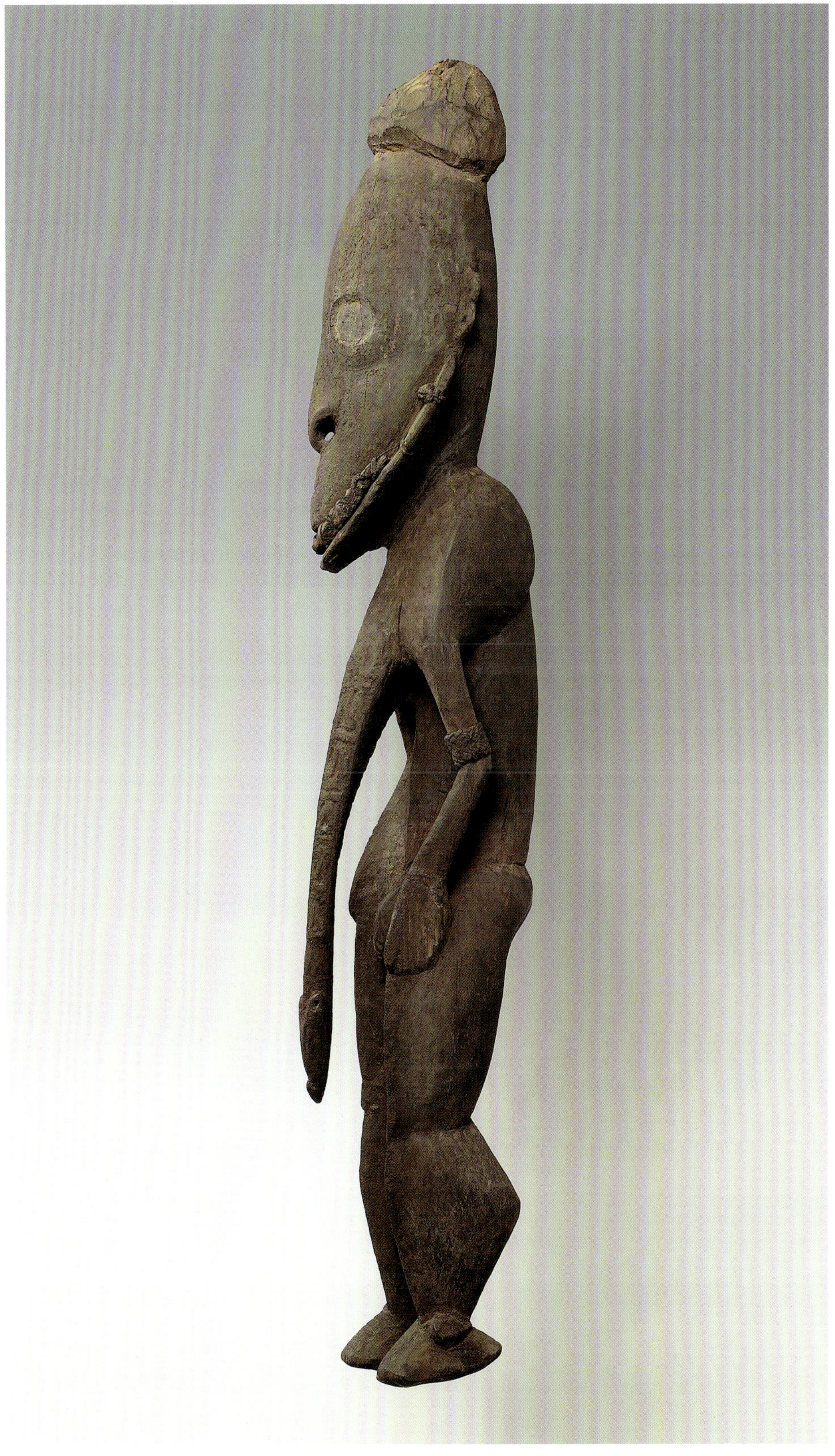

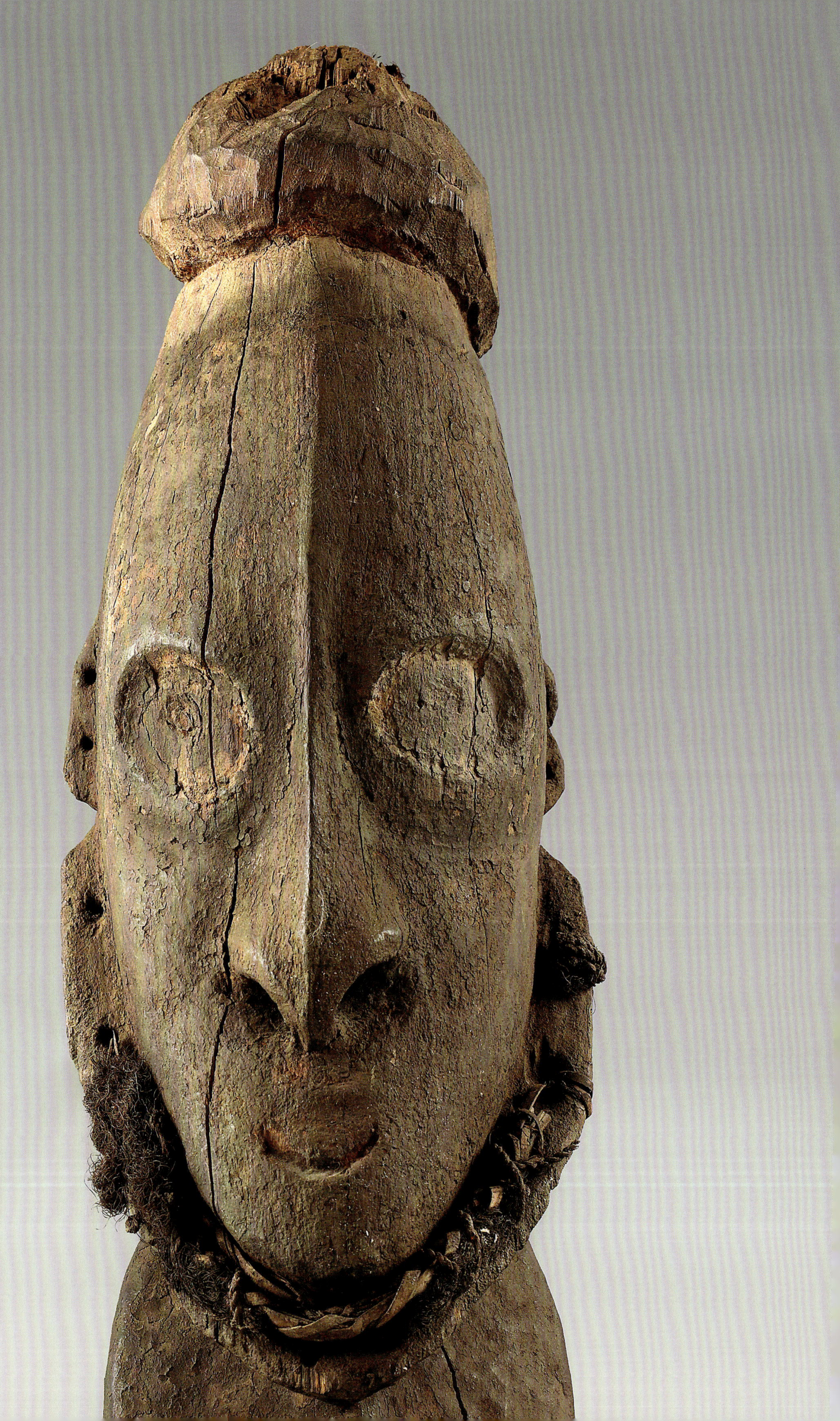

The Americas

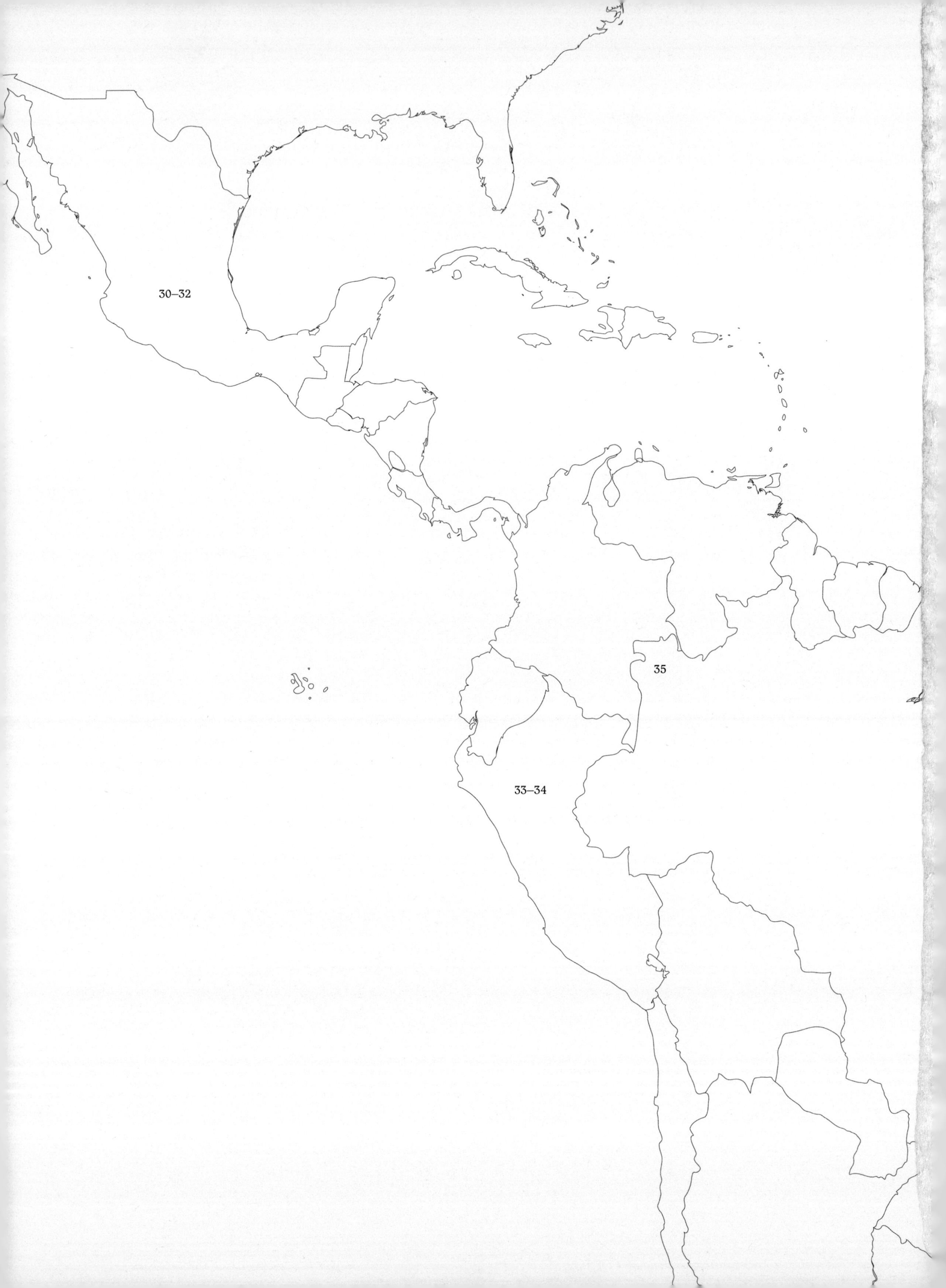

30–32
33–34
35

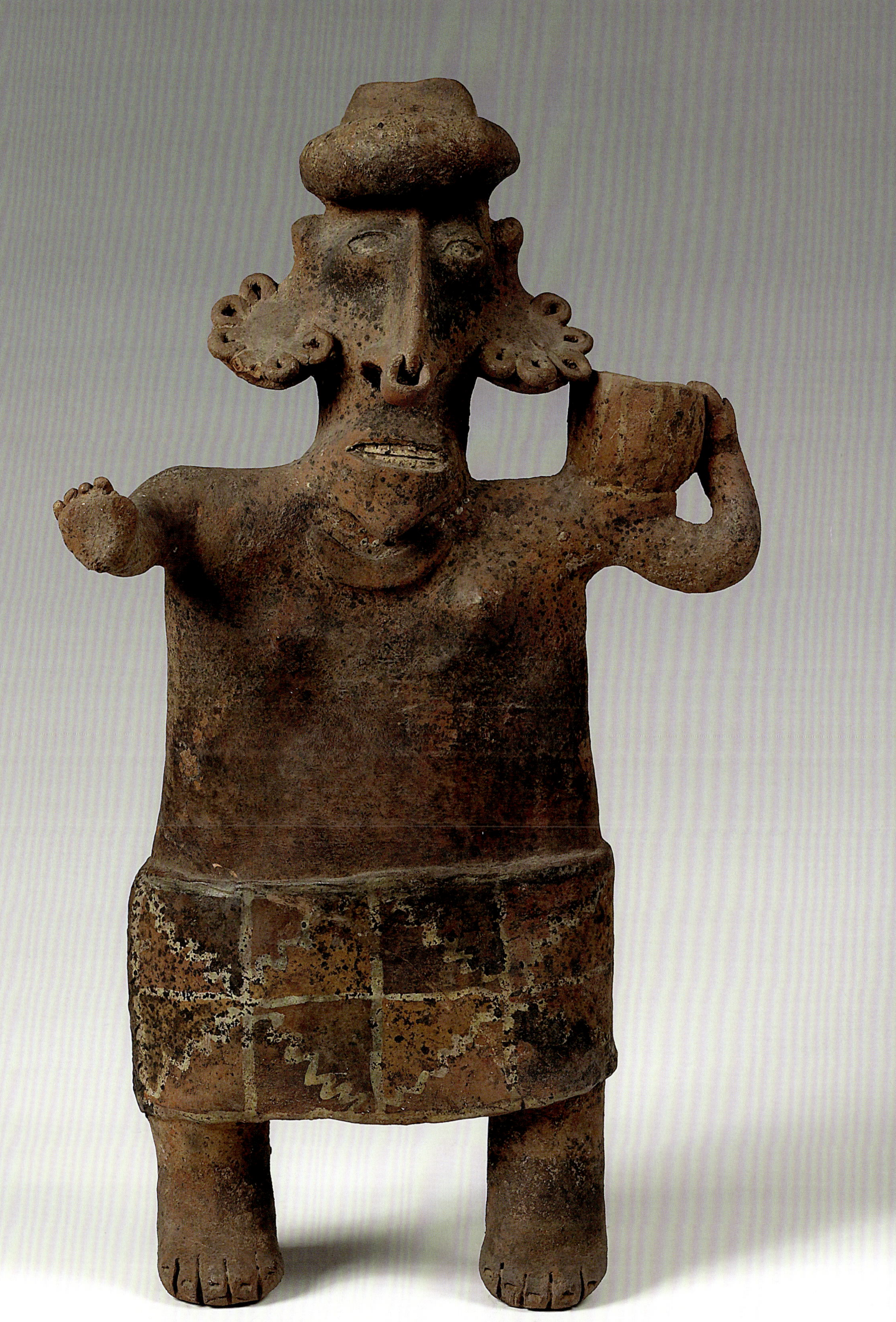

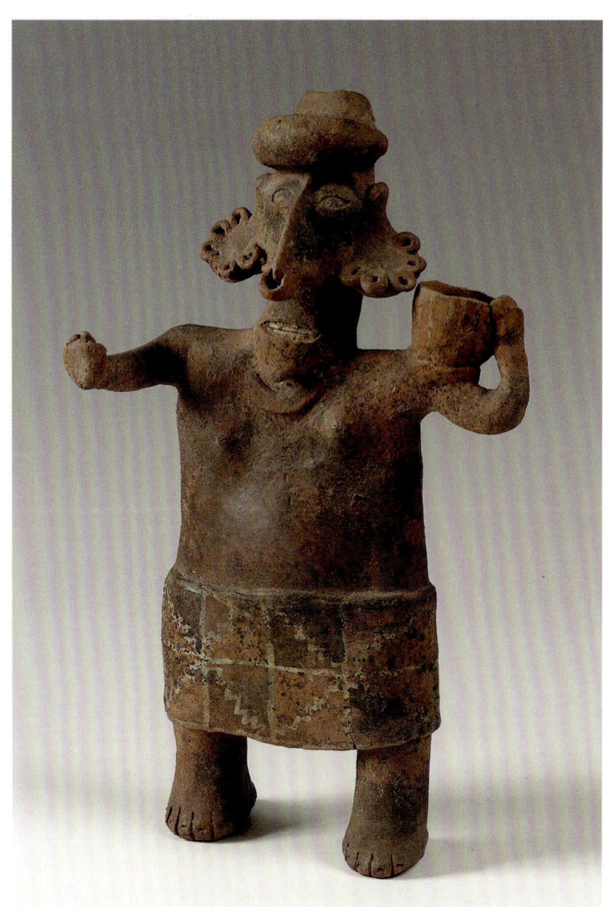

30   Female figure, 300 BCE – 400 CE
Unrecorded Nayarit artist (Ixtlán del Río culture),
ancient West Mexico
Slip-painted terracotta, 42 × 24 × 13 cm

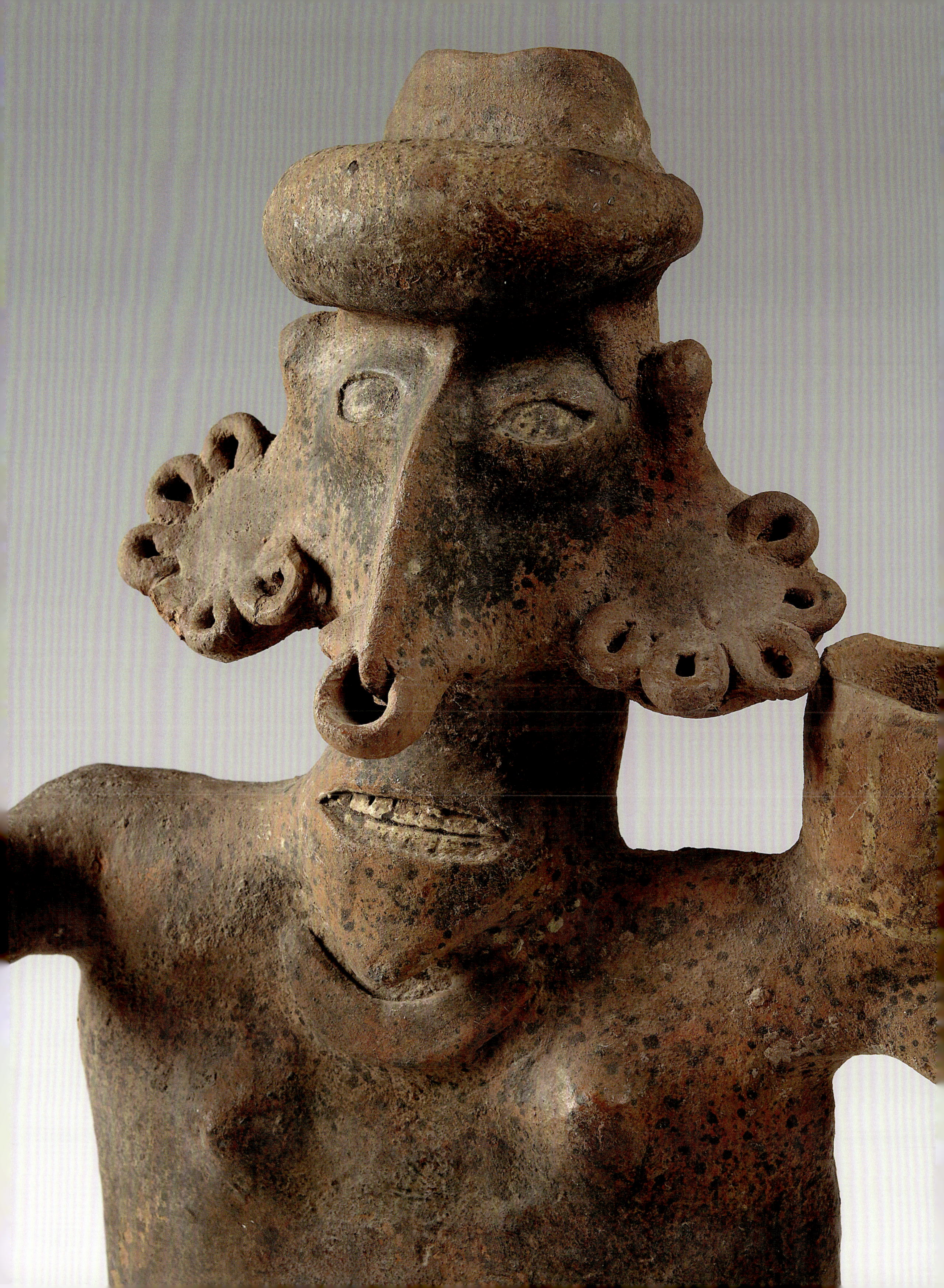

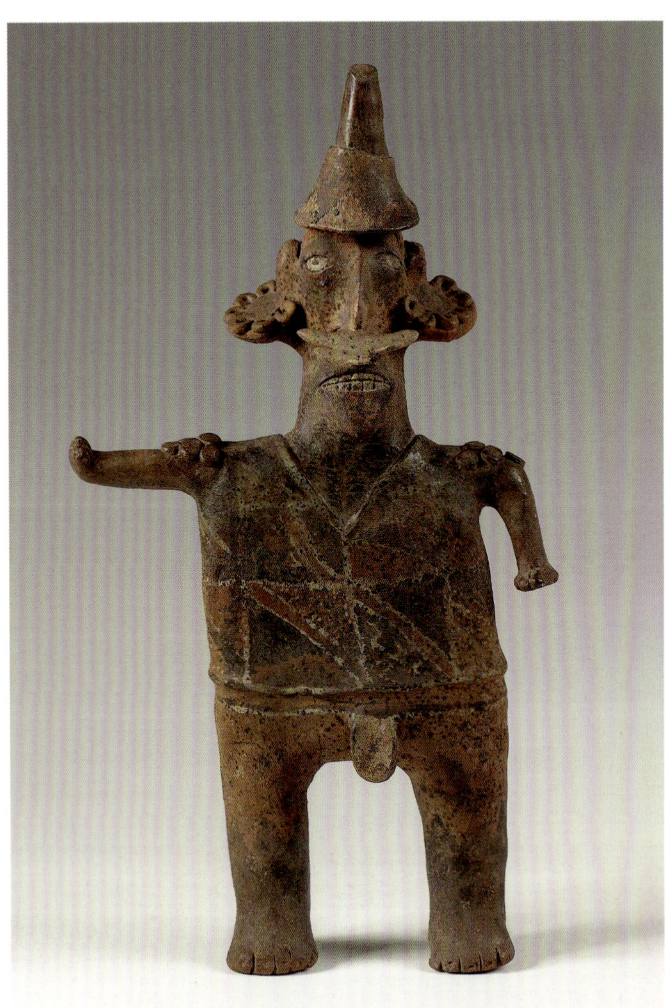

31   Male figure, 300 BCE – 400 CE
Unrecorded Nayarit artist (Ixtlán del Río culture),
ancient West Mexico
Slip-painted terracotta, 46 × 25 × 11 cm

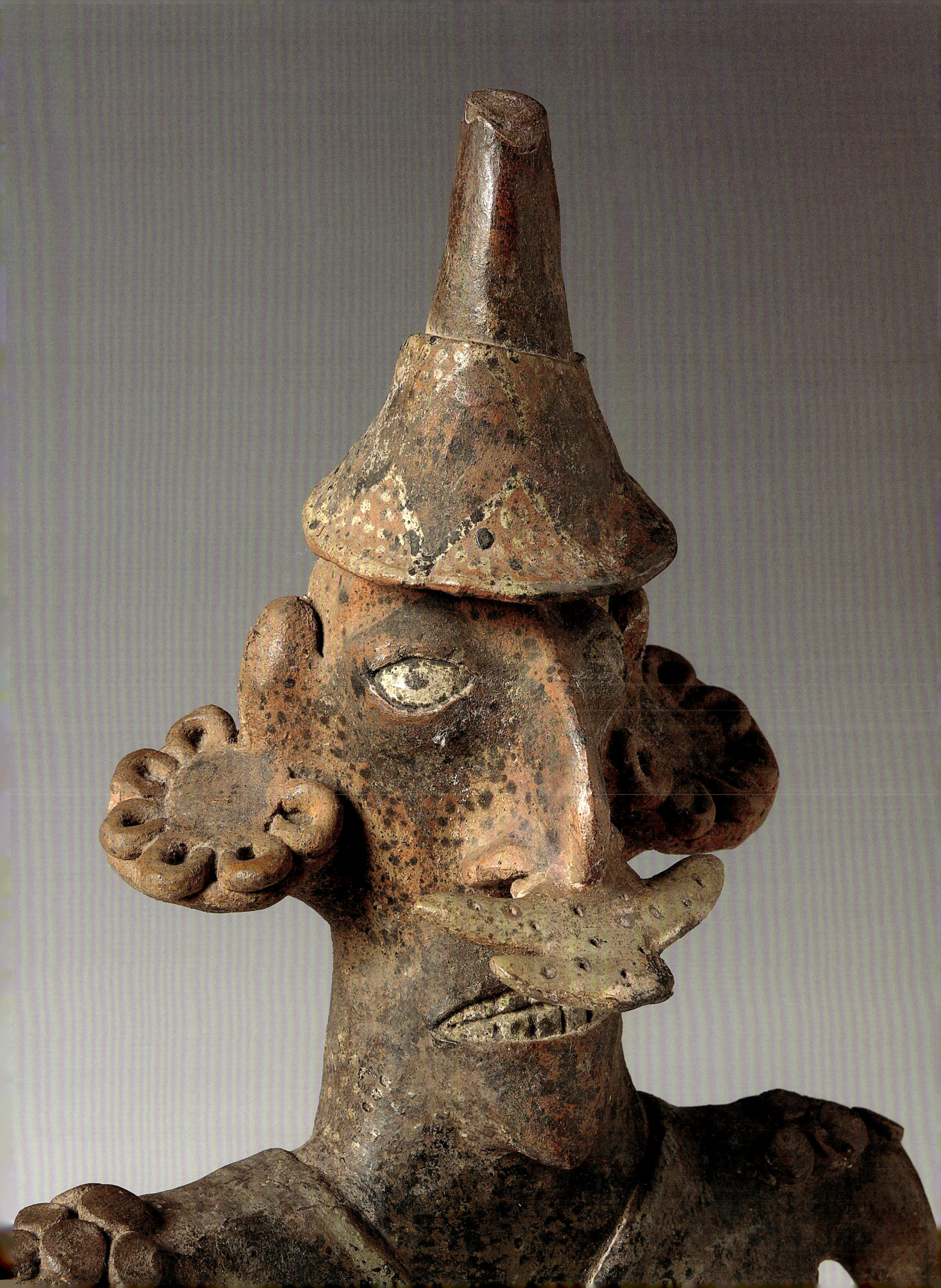

32   Marriage pair with infant, 300 BCE – 400 CE
Unrecorded Nayarit artist (Ixtlán del Río culture),
ancient West Mexico
Slip-painted terracotta, 31 × 27 × 15 cm

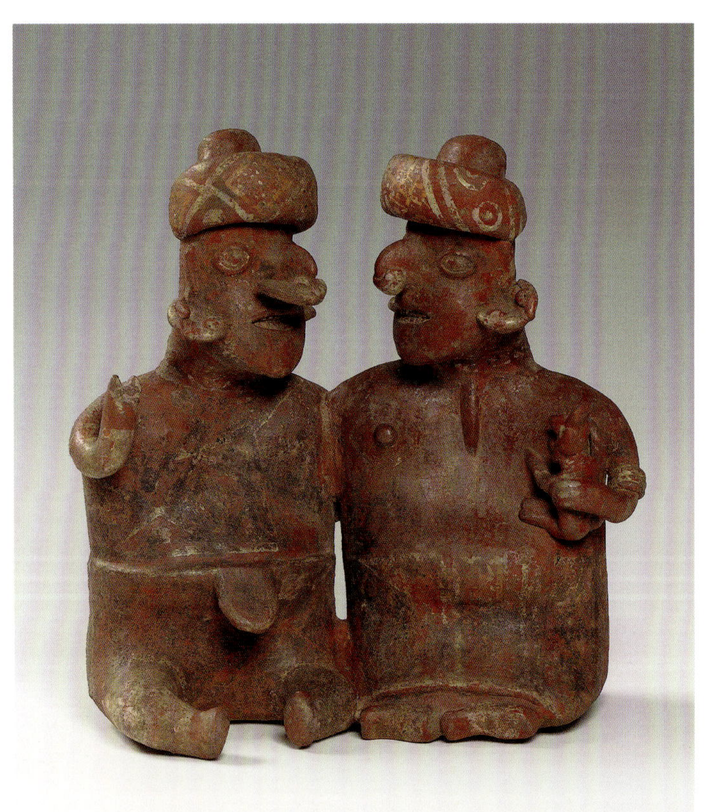
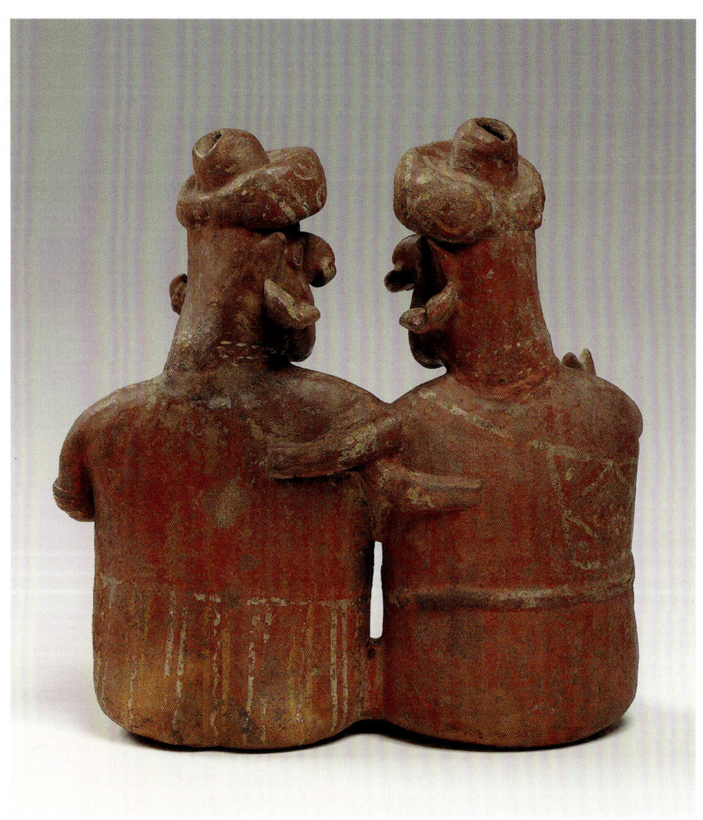

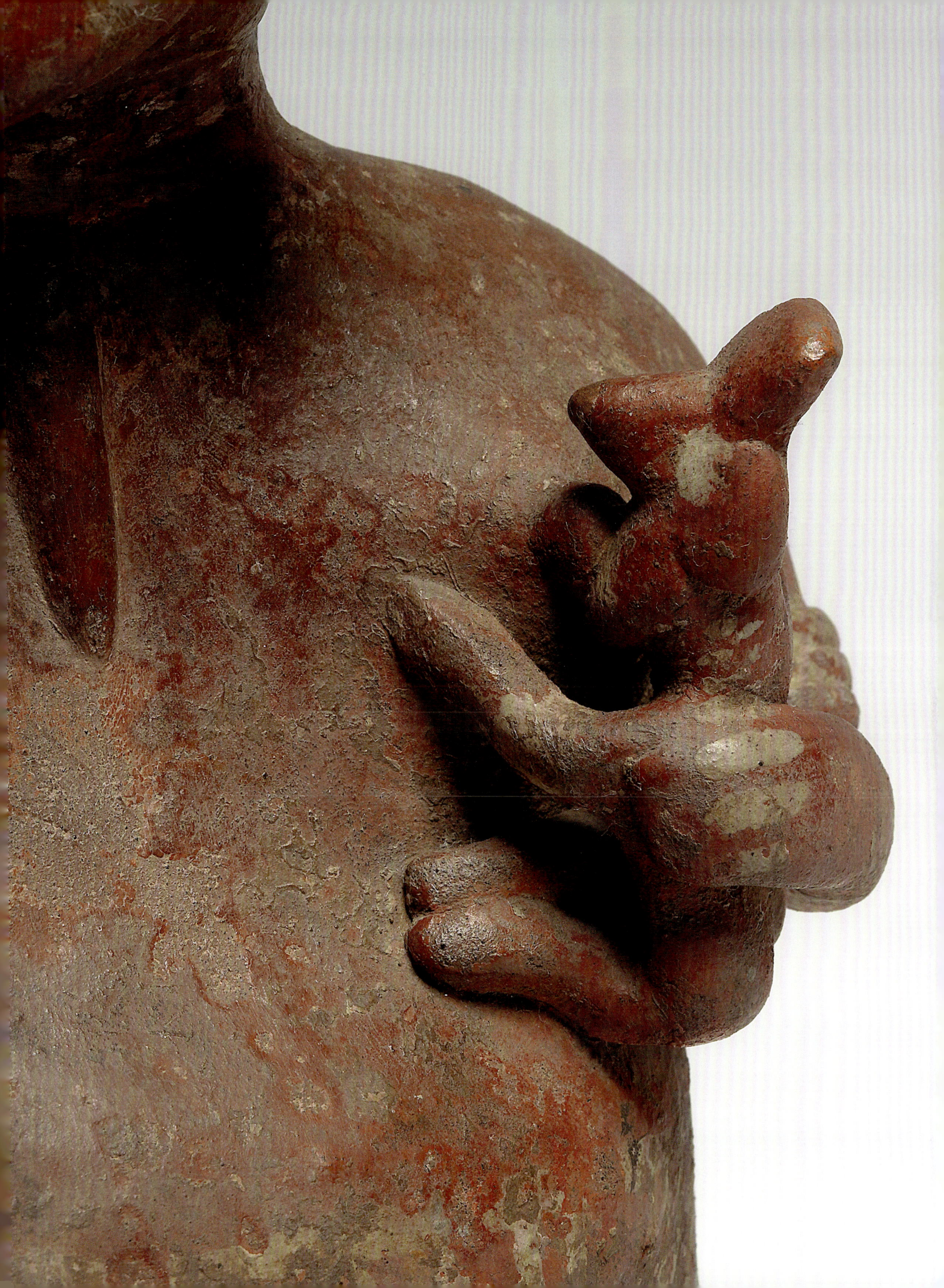

33   Three-panel mummy mask, 900–1470 CE
Unrecorded Chimú artist (Kingdom of Chimor), Northern Peru
Wood, 53 × 15 × 3 cm (left and right panels), 51 × 18 × 6 cm (middle panel)

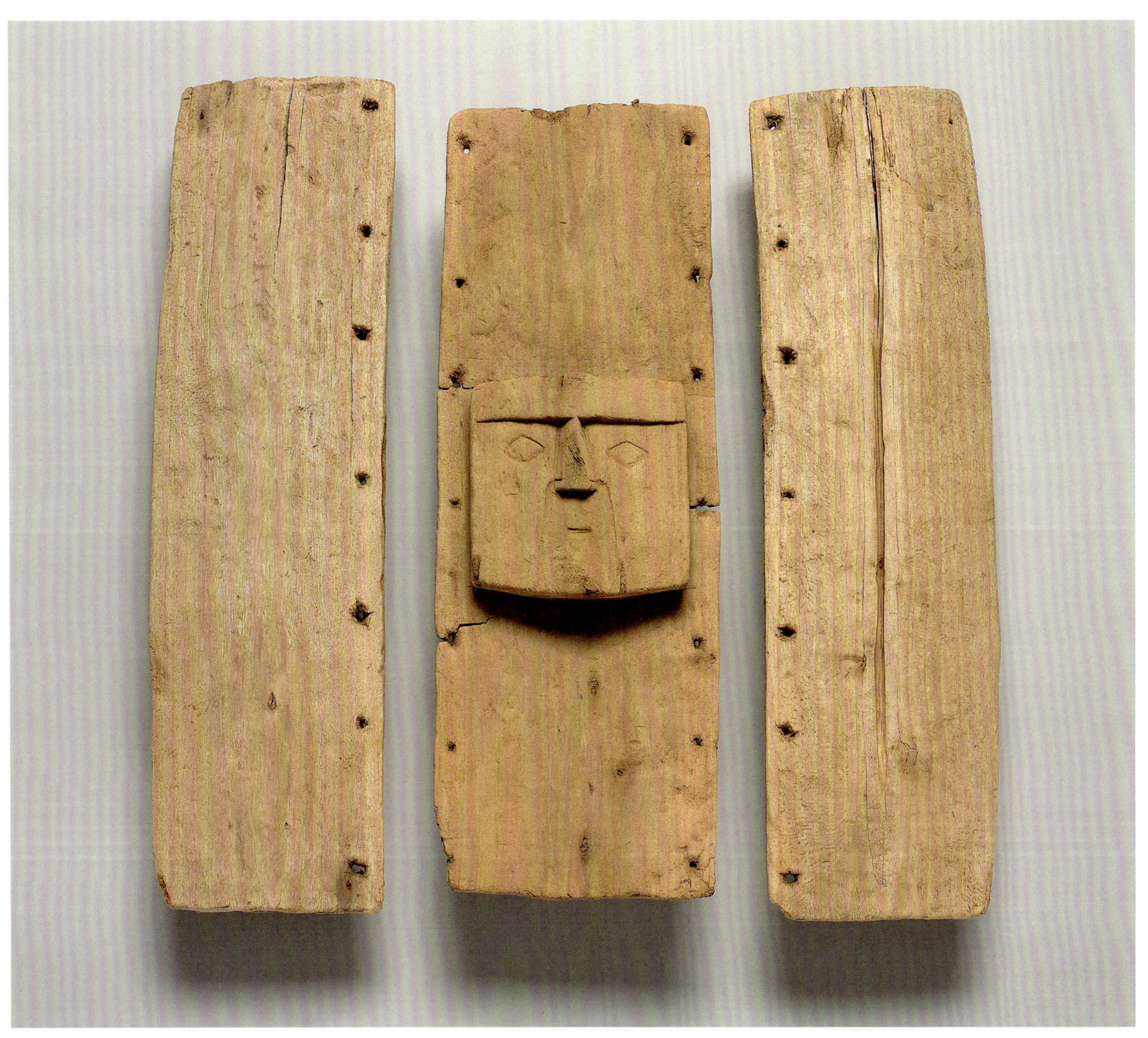

34   *Poncho* with camelids, 900–1470 CE
Unrecorded Chimú artists (Kingdom of Chimor), Northern Peru
Feathers and cotton, 80 × 80 cm

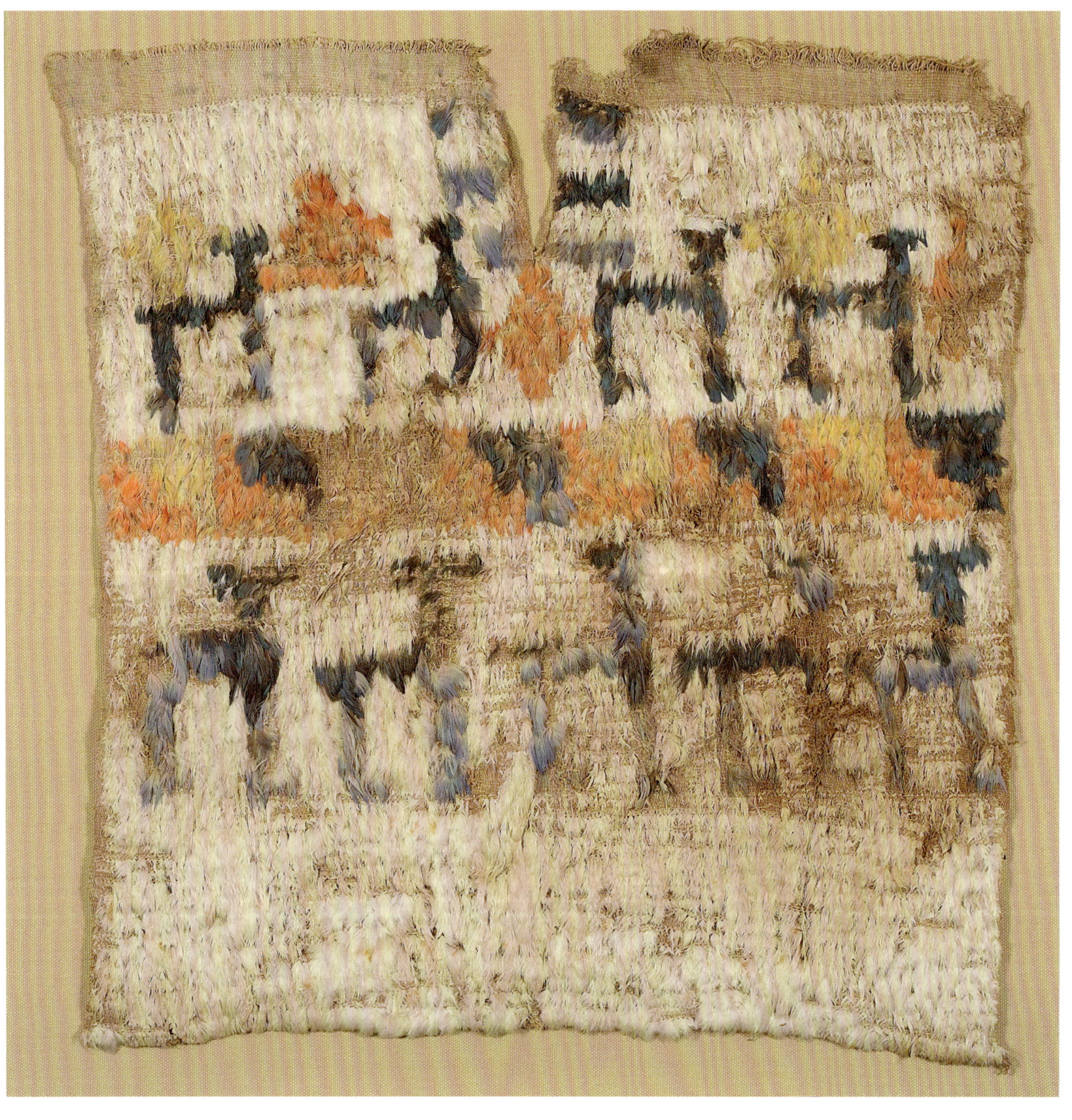

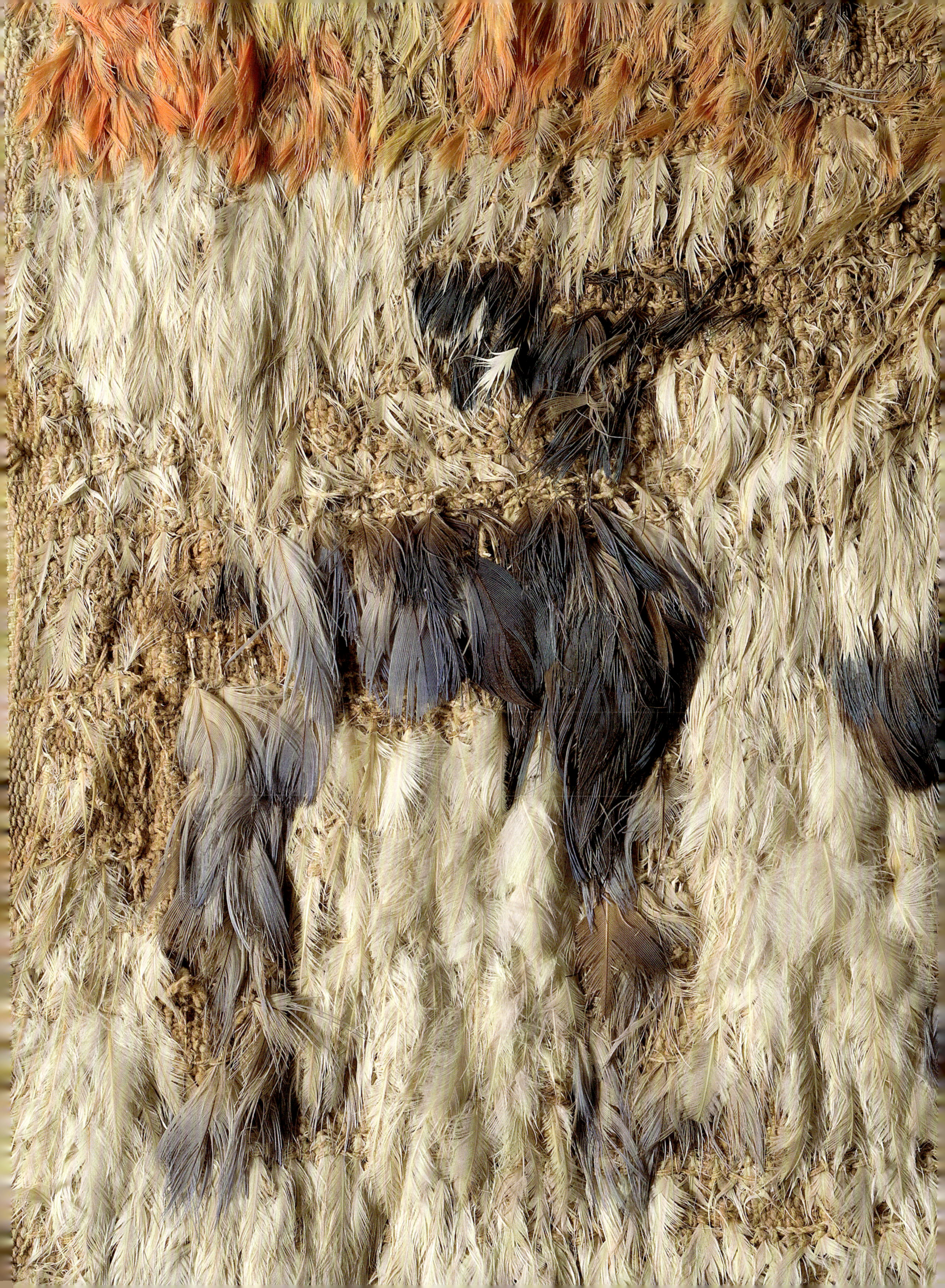

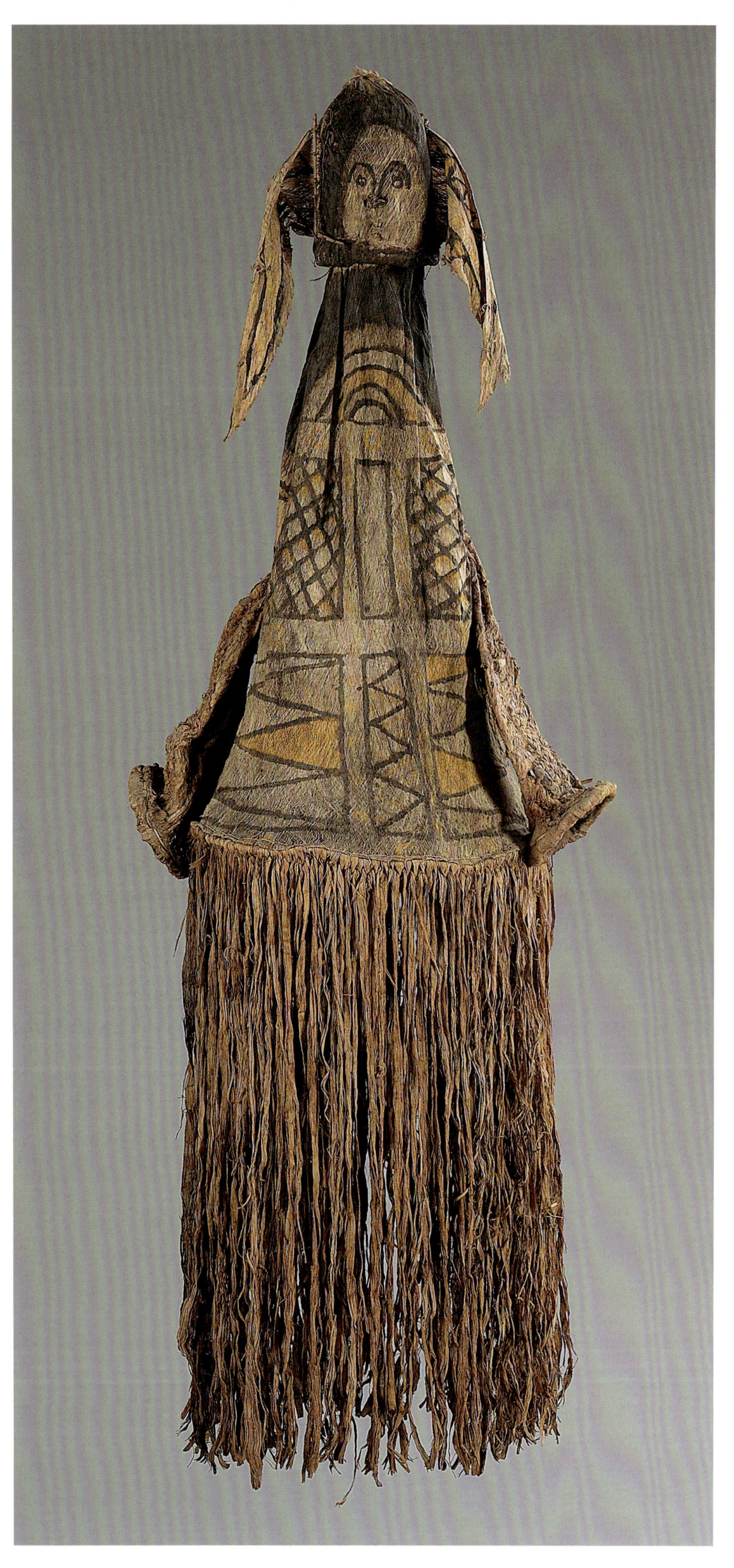

35   Bark mask, first half of the
20th century
Unrecorded Cubeo artist, Rio
Uaupés region, Northern Amazon
Bark cloth, natural pigments, and
palm thread, 140 × 55 × 35 cm

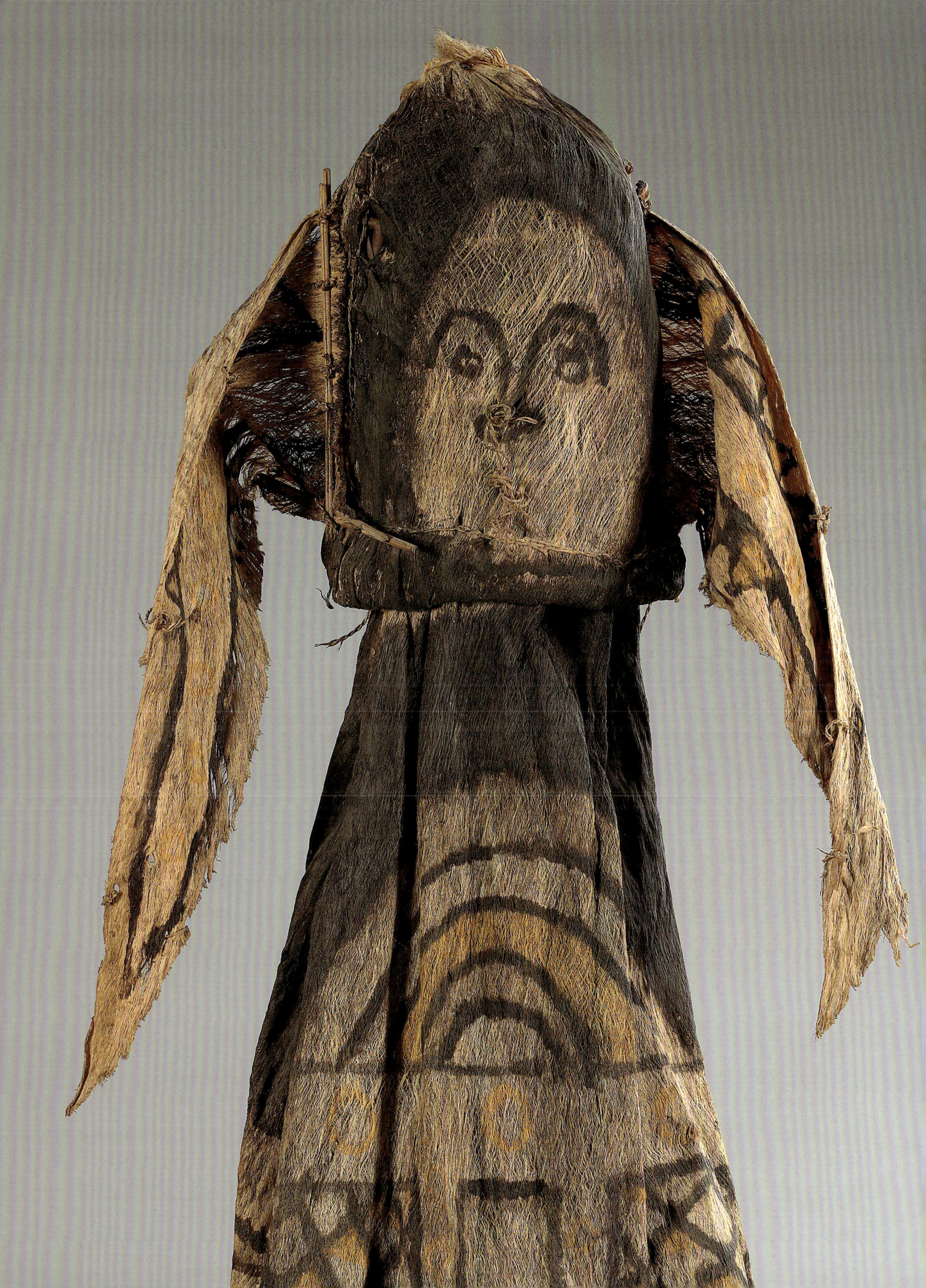

Selected Bibliography

Note to Reader: Analyses of race, colonialism, and "modernist primitivism" are ongoing and vast. They are ever-evolving in fields such as art history and anthropology and cannot be contained in a brief bibliography. The select publications listed below provide a context for those cultures represented within Peggy Guggenheim's collection, augmenting the additional references in the essay notes.

Abiodun, Rowland. *Yoruba Art and Language: Seeking the African in African Art*. New York: Cambridge University Press, 2014.

Berzock, Kathleen Bickford, and Christa Clarke, eds. *Representing Africa in American Art Museums: A Century of Collecting and Display*. Seattle: University of Washington Press, 2010.

Bourgeois, Arthur. *Yaka: Visions of Africa Series*. Milan: 5 Continents Editions, 2014.

Braun, Barbara. *Pre-Columbian Art and the Post-Columbian World: Ancient American Sources of Modern Art*. New York: Harry N. Abrams, 1993.

Braun, Barbara, and Peter G. Roe, eds. *Arts of the Amazon*. London: Thames and Hudson, 1995.

Brunt, Peter, Nicholas Thomas, Sean Mallon, Lissant Bolton, Deidre Brown, Damian Skinner, and Susanne Küchler. *Art in Oceania: A New History*. London: Thames and Hudson, 2012.

Cameron, Elizabeth. *Reclusive Rebels: An Approach to the Sala Mpasu and Their Masks*. Exh. cat. San Diego: Mesa College Art Gallery, 1992.

Campione, Francesco Paolo, ed. *Ethnopassion: Peggy Guggenheim's Ethnic Art Collection*. Exh. cat. Milan: Mazzotta, 2008.

Clarke, Christa, ed. *African Art in the Barnes Foundation: The Triumph of L'art Nègre and the Harlem Renaissance*. New York: Skira Rizzoli, 2015.

Clifford, James. *The Predicament of Culture: Twentieth-Century Ethnography, Literature, and Art*. Cambridge, Mass.: Harvard University Press, 1988.

Colleyn, Jean-Paul, ed. *Bamana: The Art of Existence in Mali*. Exh. cat. New York: Museum for African Art; Zürich: Museum Rietberg; Ghent: Snoeck-Ducaju & Zoon, 2001.

Cowling, Elizabeth. "'L'Oeil sauvage': Oceanic Art and the Surrealists." In *Art of Northwest New Guinea: From Geelvink Bay, Humboldt Bay, and Lake Sentani*. Edited by Suzanne Greub. New York: Rizzoli, 1992.

Dandrieu, Chantal, and Fabrizio Giovagnoni, eds. *Passione d'Africa: L'arte africana nelle collezioni italiane*. Milan: Officina Libraria, 2009.

Evans, R. Tripp. "Navigating the Afterlife: Two Shaft Tomb Figures from Ancient West Mexico," *Yale University Art Gallery Bulletin*. New Haven: Yale University Art Gallery, 1995–96, pp. 28–33.

————. *Romancing the Maya: Mexican Antiquity in the American Imagination, 1820–1915*. Austin: University of Texas Press, 2004.

Ezra, Kate. *Art of the Dogon: Selections from the Lester Wunderman Collection*. Exh. cat. New York: Metropolitan Museum of Art, 1988.

Flam, Jack, and Miriam Deutch, eds. *Primitivism and Twentieth-Century Art: A Documentary History*. Berkeley: University of California Press, 2003.

Foster, Hal. "The 'Primitive' Unconscious of Modern Art," *October* 34 (Fall 1985), pp. 58–70.

Gagliardi, Susan Elizabeth. *Senufo Unbound: Dynamics of Art and Identity in West Africa*. Exh. cat. Cleveland: Cleveland Museum of Art; Milan: 5 Continents Editions, 2015.

Garrigan, Shelley E. *Collecting Mexico: Museums, Monuments, and the Creation of National Identity*. Minneapolis: University of Minnesota Press, 2012.

Geary, Christraud M., and Stephanie Xatart. *Material Journeys: Collecting African and Oceanic Art, 1945–2000*. Boston: MFA Publications, 2007.

Goldman, Irving. *The Cubeo, Indians of the Northwest Amazon*. Champaign: University of Illinois Press, 1963.

Lamp, Frederick. *Art of the Baga: A Drama of Cultural Reinvention*. Exh. cat. Munich: Prestel for the Museum for African Art, 1996.

Le Fur, Yves, et al. *D'un regard l'Autre: Histoire des regards européens sur l'Afrique, l'Amérique et l'Océanie*. Exh. cat. Paris: Musée du quai Branly, 2006.

Leloup, Hélène. *Dogon Statuary*. Strasbourg: Daniele Amez, 1994.

McBreen, Ellen. *Matisse's Sculpture: The Pinup and the Primitive*. New Haven: Yale University Press, 2014.

Moseley, Michael E. *The Incas and Their Ancestors: The Archaeology of Peru*. London: Thames and Hudson, 1992.

Oles, James. *South of the Border: Mexico in the American Imagination 1914–1947*. Exh. cat. Washington, D.C.: Smithsonian Institution Press, 1993.

Paudrat, Jean-Louis. "Between the Fin-de-Siècle and the Roaring Twenties: The 'Discovery' of African Arts." In *Arts of Africa: 7000 Years of African Art*. Edited by Ezio Bassani. Exh. cat. Milan: Skira, 2005.

Peltier, Philippe, and Michael Gunn, eds. *New Ireland: Art of the South Pacific*. Exh. cat. Paris: Musée du quai Branly; Milan: 5 Continents Editions, 2006.

Peltier, Philippe, and Floriane Morin, eds. *Shadows of New Guinea: Art of the Great Island of Oceania in the Barbier-Mueller Collections*. Exh. cat. Paris: Somogy éditions d'art, The Mona Bismarck Foundation; Geneva: Musée Barbier-Mueller, 2006.

Peltier, Philippe, Markus Schindlbeck, and Christian Kaufmann, eds. *Sepik: Arts de Papouasie-Nouvelle-Guinée*. Exh. cat. Paris: Musée du quai Branly, Éditions Skira Paris, 2015.

Perrois, Louis. *Kota*. Milan: 5 Continents Editions, 2012.

Rubin, William, ed. *"Primitivism" in 20th Century Art: Affinity of the Tribal and the Modern*. Exh. cat. New York: Museum of Modern Art, 1984.

Smidt, Dirk A. M., ed. *Asmat Art: Woodcarvings of Southwest New Guinea*. New York: George Braziller, 1993.

Spitta, Sylvia. *Misplaced Objects: Migrating Collections and Recollections in Europe and the Americas*. Austin: University of Texas Press, 2009.

Stanley, Nick. *The Making of Asmat Art: Indigenous Art in a World Perspective*. Canon Pyon, UK: Sean Kingston Publishing, 2012.

Stepan, Peter. *Picasso's Collection of African and Oceanic Art: Masters of Metamorphosis*. Munich: Prestel, 2006.

Stone-Miller, Rebecca. *Art of the Andes from Chavín to Inca*. London: Thames and Hudson, 1995.

Townsend, Richard F., ed. *Ancient West Mexico: Art and Archaeology of the Unknown Past*. Exh. cat. Chicago: Art Institute of Chicago, 1998.

Tythacott, Louise. *Surrealism and the Exotic*. London: Routledge, 2003.

Van Damme, Annemieke, and David A. Binkley. *Spectacular Display: The Art of Nkanu Initiation Rituals*. Exh. cat. Washington, DC: Smithsonian National Museum of African Art; London: Philip Wilson Publishers, 2001.

Veys, Fanny Wonu. "Papua Collections in the Netherlands: A Story of Exploration, Research, Missionization and Colonization." *Pacific Presences: Oceanic Art and European Museums*. Edited by Lucie Carreau, Alison Clark, Alana Jelinek, Erna Lilje, and Nicholas Thomas. Vol. 1, pp. 127–68. Leiden: Sidestone Press, 2018.

Wolff, Norma H. "'A Matter of Must': Continuities and Change in the Adugbologe Woodcarving Workshop in Abeokuta, Nigeria." In *African Art and Agency in the Workshop*. Edited by Sidney Littlefield Kasfir and Till Förster. Bloomington: Indiana University Press, 2013.

Zarur, Elizabeth. *Fiber and Feathers: Native Baskets of North America and Featherwork of South America*. Exh. cat. Norton, Mass.: Beard Gallery, Wheaton College, 1993.

Contributors

Christa Clarke is an Independent Curator/Scholar, Arts of Global Africa, and Affiliate, Hutchins Center for African & African American Research, Harvard University (Cambridge, Mass.).

R. Tripp Evans is Professor of the History of Art, and Co-Chair, Department of Visual Art and History of Art, Wheaton College (Norton, Mass.).

Ellen McBreen is Associate Professor of the History of Art, Department of Visual Art and History of Art, Wheaton College (Norton, Mass.).

Fanny Wonu Veys is Curator, Oceania, National Museum of World Cultures, Amsterdam (Tropenmuseum), Berg en Dal (Afrika Museum), Leiden (Museum Volkenkunde), and Rotterdam (Wereldmuseum), The Netherlands.

Published on the occasion of
*Migrating Objects: Arts of Africa, Oceania,
and the Americas in the Peggy Guggenheim
Collection*

Organized by the Curatorial Advisory Committee:
Christa Clarke, R. Tripp Evans, Ellen McBreen,
and Fanny Wonu Veys with Vivien Greene

Peggy Guggenheim Collection, Venice
February 15 – June 14, 2020

ISBN 978-88-297-0485-9

Peggy Guggenheim Collection
Dorsoduro 701
I-30123 Venice
www.guggenheim-venice.it

Marsilio Editori SpA
Santa Marta, fabbricato 17
I-30123 Venice
www.marsilioeditori.it

Available through
ARTBOOK | D.A.P.
75 Broad Street, Suite 630
New York, NY 10004
USA

Design
Neil Donnelly
Ben Fehrman-Lee

Editorial
Anne B. Barriault

Typeset in Magister
Printed in Italy by Conti Tipocolor

Photographs of artworks in the Peggy Guggenheim
Collection are by Paolo Manusardi.

Front endsheet
Dealer Hélène Leloup in Guinea loading Baga
sculptures, including a *D'mba* headdress, onto the
back of a truck, ca. 1956. Courtesy Hélène Leloup

Back endsheet
Peggy Guggenheim in the foyer of Palazzo Venier
dei Leoni, Venice, 1960s. From left: *Developable
Surface* (*Surface développable*), 1941, Antoine
Pevsner; *D'mba* headdress, probably first half
of 20th century, unrecorded Baga artist, Guinea
(Pl. 13); *Bowl of Grapes* (*Le Compotier de raisins*),
1926, Georges Braque. Suspended from ceiling:
Arc of Petals, 1941, Alexander Calder. Archivio
Cameraphoto Epoche, Solomon R. Guggenheim
Foundation, Venice, Gift, Cassa di Risparmio di
Venezia, 2005

Introduction, p. 13
Photo: Tony Vaccaro/Hulton Archive/Getty Images

Fig. 1, p. 19
© 2019 Foto Scala, Florence/bbk Bildagentur für
Kunst, Kultur und Geschichte, Berlin

Fig. 5, p. 25
Photo © RMN-Grand Palais (Musée national
Picasso-Paris). Photo: René-Gabriel Ojéda

Fig. 6, p. 25
© 2019 Image copyright The Metropolitan
Museum of Art/Art Resource/Scala, Florence

Fig. 7, p. 27
© 2019 Digital image, The Museum of Modern Art,
New York/Scala, Florence

Fig. 9, p. 28
Photo © Centre Pompidou, MNAM-CCI
Bibliothèque Kandinsky, Dist. RMN-Grand Palais
/ Fonds Man Ray

Fig. 10, p. 28
Archivio Cameraphoto Epoche, Solomon R.
Guggenheim Foundation, Venice, Gift, Cassa di
Risparmio di Venezia, 2005

Fig. 12, p. 31
© 2019 Foto Scala, Florence/bpk, Bildagentur für
Kunst, Kultur und Geschichte, Berlin

Fig. 13, p. 38
© 2019. Image copyright The Metropolitan
Museum of Art/Art Resource/Scala, Florence

Fig. 14, p. 40
Photo © Columbia/Kobal/Shutterstock

Fig. 15, p. 40
© 2019 Image copyright The Metropolitan
Museum of Art/Art Resource/Scala, Florence

Fig. 16, p. 42
Courtesy Hélène Leloup

Fig. 17, p. 47
Purchase, Solomon R. Guggenheim Foundation,
Venice, 2007

Fig. 18, p. 49
Collection Nationaal Museum van Wereldculturen.
Coll. no. RV-10387-41

Fig. 19, p. 52
Collection Nationaal Museum van Wereldculturen.
Coll. no. TM-20017133

Fig. 20, p. 52
Archivio Cameraphoto Epoche, Solomon R.
Guggenheim Foundation, Venice, Gift, Cassa di
Risparmio di Venezia, 2005

Fig. 21, p. 54
Courtesy Nationaal Museum van Wereldculturen

Fig. 22, p. 60
Archivio Cameraphoto Epoche, Solomon R.
Guggenheim Foundation, Venice, Gift, Cassa di
Risparmio di Venezia, 2005

Fig. 24, p. 62
Archivio Cameraphoto Epoche, Solomon R.
Guggenheim Foundation, Venice, Gift, Cassa di
Risparmio di Venezia, 2005

Fig. 25, p. 62
Archivio Cameraphoto Epoche, Solomon R.
Guggenheim Foundation, Venice, Gift, Cassa di
Risparmio di Venezia, 2005